The Discourse of Europe

Discourse Approaches to Politics, Society and Culture (DAPSAC)

The editors invite contributions that investigate political, social and cultural processes from a linguistic/discourse-analytic point of view. The aim is to publish monographs and edited volumes which combine language-based approaches with disciplines concerned essentially with human interaction – disciplines such as political science, international relations, social psychology, social anthropology, sociology, economics, and gender studies.

General Editors

Ruth Wodak and Greg Myers
University of Lancaster

Editorial address: Ruth Wodak, Bowland College, Department of Linguistics and English Language, University of Lancaster University, LANCASTER LA1 4YT, UK
r.wodak@lancaster.ac.uk and g.myers@lancaster.ac.uk

Advisory Board

Volume 26

The Discourse of Europe. Talk and text in everyday life
Edited by Sharon Millar and John Wilson

The Discourse of Europe

Talk and text in everyday life

Edited by

Sharon Millar
University of Southern Denmark

John Wilson
University of Ulster

John Benjamins Publishing Company

Amsterdam / Philadelphia

^{TM} The paper used in this publication meets the minimum requirements of
American National Standard for Information Sciences – Permanence of
Paper for Printed Library Materials, ANSI z39.48-1984.

Library of Congress Cataloging-in-Publication Data

The discourse of Europe : talk and text in everyday life / edited by Sharon Millar, John
    Wilson.
      p.   cm. (Discourse Approaches to Politics, Society and Culture, ISSN 1569-9463 ; v. 26)
    Includes bibliographical references and index.
        1. Europe--Languages. 2. Discourse analysis. 3. Ethnicity--Europe. I. Millar,
        Sharon. II. Wilson, John, 1954-
      P380.D57   2007
    401'.41094--dc22   2007029434
    ISBN 978 90 272 2717 1 (Hb; alk. paper)

John Benjamins Publishing Co. · P.O. Box 36224 · 1020 ME Amsterdam · The Netherlands
John Benjamins North America · P.O. Box 27519 · Philadelphia PA 19118-0519 · USA

Table of contents

Introduction

John Wilson and Sharon Millar
University of Ulster / University of Southern Denmark

Background

This book[1] brings together a series of articles which explore the way in which the talk and text of everyday interaction in Europe might help us understand what Europe means to a range of its citizens. The concept of Europe is far from straightforward, but in the last decade attempts to discuss Europe within a range of frameworks and disciplines have been prominent. Perhaps this is because the general concept of Europeanisation, as found particularly within the work of the EU, has been central. As the EU has grown to some 27 members, it is not surprising that we should want to reflect on what exactly Europe is and where it is going (Strath 2006). Such reflections have tended to produce as many answers as there are states, and the concept of Europe is now of interest not only for European societies, but also beyond elsewhere in the world where concerns about trade blocks or NATO might seem significant.

Europe is not a single concept, anymore than an individual nation state is a single concept. Within any state, historical, cultural, social, legal, ethnic or economic dimensions could be explored, and equally any of these dimensions could be applied to Europe (see, for example, Holmes and Murray 1999; Pagden 2002; Shore 2000). So which are we targeting in this volume? The answer is the one or ones which are of interest to our informants. In focusing on talk and text, we are not determining a priori the limits of topics or debate. In what follows we will find, inter alia, issues of identity, youth perspectives on Europe, border issues as well as questions of ethnicity, politics and minority languages. This should not be surprising, however, since debates on Europe are frequently pragmatic debates

1.   The chapter in this book emerged orignally from a conference on European Narrative, organised by John Wilson and funded by the European Science Foundation research conference programme, EURESCO.

on what impacts on peoples' lives. While issues of everyday life, writ small, may not have the theoretical sophistication of the academic or politician, the actual concerns, worries and fears look remarkably similar and they demand attention within fully democratised systems (see Wodak 2006).

Similar to the comments above, Malborg and Strath (2002) suggest that there is no one meaning of Europe, but a multiplicity of meanings. They go as far as to suggest that Europe is an imaginary discursive construction; it has emerged out of nation state debates within the imaginary frame of a European identity. While we agree that Europe is a discursive construct, the term 'imaginary' is perhaps overstating the position. The very issue of an individual's identity could be treated in the same way, since one has many identities, but this does not suggest that one does not have some general sense of self as a general template. This general sense is an amalgam of a range of senses of identity, and at a number of levels it makes sense to talk of John Wilson's identity or Sharon Millar's identity, without being able to conclusively and objectively state that it is X or Y.

Roberts (1996:xv) in his history of Europe reminds us that in trying to define Europe we must be "...cautious about its meaning". He goes on to say:

> We still do not easily agree on who are Europeans or (if we think we can answer that question) what it is that they share. The answer must be 'different things at different times'.

And what is it that Europeans share at this time? Again this would not be a simple question to answer. However, with the enlargement of the European Union to 27 states as of January 2007, and with Turkey waiting in the wings, a cautious answer would be a wish to develop a politically strong and economically successful union of independent states, i.e. a process of Europeanisation. For us then, Europe and the EU, while not coterminous, have become central in the minds of Europeans as a sense of what Europe is. This may be for either positive or negative reasons, but of the many senses one can have of Europe, primary is the interrelation between state and union, even for those like Switzerland and Norway who, while not full members, take cognizance of the political and economic context of the EU.

Hence, in what follows the chapters deal with issues the shadow of the EU, even when the arguments seem to be central to national or regional issues.

Europe, state and the individual

Following the Nice European Council meeting in December 2000, Europe's political leaders initiated a debate which became entitled 'The Future of Europe.'

There were to be three phases of debate. The first ended with the Laeken Declaration on the Future of the European Union. The second phase was a Convention set up in 2002 that paved the way for the next Intergovernmental Council (IGC) in 2004, which would not only agree a new treaty for Europe but also do so within the context of the establishment of a European Constitution, a constitution finally agreed in June 2004. We seemed to be approaching, as Joschka Fischer, the German Foreign Minister, put it in a speech delivered in 2000 – "the finality of European integration"(Fischer 2000).

While there may be a political logic here (see Habermas 2004), the problem is that the constitutional debates on Europe often operate at a level which the 'person in the street' finds difficult either to understand, or to care about. The reality is that European debates take place at a variety of levels simultaneously and often without touching each other. This is why so often the same issues and questions come back again and again in different formats and in different conceptual guises. While at one level one might talk of 'the finality of European integration', at another level there are recently established research projects financed by the Economic and Social Science Research Council in the United Kingdom that explore questions such as 'One Europe or Several'(e.g. Brown 2006). Equally, regionalisation in forms such as UK devolution further advance national and regional identities against the backdrop of a European polity debating federation or confederation.

Within such a context we are reminded of Shore and Black's (1994: 275) comment that many European Commission documents highlight the European concept in terms of a "people" – "a union among peoples", a "Citizen's Europe", "a Peoples' Europe". Yet, as Shore and Black correctly point out, despite such aspirations most studies have been focused on "…policies, legislation and institutional questions" (276). In response, and somewhat surprisingly, Shore and Black then proceed to look at what they call the "institutions", in this case the "institutions of culture" (p. 276). Once again, and in line with their own initial premise, there is no sign of the 'peoples' of Europe, whom we take to be the individuals and groups living and working within the European Union.

As noted above, the aim of this book is to look at the discourse of a cross section of the 'people of Europe', and to consider how they view, or act at, being European in local and national contexts as they reflect on their own identities and those of others. Our primary focus is the discursive language used to express different positions and views of self and other. We want to do this neither against some constraining theory of discourse (in the sense that to follow a single theory one must exclude other possibilities), nor any limiting political ideology. We want only to reflect on the discourse (and in some cases the lack of this: what is not said may also be meaningful) by bringing language analysis to the fore through the exploration of a range of concerns and issues operating within samples of the everyday life of Europe and Europeans. Ultimately, we argue that it is here, not in political edicts or treaties, or constitutions, that what is Europe or what is European will be decided and defined.

What is it to be European?

This is a complex and multifaceted question which may be answered in a variety of ways. It is a problematic issue because all attempts to define the general concept of 'identity' indicate that the term is made up of several layers of different forms of 'identities'. This may include, inter alia, social, personal, family, professional, geographical and national identity. In such a context then, what is it to be European, to have a European identity? Recently, James Kurth (2006) gave an insightful account of European identity in terms of the dialectic of great wars. Specifically, he argues that great wars often emerge out of forms of conflict of identity, and the result of such wars is a transformation of those identities. He suggests that a premodern Europe was essentially Christian, but that the beginning of the modern era produced a protestant reformation which led to the thirty years war, which in turn created as an output not only Protestant and Catholic identities, but emergent, secular, non-Christian identities. These secular alternatives then led in turn to the creation of specific political philosophies, such as liberalism, socialism, and nationalism. Such products of enlightenment in their turn created conflicts of their own, and from these liberalism became transformed into democracy, socialism into communism, and nationalism into fascism. With these, of course, we have the great conflicts of the twentieth century, spectacularly exemplified by the Second World War. It was the sheer scale of the consequences of this war that led, according to Kurth (2006: 544), to the triumph in Europe of a strong form of liberal identity, one predicated on an open society, free market capitalism and a focus on individualism, what he called a "hyperindividualism".

Like all broad assessments, there is much that one might challenge here, or much that could be said to be overly simplistic in terms of its representation. Yet there is also something generally correct in Kurth's view and also much that assists us in understanding why answers to the question of what it is to be European or have a European identity is not only multifaceted, but also contextually and historically sensitive. Consider, for example the ongoing debate on Turkey's membership of the European Union. The essentially Christian nature of Europe noted by Kurth has been a stumbling block for some members of the Union. Gole (2005: 1) suggests that many Turks see candidacy for the European Union as "..a continuous and almost "natural" outcome of their history". This would not sit easy with most European views or with Kurth's analysis. Or consider, Kurth's assessment of an emergent 'hyperindividualism' which suggests for example a self-centred philosophy for Europeans, one which may be seen in the welfare state, immigration, and falling birth rates. But we want to suggest that, as has always been the case, there is not one identity category available at any one time but several, all of which may or may not reflect a 'hyperindividualism'. The sense of a European Union, for example, which develops a transnational perspective, might be exactly what an immigrant needs in order to resolve their problems of citizenship (Europe), state, (residence), and country of origin. Here, a shared sense of a single vision of Europe (at some levels) beyond national boundaries becomes attractive. Equally, for the ordinary individual at the levels of law or economics, choices can be made to transcend national limits (European Court, EU trade laws) for one's own needs. This may be hyperindividualism, but it is certainly a pragmatic reaction to available circumstances. For many then, being European or having a European identity may simply reflect a personal, needs-based analysis.

There is little doubt that however we view Europe and European identity, the question of European identity has been a topic of significant interest in the last decade. This is in part a consequence of the recent and continuing growth of the EU since European identity, at an official level at least, was always intimately tied to the coordination and development of the member states (again a pragmatic issue). As long ago as 1973 at the Copenhagen summit, the then nine member countries issued a text entitled *Declaration on European Identity*. In section 22 it is noted that:

> The European identity will evolve as a function of the dynamic construction of a United Europe. In their external relations, the nine propose progressively to undertake the definition of their identity in relation to other countries.

This approach suggests, as for other forms of identity, that it will be progressively constructed out of a clear view of what European identity is not – i.e. it is the differences between Europe compared with other countries that provide the definition of what it is to be European. Hobsbawn (1990) has noted that this is the natural history of identities, i.e. that they develop to separate one group or nation from another. Bauböck (1997) goes one step further arguing that the project of building a common European fatherland, when based on an "ethno-cultural Euro nationalism", requires for its success not just the presence of the 'other', but the *threat* of the 'other'. He believes that such a threat does not exist in reality, but acknowledges that "Euro-chauvinism and xenophobia appear as very real side-effects of the imaginary project of European nation-building", with the 'Orient', including Islamic fundamentalism, being created as the external threat. Certainly when Europe is defined in civilisation terms as a shared cultural heritage (e.g.

classical learning, Christianity, the Enlightenment), it is possible to exclude the Judaic and Islamic worlds from this cultural community (Asad 2002).

The official, institutionalised EU approach to European identity has always attempted to avoid the problems of national identity in that nationalisms are not challenged or forced into a form of integrationist identity which blurs any nation's independence. However, the idea that the EU *is* a threat to the concept of the 'nation' is one that has assumed a central importance in considering the potential emergence of a European identity (see Fossum 2003). Yet with the continuing growth of the Union, and the expansion of movement across borders, it may be that national identities are reaching a level of maturity wherein one can be European without any sense of loss of national identity. For instance, in a review of Eurobarometer data (data on attitudes to Europe collected by the European Commission on a regular basis) van der Veen (2002: 1) suggests that:

> ...cross national differences in the strength of a European identity are not related to a fear that the national identity might be displaced or replaced by the European identity. Instead, they may be explained in part by differences across member states in the shares of their population that have lived and/or studied in another member state.

It seems then that ones sense of place is affected by ones geographical and social mobility, and the incumbent experiences gained therein. This can be seen in the figures from Eurobarometer 65 (2006). Attachment to Europe varies by country, as one would expect: the overall EU level is 63%, but, at the lower end of the scale, we have 46% for the UK, 43% in Greece, 42% in Lithuania, 38% in Estonia and just a quarter (27%) of the people in Cyprus. But most significant, in light of the comments above, is that attachment is affected also by age, education, employment and other social factors. Of those educated to age 15 or below, the figure is 36%, compared to 59% for those educated to 20 or above. For managers and the self-employed, the figures are 68% and 58%, respectively. In such a varied context of views, beliefs and attitudes, it is difficult to talk of a single European identity or of being European.

In the end, we suggest that it is a common sense view of pragmatic utility that centres what it is to be European, and this is something which is continually fluid and shifting within ever changing social, historical and political circumstances. But how then does one get a sense of these shifting boundaries of self and other in Europe? Research on Europe is awash with questionnaires, surveys, focus group studies and so on, which attempt to tackle such an issue. However, there is much less qualitative work, and almost nothing on how peoples' sense of themselves within Europe is reflected in their everyday communication. Perhaps here we might find some insight to what it is to be European, by considering what Europeans talk about.

Europe? What's the answer? What's the question?

Former Vice-President of the United States, Dan Quayle is reputed to have told his audience that "We have a firm commitment to NATO, we are a part of NATO. We have a firm commitment to Europe. We are a part of Europe". At the time, this was taken as yet another example of the Vice-President's rather dubious intellectual abilities. But why should this be so? Friedrich (1969: 1) states:

> There always has been a European Community. It is the community which has been the carrier of what is called European culture or civilization...Neither Russia nor America nor the British settlements of European stock can be excluded from it.

In similar vein, 'Anthony', participating in an online, youth discussion forum in 2003 on 'What does European identity mean?', tells us that "Americans & Australians do have this convenient way of forgetting that in the end they're a bunch of exiled Europeans" (http://www.transeuth.org/link.asp?TOPIC_ID=31). In contrast to such talk of Europeans in faraway places, there are those in the European Union who debate the possible accession of Turkey to the EU not only in political and economic terms, but also in terms of the question 'is Turkey actually part of Europe'? The point, of course, as we have already noted, is that the concepts of 'Europe' and 'European' can be understood in a myriad of ways: geographical (the source of Dan Quayle's problem, and, for some, Turkey's problem) cultural, intellectual, political, economic, historical, psychological and so on. For this reason, we do not wish to begin with some a priori objectified and agreed definition of what Europe is and then set this up against the context of everyday talk and text. As argued by Herzfeld (2002: 145), "the "idea of Europe" has percolated through the complex populations of the European continent and is "refracted" through the prism of daily interaction". Our interest concerns not only how people understand and construct the concept of Europe in everyday discourse, but also whether this concept has any significance for people at all. For instance, Pagden (2002: 24) claims that "for most in today's Europe, "Europe" has as much resonance as "France" or "England" or "Castile" would have had for a sixteenth-century farmer".

For us then, Europe is not a pre-determined entity waiting to be discovered, but something that is socially and discursively 'constructed'. The term 'construction' has become particularly prominent in recent times and within a variety of disciplines (see Christiansen, Jorgensen and Wiener 2001; de Cillia, Reisigl, and Wodak 1999; Gergen 1999; Hacking 1999; Kratochwil and Ruggie 1986; Parker 1989). Our view of 'construction' is in line with a classical pragmatic position (exemplified in the work of Rorty 1998) that 'social practices' are matters concerned with the 'utility' of belief, rather than any direct or objective correspondence between language and the world. We agree with Ruggie (1998: 33) when he says:

> ...Constructivists hold a view that the building blocks of international reality are ideational as well as material; that ideational factors have normative as well as instrumental dimensions; that they express not only individual but also collective intentionality; and that the meaning and significance of ideational factors are not independent of time and place.

We treat our approach as one of 'discursive construction' where the term 'discourse' refers directly to linguistic formats utilised to create ways of representing particular positions, views, beliefs and emotions (see Hall 1992). But this need not imply or indeed exclude any specific theoretical position on such construction. For instance, a number of the chapters in the volume are concerned with narrative, be this in the specific sense of a 'story' or more generally as exposition or opinion, but they approach this from varying perspectives, such as structural narrative analysis, critical discourse analysis, linguistic bias model, and classical rhetoric. All of these approaches, however, are used to illuminate how identities are constructed and how positions are taken in relation to self and other. Primacy is given to language in action, that is language as used by individuals and groups in a variety of contexts and in a range of modalities and media (written vs. spoken, print vs. broadcast), as opposed to questionnaire responses, formal interviews, or experimental contexts. What people do in language is where we wish to look for 'Europe', or in some cases for the explicit lack of 'Europe'. It is here that we see contestation and reflection about being European, about being an ethnic or minority group within Europe, about the relevance of Europe and about individual responsibilities of being a citizen of Europe. These are some of the issues we touch upon in this volume and we will do so through an analysis of the how the question and answer of Europe is constructed in a variety of linguistic contexts.

The people's voice

As we have stated above we wish to place central the 'people' of Europe, but what or which people? First, we are not intending to imply some special sense of the 'ordinary' people, or some 'natural' discourse. Both the terms 'ordinary' and 'natural' are themselves constructed entities. There is often a tendency to think of 'natural' speech (see Wilson 1987; Wolfson 1976) as 'ordinary conversation' and everything else as formally constructed language. Yet, it is surely true, in one sense, that a political speech delivered by a politician is in some ways an 'ordinary' and indeed quite a 'natural' event for them, whereas, for the same politician holding a conversation with an unemployed mother about the merits of living on welfare benefits might be anything but 'natural' or 'ordinary'. By the 'people' and 'the people's voice' we mean simply that they are not direct protagonists for Europe, i.e. the Commissioners, the civil servants, or the international lawyers. They may, however, be politicians where the central concern could be European politics, such as further EU integration, or local and national politics. In the latter case, Europe may be directly or indirectly accommodated, e.g. politicians may wish to position themselves by attacking Europe, or they may talk of it only indirectly in terms of everyday political issues such as education, health, tax etc.

The people's voice does not find expression in a vacuum, but is articulated within specific spatial coordinates – those physical, social and perceived spaces, which together combine to create spatiality, what Britain (2002: 604) sees as perpetually in motion, "always in a state of linguistic "becoming"". In terms of physical space, this volume can only offer selective geographical coverage: Denmark, England, Greece, Italy, the Netherlands, Northern Ireland and Poland. Within this arena, the focus varies from specific localities, e.g. the city of Birmingham, or the region of Trieste, to a broader, country-wide perspective, e.g. particular actors in Denmark, Greece and Italy. In some cases, the physical space is not the most salient, e.g. the Netherlands merely provides the backdrop for the foreign exchange students discussing citizenship in Barnhurst's contribution. This physical space could be discursively constructed into perceived space along differing dimensions, such as north/south, east/west, centre/margin. For instance, Herzfeld (2002: 145) refers to "a view from the margins", i.e. the political and geographical margins of Europe and suggests that when working in less "mainstream European sites", one finds the "tension between "being European" and "being other than European" is already in place – indeed, is a staple of everyday conversation and media attention" (147). In the spirit of this volume, however, we must refrain from defining space for others and allow the people themselves to construct their own perceived space along the dimensions of relevance to them. For instance, as noted by Nikolaria (this volume), Greece is sometimes seen by Greeks as being in the centre of Europe and other times as at the margin. No doubt with EU enlargement, the dimensions of perceptual space will continue to alter.

In terms of social space, the voices of the people considered in this volume represent a broad spectrum: young and old, male and female, with varying degrees of education and coming from various social and ethnic backgrounds. As already noted, a sense of European identity seems to tie into the social characteristics of the individual. However, we do not claim that the talk and text analysed here are in any strict sense representative of the people of Europe or a particular member state.

Finally, turning from dimensions of spatiality to temporality, all of the chapters are historical since the data are embedded in specific moments and events in the past. While they must be understood in their contemporary contexts, the analyses nonetheless can inform current debates since in focus are the general processes of identity construction and positioning. Moreover, as diachronic snapshots, the chapters contribute to an understanding of the development of, and changes in, identities within the European arena over time.

Overview of chapters

The volume begins with Barnhurst's chapter on 'A Phenomenology of Citizenship among Young Europeans'. He notes the gap between the theoretical ideal of citizenship, that of the rational, active, engaged individual, as articulated by progressive thinkers such as John Dewey, and the experience of citizenship as narrated in the life histories written by mainly young Europeans. These narratives reveal that, for the young, political discourse in the media is a fringe condition, made sporadically salient by specific events, conflicts and personalities. Emotion rather than rationality can hold sway. Consequently, a new ideal of citizenship is needed, one which takes account of emotionally experienced identity. Moreover, Barnhurst suggests conditions that might encourage the renewal of citizenship, such as free and open distribution of political ideas via for example the Internet, and the presentation of clear political options.

While Barnhurst considers political communication from the perspective of citizens' experiences, i.e. the receivers, noting in passing the potential significance of the Internet for renewing citizenship, Cortini and Manuti in 'The Narrative Bias: Political Marketing on the World Wide Web' focus on the effects the Internet has had for political communication itself as sent via the web pages of the main political parties in Italy before regional and national elections in 2000 and 2001, respectively. Of interest are the discursive and argumentative structures employed to describe self and other, with one recurring narrative device, the competitive narrative, being particularly scrutinised. The theoretical and analytical frameworks used are the Linguistic Intergroup Bias (LIB) Model, a model which adds a linguistic perspective (in terms of level of language abstraction) to social identity theory (as developed by Henri Tajfel and colleagues), as well as content analysis and critical discourse analysis. The authors conclude that web-based political communication does not follow in all cases the predictions of the LIB model and that the web pages blend the objectivity of the political proposal with the subjective needs of the electorate, in other words political communication has features of advertising discourse. Interestingly in this marketing discourse, the concept of Europe, when mentioned, was used as a rhetorical strategy to legitimise political claims and objectives.

Toolan in 'Are Brummies Developing Narratives of European Identity?' broaches the issue of whether English people, in this case callers to a local radio programme in Birmingham, have any sense of European identity. Arguing that if Europe is part of individual identity, it must at least be in the background of some of the narratives an individual tells, he adopts a naturalistic, overhearing technique to discover that most callers make no spontaneous reference to Europe or Europeanness, be this positive or negative, with the exception of one. The sample is limited and not representative, acknowledges Toolan, and one cannot simplistically conclude that most of these people have no orientation towards Europeanness. Nonetheless the bottom-up methodology is likely to reveal more about folk identifications than top-down investigations of discourse in the national media.

Like Toolan, Galasinska and Galasinski to a great extent search in vain for a European identity in their chapter 'Rejecting an identity. Discourses of Europe in Polish border Communities'. Adopting techniques of critical discourse analysis, they note a strong national dimension to narratives about the European Union elicited from the inhabitants of the Polish border community of Zgorzelec. Apparent too is a tendency towards self-criticism as a group (Poles as backward, lazy etc.), where Polishness is viewed as clashing with any notion of European identity, although there are signs that the latter finds some favour amongst the younger generation. The conflict between national and European identities is also noted by Millar in 'Rhetoricians at Work: Constructing the European Union in Denmark'. Using precepts from classical rhetoric, she examines the argumentative strategies used in letters-to-the-editor written by Danes during the run-up to the 1992 referendum on the Maastricht treaty. No-voters construct Danishness and Europeanness (in the sense of the EU) as mutually exclusive while yes-voters permit compatibility, although in neither case is European identity specified in any concrete terms.

Nikolarea in 'Narratives of Greek Identity in European Life' considers the dynamics of Greek identity in relation to European, or put another way, how self relates to other. Within a Bakhtinian framework, she examines texts from academia, government, and banks to chart the gradual 'Europeanisation' of Greeks, but notes that Greek and European identities do not always co-identify. Supranational economic policies, such as monetary union (the Euro), may help construct the illusion of an EU identity, but supranational politics, especially at times of crisis (for example in the Balkan region), may destabilise any such unitary identity which is subjugated to the needs of national identity.

Relations between self and other are also the focus of Sbisa and Vascotto's chapter on 'How to Conceive the Other's Point of View: Considerations from a Case Study in Trieste'. Here, however, the concern is with majority-minority relations within the same territory, i.e. Italian-speaking and Slovene-speaking groups in the Italian region of Trieste. An examination of descriptions of the local territory given by schoolchildren revealed that awareness of the composite nature of the population differed between the two groups, but in both cases awareness of the presence of the other was low. The authors argue that management of identity differences in Europe of whatever type, linguistic, cultural, ethnic and national, requires an awareness and understanding of the 'other' that is best approached from within Wittgenstein's family resemblances paradigm rather than from any idealised notion of perfect delimitation.

The theme of minority difference continues in Wilson and Stapleton's chapter on 'Narratives on Lesser-Used Languages in Europe: The Case of Ulster Scots'. Management of linguistic difference has been a concern of the European Union, which promotes language diversity between and within member states. The authors examine the personal narratives on language of people in Northern Ireland who consider themselves to be Ulster Scots in order to understand both local issues of minority identity and language as well as general issues of European minority linguistic identity. They find that being Ulster Scots has no linguistic requirement (i.e. actually speaking Ulster Scots), but the language is symbolically important to identity. The role of Europe in recognising minority languages is viewed with a certain scepticism.

Although the chapters deal with varying issues in differing locations, it is possible to identify a number of common threads among the contributions. One such thread is the significance of the affective dimension for identity. Barnhurst argues for a new approach to citizenship that takes account of the emotional experience of identity; Cortini and Manuti point out the importance of the subjective needs of the voter, as opposed to objective policy statements, in political rhetoric; Millar observes the power of emotion in relation to national symbols and collective memories and, like Galansinska and Galasinski as well as Toolan, notes that Europe often provokes negative sentiment, if any at all; Wilson and Stapleton report the attachment of the Ulster Scots minority to "the words". That emotion should be so significant for identity is in itself not a revelation, but it is problematic for those who attempt to construct European identity and citizenship at a more macro level without reference to the affective dimension. For instance, Habermas (1992) espouses a programme of 'constitutional patriotism' where allegiances and identities are not grounded on any sense of shared cultural values, but on shared constitutional principles. Indeed, since October 2004 the EU has had a constitution based on values such as liberty, equality, democracy, and respect for human rights, although this as yet has not been ratified by all member states. However, such principles or values are themselves imbued with strong emotion and can be constructed very differently according to viewpoint. For instance, the euphemistically named 'democratic deficit' of the EU (d'Appollonia 2002) has been referred to in considerably more emotive terms by some of its Danish citizens, e.g. as bureaucratic dictatorship. In an attempt to address the deficit issue, the constitution stresses the importance of participatory democracy and citizenship, but, arguably, until the emotional aspects of identity and citizenship are addressed, the extent of citizen engagement with the EU and its institutions is unlikely to be overwhelming.

A further problem for any project of Europeanisation is the complexities of identity itself. Most of the contributions to this volume touch on the different contexts in which identities locate themselves – local, regional, national, glocal, global – and the tensions that often arise as a result. The various types of attachment that the individual and the collective may feel require, following Sbisà and Vascotti, management and not just acknowledgement. A crucial issue is the recognition and understanding of the 'other' and their point of view, not always apparent even in the same territory. Yet who this 'other' may be tends to fluctuate and, in the case of European identity, may even be difficult to define. In some cases, as reported by Galasinska and Galsinski in Poland, and Millar in Denmark, the 'other' may be Europe itself, constructed in opposition to national identity; in the case of Greece, Nikolarea shows that it is sometimes the nation that is seen as the 'other' in relation to the EU and sometimes vice-versa. Increasingly, research suggests that for many national identity and European identity are becoming compatible, but it is still not clear what the latter actually is. A more recent candidate for an 'other' in relation to European identity is the Islamic world. Such 'othering' processes have little to do with understanding the other's point of view but have more in common with the competitive characteristics of political rhetoric noted by Cortini and Manuti. How one reconciles the creation and maintenance of the 'other', so necessary for identity construction, with the management of difference is the eternal question. The EU has generally relied on political solutions, but, as Wilson and Stapleton found, the political management of linguistic difference does not necessarily address the cultural issues, although it can open up new narrative spaces where these can be tackled.

Another enduring problem for European identity is group internal rather than external. As Nikolarea notes, policies of economic union can function as a centripetal force for European identity, but international political crises can operate as a centrifugal force, wreaking havoc on any idea of a unified European entity. Finding "something" to hold these opposing forces together is, for Niko-larea, the future challenge. In similar vein, an article from January 4th 2007 in the online edition of the British newspaper 'The Guardian' (www.guardian.co.uk/eu/story/0,,1982466,00.html) concludes that the newly enlarged European Union is "27 states in search of a story" since it lacks a cohesive political narrative to link past with future now that the memory of World War II is fading in political and public consciousness. Ironically too, the logo designed by a Polish student for the 50th anniversary celebrations for the Treaty of Rome has met with objections. The logo, made up of different letters, typescripts and accents from varying European countries reads "Tögethé® since 1957", but has been criticised, amongst other things, for being in English. It would seem that "togetherness" is best left as a linguistically unexpressed aspiration.

It may be that the understanding of European identity in terms of pragmatic individualism, as discussed above, holds the key. Europe exists in the context of the individual and may find favour or not depending on its perceived utility to the self and one's group, as exemplified by the following 15 year-old from Scotland writing online in 2003 for a BBC youth news programme (http://news.bbc.co.uk/cbbcnews/hi/club/your_reports/newsid_2969000 /2969810.stm); for him, a United Europe is a great idea for the very simple reason that it would be "cool" to go on holiday without a passport.

References

Asad, Talal. 2002. "Muslims and European identity: Can Europe represent Islam?" In A. Pagden (ed.), 209–227.

Bauböck, Rainer. 1997. "Citizenship and national identity in the European Union". *The Jean Monnet Working Papers* No. 4. Available at <http://www.jeanmonnetprogram.org/papers/97/97-04-.html>. Accessed 8 January 2007.

Britain, David. 2002. "Space and spatial diffusion". In *The Handbook of Language Variation and Change*, J. Chambers, P. Trudgill & N. Schilling-Estes (eds.), 603–637. Oxford: Blackwell.

Brown, Derek. 2006. "One Europe or several. Mapping the new Europe". ESRC. Available at <http://www.esrcsocietytoday.ac.uk/ESRCInfoCentre/about/CI/CP/the_edge/issue11/oneeuropemapping_2.aspx>. Accessed 8 January 2007.

Christiansen, Thomas, Jorgensen, Erik.K. and Wiener, Antje. 2001. *The Social Construction of Europe*. London: Sage.

d'Appollonia, Ariane. 2002. "European nationalism and European union". In A. Pagden (ed.), 171–190.

Fischer, Joschka. 2000. "From union to federation: Thoughts on the finality of European integration". Speech delivered at Humbolt University, Berlin. Available at <http://www.europa.eu/constitution/futurum/documents/speech/sp120500_en.pdf>. Accessed 8 January 2007.

Fossum, John Erik. 2003. "The European Union: In search of an identity". *European Journal of Political Theory* 2(3):319–340.

Eurobarometer 65. 2006. Available at <http://ec.europa.eu/public_opinion/archives/eb/eb65/eb65_en.htm>. Accessed 8 January 2007.

Friedrich, Carl. 1969. *Europe. An Emergent Nation?* New York: Harper & Row.

Gergen, Kenneth. J. 1999. *An Invitation to Social Construction*. London: Sage.

Gole, Nilfuer. 2005. "Europe – An Identity or a Project?". Available at <http://www.signand-sight.com/features/514.html>. Accessed 8 January 2007.

Habermas, Jürgen. 1992. "Citizenship and national identity: Some reflections on the future Europe". *Praxis Internationale* 12(1):1–19.

Habermas, Jürgen. 2004. *America and the World: A Conversation with Jürgen Habermas – with Eduardo Mendieta*; translated by Jeffrey Graig Millar. Available at <http://www.logos-journal.com/issue.3.3/Habermas-interview.htm>. Accessed 8 January 2007.

Hacking, Ian. 1999. *The Social Construction of What?* Cambridge, MA.: Harvard University Press.

Hall, Stuart. 1992. *Representation*. Berkshire: Open University Press.

Herzfeld, Michael. 2002. "The European self". In A. Pagden (ed.), 139–170.

Hobsbawn, Eric. 1990. *Nations and Nationalism since 1780: Programme Myth and Reality*. Cambridge: Cambridge University Press.

Holmes, Leslie and Murray, Philomena. 1999. *Citizenship and Identity in Europe*. Aldershot: Ashgate.

Hug, Simon. 2002. *Voices of Europe*. Lanham: Rowman & Littlefield.

Kratochwil, Friedrich, and Ruggie, John Gerard. 1986. "International organisation. A state of the art on the art of the state". *International Organisation* 40: 753–75.

Kurth, James. 2006. "Europe's identity problem and the new Islamist war". *Orbis*, Summer 2006: 541–554.

Malborg, Mikael Af and Strath, Bo. 2002. *The Meaning of Europe: Variety and Contention Within and Among Nations*. Oxford: Berg.

Pagden, Anthony. 2002. "Introduction". In A. Pagden (ed.), 1–32.

Pagden, Anthony. (ed.). 2002. *The Idea of Europe. From Antiquity to the European Union*. Cambridge/Washington: Cambridge University Press/ Woodrow Wilson Center Press.

Parker, Ian. 1989. *The Crisis in Modern Social Psychology – and How to End It*. London and New York: Routledge.

Roberts, J.M. 1996. *The Penguin History of Europe*. Harmonsworth: Penguin.

Rorty, Richard. 1998. *Truth and Progress: Philosophical Papers Vol 3*. Cambridge: Cambridge University Press.

Ruggie, John Gerard. 1998. *Constructing the World Polity: Essays on International Institution-alisation*. New York: Routledge.

Shore, Cris. 2000. *Building Europe: The Cultural Politics of European Integration*. London: Routledge.

Shore, Cris and Black, Annabel.1994. "Citizen's Europe and the construction of European iden-tity". In *The Anthropology of Europe. Identities and Boundaries in Conflict,* J. Goddard, R.L. Lobera and C. Shore (eds.), 275–298. Oxford: Berg.

Strath, Bo. 2006. "Future of Europe". *Journal of Language and Politics* 5(3): 427–449.

Wilson, John. 1987. "The sociolinguistic paradox: Data as a methodological product". *Language and Communication* 7(2):161–177.

Van der Veen, Maurits, A. 2002. "Determinants of European identity: A preliminary investigation using Eurobarometer data". Available at <http://www.isanet.org/noarchive/vanderveen.html>. Accessed 8 January 2007.

Wodak, Ruth, De Cillia, Rudolf, Reisigl, Martin, and Leibhart, Karin. 1999. *The Discursive Construction of National Identity*. Edinburgh: Edinburgh University Press.

Wodak, Ruth. 2006. "Preface". *Journal of Language and Politics* 5(3):299–303.

Wolfson, Nessa. 1976. "Speech events and natural speech: Some implications for sociolinguistic methodology". *Language in Society* 5(2):189–210.

A phenomenology of citizenship among young Europeans

Kevin G. Barnhurst
University of Illinois at Chicago

Introduction

Young adults in Europe and America are often described as apathetic, dispirited citizens. Scholars usually study the problem using evidence from voting patterns, attitude surveys, and audience statistics. The data accumulated in the past century suggest that the young have limited interest in being productive, efficient citizens involved in rational deliberation or instrumental political activity. They fall short on each of the three standards for citizenship that thinkers developed a century ago, by the end of the Progressive Era in America: a willingness to take responsibility for the collective well-being, a commitment to sociability as the tool for building unity within the community, and engagement in the processes of political communication. When he summarized the theory of rational and active citizenship, the pragmatist philosopher John Dewey (1927) aimed at a remedy for the problems of democracy, but the theory became disconnected from the experience of citizens.

Reformers in America did not set out to create a new definition of citizenship, but their reforms inadvertently created a national legal category. They presented themselves as exemplars of citizenship, and their policy successes from the local to the national level showed what a community of model citizens could accomplish. In Europe sociologists of the period accepted a similar definition of citizenship, but despite its eventual widespread acceptance in theory, ordinary members of the population, by every measure, fell short in practice. The theory set up an unreachable ideal that devalued how the people enact citizenship in daily life. After a century of evidence showing the inadequacy of citizens, especially the young, it seems time to reassess.

This essay analyzes life histories written by young adults principally from Europe, to see how their accounts describe and explain their own citizenship. The reading presented here examines their accounts in light of ideas from pragmatic and progressive thought developed a century ago and employs techniques of phenomenology developed during the same period, at the time the ideal of citizenship emerged. The resulting critique questions the widely accepted ideal of citizenship and points to the ways that young adults describe their experiences with the media and politics, with the aim of exploring how they re-imagine citizenship. Recent attitude surveys on the participation of European youth in politics continue to encourage citizenship education, but researchers now cite benefits in two directions – for the nation and for the European Union – when the young become politically involved (see, e.g., Dell'Olio 2005; Jamieson et al. 2005).

Ideal citizenship

Since the Progressive Era, citizenship has been held up as a shining ideal. Its best known proponent, John Dewey, outlined in *The Public and Its Problems* three vital characteristics of citizens: responsibility, sociability, and communication. The citizen on one hand carried the legal duties to vote, serve on juries, and otherwise act as the ultimate repository of power, with all the moral weight those obligations imply. Dewey (1927: 147) called on the individual to take "a responsible share... in forming and directing activities" and on groups to facilitate individual responsibility by working toward the "liberation of the potentialities of members". Ideal citizenship stood not only for bearing the legal charge to serve the public but also for fulfilling the civic demands of community, with expectations for active "participation in family life, industry, scientific and artistic associations". Dewey (1927: 148) went on to say that "democracy is not an alternative to... associated life. It is the idea of community life itself". Community formed the central vision of Progressive Era democratic thinking (Royce 1969), and Dewey (1927: 149) attacked any ideals not springing out of community (such as fraternity, liberty, equality) as "hopeless abstractions". The fulfillment of legal responsibilities and the enriching experience of community life, through "participation in activities and sharing in results", in Dewey's words, depended upon the third characteristic: "communication as a prerequisite" (1927: 152). The role of communication in expressing public opinion and informing the voter was central to Progressive thinking about citizenship (Beard and Beard 1931; Godkin 1896, 1898). Communication was so central to Dewey's sense of democracy that he quoted Carlyle: "Invent the printing press and democracy is inevitable" (in 1927: 110).

Progressive thinkers had invented ideal citizenship unintentionally, as a by-product of other crusades. Writing in 1910, Charles W. Beard (1949) observed that the original framers of the US Constitution distinguished the citizen from the mere resident and left to the states the question of whom to consider citizens. The Progressive movement grew indirectly out of abolitionism, which a generation of reformers (called the Mugwumps) saw as a triumph of moral citizen action. The abolition of slavery resulted in the creation of universal citizenship. The Fourteenth Amendment made citizens of "all persons born or naturalized in the United States", effectively nationalizing what the Constitution left to the states and creating the modern legal definition of citizenship (Beard 1949: 77). The Progressives did not know quite how to define that creation in practice. E. L. Godkin, the editor of *The Nation* and a leading thinker of the post-Civil War reform movement, supported democracy against its critics but tended to describe citizens in the image of himself: educated men accustomed to prolonged discussion and book reading (see, for example, his essay, "The Duty of Educated Men in a Democracy", Godkin 1896). Reforms of the civil service, municipal government, and child labor set a high standard for what such citizens could accomplish. Woodrow Wilson (1961) elevated a free, educated, and thoughtful expression of the popular will of citizens to the highest status, as the first of four essential elements of constitutional government, followed by the legislative, executive, and judiciary bodies.

In reform thought, the citizen, after adopting service to the united community as an ideal (Royce 1969), begins by paying close attention to political events as reported through various media (Godkin 1898), and that leads inevitably into further purposive activity (Godkin 1896). The successes of the reformers illustrated those activities: formulating sensible opinions as members of the public and expressing those views to elected officials, taking part in open debate of the issues through speeches and publications, serving in groups to solve problems and select candidates, and joining when necessary in acts of civil demonstration and disobedience. The ideal citizen is a reformer at every level and at all times or, in other words, is made in the image of someone like Jane Addams. To fulfill the ideal, a citizen might not have to lay aside all other earthly endeavors but would spend each waking hour in civic-minded attentiveness. Thinkers in Europe of the era had a similar take on citizenship. Max Weber described two avenues to Politics as a Vocation (the title of his well-known essay). Elected officials may live *off* politics, he wrote, but anyone can live *for* politics: "He who lives 'for' politics makes politics his life, in an internal sense... he nourishes his inner balance and self-feeling by the consciousness that his life has *meaning* in the service of a 'cause'" (Weber 1958: 84).

It is beyond the scope of this essay to describe the historical course followed by the notion of active, rational citizenship. It seems clear, however, that by the end of the Progressive Era, "the discourse of citizenship and citizenship ideals was transformed" (Schudson 1998: 147). The ideal of the informed citizenry also emerged in the thought of leading sociologists and philosophers during the key period around the turn of the century, and from there entered the popular imagination in Europe and America. By the mid-twentieth century, political scientists delineated the ideal into a hierarchy of instrumental activity, ranging from voters at the base (who perform the narrowest legal duty) to full-time politicians and activists at the pinnacle (Milbrath 1965). Theorists found themselves struggling with the odd concern that a society where all citizens reached or approached the ideal might become unstable from so much political activity (e.g., Lerner 1966). Could there be too active a citizenry or, in effect, too much citizenship?

The concern over the ideal was tempered by complaints – most of them originating in the late nineteenth century – about the performance of ordinary individuals as citizens. Godkin and his peers saw themselves as heirs to the founding American generation of aristocratic leaders and distinguished themselves from the ordinary mass of citizens enfranchised over the course of the republic's first century (see Beard and Beard 1931; Godkin 1898). In his collected essays, *Problems of Modern Democracy,* Godkin (1898) noted the low levels of public knowledge (which he elsewhere called "democratic ignorance", 1896: 87), as well as the indolence and corruption of voters and their reliance on political parties and party bosses for personal comfort and profit. In theory, "Every man was supposed to be intensely occupied with public affairs, to be eager to vote on them, and to be quite able to vote intelligently" (1896: 297), but in fact, Godkin (1896: 289) observed, "a very large proportion of the voters are not interested in public questions at all, or their feeble interest has to be aroused and kept awake. Another large proportion do not desire to give themselves the trouble to vote".

Dewey (1927: 169) later noted how the "inertia, prejudices and emotional partisanship of the masses" make the people slaves to habit, which William James called "the enormous fly-wheel of society" (quoted in Dewey 1927: 159). Dewey was, of course, echoing Lippmann (1922: 229–30), who condemned the public for "apathy, preference for the curious trivial as against the dull important, and the hunger for sideshows" and expressed despair over "the failure of self-governing people to transcend their casual experience and their prejudice". Dewey (1927: 116) observed that "the Public seems to be lost; it is certainly bewildered". Citing Lippmann, he decried the shrinking numbers of voters and the paucity of political conversation that most of the public "dismissed with a yawn" (1927: 132).

As a remedy, reformers called for improvements in the press and in the measurement of public opinion (Beard and Beard 1931; Godkin 1898), but as the century progressed, research showed that citizens consistently fell short of the ideal.

Voters did not have much knowledge of the workings of government or of current issues and the actions of elected officials (Berelson, Lazarsfeld, and McPhee 1954; Converse et al. 1972; Campbell et al. 1976; Nie, Verba, and Petrocik 1979). Voters spent little or no time in the work of informing themselves. With rare exceptions, they were not particularly active in political matters. They have in recent decades joined community organizations in smaller numbers (Putnam 1995). They do not debate but instead work to avoid politics in conversation (Eliasoph 1998). In the United States, often a majority does not vote. Cultural analyses reiterate the description of citizens as incompetent and infantile (Berlant 1996). The evidence amounts to an attack on the people, and among them young citizens fare the worst. They have abandoned newspaper reading at an increasing rate (Bogart 1989), and, instead of informing themselves by any other means, they appear to adopt a stance of cynicism founded on ignorance (Craig and Bennett 1997; Rushkoff 1994).

The ideal of citizenship developed by the close of the Progressive Era required levels of commitment to political activity that amounted to more than full-time work. Schematically, it places active citizenship squarely within politics (see Figure 1). The reformers and their successors in thinking about citizenship condemn political parties and other institutions for acting without citizen involvement. They chastise ordinary individuals for building an identity largely outside the zone of politics and for seeing involvement as citizens as limited. The theorists also censure the media for ignoring rational politics in favor of emotion-driven and largely apolitical contents (Godkin 1898; Lippmann 1922), which become the primary source of political knowledge for the voters. They reprimand voters in

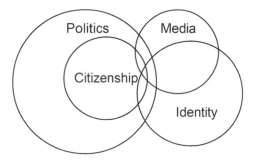

The ideal of citizenship as conceived by the Progressives, compared to their critiques of politics, the media, and the identity of the ordinary voter.

Figure 1. Ideal citizenship

turn for paying too much attention to trivial content in the media and too little attention to other sources of serious political discussion.

Since the mid-twentieth century, scholars have attempted to adjust or salvage the Progressive ideal of citizenship. The typical move has been additive, to subscribe to the active-rational citizen model while proposing that it exists in a mixture with something called the *subject* (as in "royal subject") or *parochial* model of passive citizenship (Almond and Verba 1963; see also Newman, Just and Crigler 1992). Although it attempts to balance the contradictory needs of democratic governments – to govern citizens and yet to receive legitimacy from them – the additive remedy sets aside, without effectively removing, the need to rethink citizenship. The data accumulated in the past century suggest that for most individuals, citizenship has little to do with productive efficiency, instrumental activity, or rational deliberation.

This chapter presents another view, using ideas that key thinkers developed during the era that defined the citizenship ideal: the pragmatists William James and John Dewey, the sociologist Max Weber, the phenomenologist Edmund Husserl, and Alfred Schutz, who combined phenomenology and sociology. Their thinking emerged partly in response to and incorporated elements from turn-of-the-century reform movements (James, for example, called Godkin the most influential thinker of the era). Their writings point to methods for analyzing the subjective experience of citizens in modern democracies, based on concepts that stand in sharp contrast to the assumptions usually applied in market or voter surveys.

After reviewing the literature for discussions of citizenship, I set out to test it against the lived experience of citizens by examining narrative accounts of citizenship a century after it was redefined. In the spring of 1998, nineteen citizens living and studying in Europe wrote brief life histories of their experiences with politics and the media. Roughly balanced by gender, the group included young adults, ages 18 to 29, and two older adults. Most came together in the Netherlands and were citizens of, native to, or long resident in one of ten European Union states. Six came from the Americas, and three came from nearby states in Europe and the Middle East. For each region, some were children of immigrants, and some were members of the working class.

Specifically, the group included 11 women and 8 men, whose average age had a mode of 24 and a mean of 25, including the older adults. Most were enrolled in the Access Program of the University of Amsterdam or held EU Erasmus scholarships, but three participants living in Spain were not involved in those programs. The Europeans haled from Austria, Belgium, Denmark, France, Germany, Italy, the Netherlands, Norway, Spain, and the United Kingdom. The nearby states were Bulgaria, Lithuania, and Israel, and the Americans came from the mainland

United States, Canada, and Puerto Rico (one participant held dual citizenship in Canada and the United Kingdom). The US participants included a Midwesterner from a working-class family and a New Yorker of a family that might be considered from the intelligentsia. (Eight of the Amsterdam life history essays are available on line: http://www.uic.edu/depts/comm/lifehist/).

The analysis of the life histories followed an inductive process adapted from the Chicago School sociologist Herbert Blumer (1933). After a collaborating researcher gathered the group of documents, each investigator initially read every essay and independently compiled a list of observations about the use of language and recurring themes. From these lists, we constructed an annotated inventory, which a graduate student then used to examine each essay for the presence or absence of the observations and to select illustrative examples. At the same time, we mapped the narrative structure of each essay, dividing it into its constituent stories (the essays typically recounted between five and seven of these) and indicating the elements of each one (based on the structures proposed by Labov 1972, as elaborated in Reissman 1993). Based on these analyses, I built a composite narrative. We then met with the entire group of participants and presented to them the initial analyses for their approval. Based on their input, I made adjustments in the analysis to produce the present chapter, which includes specific examples, direct quotations, and significant variations. In short, the following analysis is based on observations about which the participants and the three researchers first reached consensus.

It is important to note that the participants, as a group of varied individuals, were unusually articulate. In fact, they make the most likely candidates for the high levels of involvement envisioned for ideal citizens. Although they come from many distinct backgrounds and life experiences, they came to politics and treat citizenship in similar ways, which the political socialization literature would describe as typical (see Conover and Searing 1994): They think through their political involvement, react for and against certain kinds of policies, rely on talk with friends more than on the media for political information, and describe political choices that seem reasonable. Nevertheless, this analysis attempts to highlight another dimension to their narrative accounts, another side that survey research on political socialization would tend to dismiss.

Their life-history accounts share that side with hundreds of similar documents collected over the past two decades (Barnhurst and Wartella 1991, 1998; Barnhurst 1998, 2000). These young citizens at the end of the twentieth century are clearly familiar with the rational, model citizen, but they point out how their own encounters with citizenship differ from the ideal. First, they do not usually experience the media and political life as rational activities. Although phenomenology, psychology, and sociology a century ago held tenaciously to rationality, scholars did acknowledge a large (and largely unexplored) region of human experience outside the zone of reason. Second, rather than a focus of intentional thought and action, the young adults experience citizenship and the media as a condition very close to what James (1890) called the fringe. Scholars a century ago treated the fringe as a residual category, but they did make initial attempts to name and describe it. Finally, the young citizens' experiences of media and politics at the century's end appear to depend on emotion, a key ingredient anticipated by scholars of the earlier period.

Individuals from Europe and the Americas, in different detail but with similar challenges, reflect the concept of citizenship and its closely related ally, identity. The European Union seeks identity citizenship as a means to bind the Union itself. As noted previously, the American ideal of citizenship was a creature of the national constitution, which left to the states the task of working out the legal details. Likewise, the Union seeks a European identity that sits steady alongside national and other regional identities. Just as the United States seeks unity through diversity, the European Union aims to maintain the balance between supranational and national needs. In a comparison of the concept of cultural citizenship and European identity, Juan M. Delgado-Moreira (2000: 23) suggests that cultural citizenship is the "right to cultural difference and participation in Democracy", but European identity imposes the "need to combine national identities in a concentric system under a shared global identity". The same problem arises for a United States with multiple ethnicities but a shared sense of national self.

Media as fringe condition

In his *Principles of Psychology,* James (1890) defines meaning as thought's object: "all that thought thinks, just as thought thinks it" (quoted in Wilshire 1968: 120). The ultimate object (what Husserl 1927, calls *noema*) James defines as a pervasive sense of the world's presence, occupying the outer fringe of all thought and providing a necessary precondition for thought. The fringe exists at the margins, in unfocused awareness, not at the center of attention and judgment. Ordinary citizens since the Progressive Era have come under reproach for leaving too much of politics and serious political analysis in the fringe, while focusing attention on facile media content. Godkin (1898) complains that reading papers is all the new generation of citizens do to inform themselves. In life history accounts, young adults often begin with the observation that the media existed as a fringe condition of their early lives (Barnhurst and Wartella 1998).

In typical fashion, a male in his early 30s from Germany begins his life history by writing, "I cannot remember when I watched the evening news for the first time, but I know that my parents watched regularly". He then turns to the moment when watching news came into focused attention:

> I remember that I was around five or six years old when my grandmother was shocked during a visit that "the child" was allowed to watch those horrible pictures about the things happening in the world, and from that time on I wasn't allowed to watch the news for a couple of years. – Clemens Schoell

Note how the intervention of authority separated out Schoell from the ordinary flow of his world and placed him in a separate and subordinate category – the child (in quotation marks) – before banishing him. Phenomenologically, a person's experience of the world has these two aspects, a "general indeterminate sense" and a "sense determining itself according to particular realities" (Husserl 1927:27). The room I am sitting in (my kitchen in Chicago) provides a fringe condition (dishes in the drain, spring sunshine reflecting across the wall) for this moment's particular reality (that of my role as writer, operating a computer and focusing on life-history typescripts). At another time (doing the dishes or wiping the walls), I place the room itself in focus, its condition becoming the particular reality (that of my role as scrub-man cleaning the kitchen).

To come to know the world in consciousness, Husserl suggests, individuals must put brackets around some portion of it. James (1890) argues that one becomes aware of the fringe only when expectations of it are disappointed. A 24-year-old from Austria introduces her life history with a brief story about ill health pushing media into her zone of awareness:

> "Am dam des" was the name of an Austrian TV show that I got to watch only when I was home during the day, which was normally when I got my annual cold. Enjoying that treat of getting to watch TV in the middle of the day is about my first media memory. – Ulla Gahn

Periods of watching television clearly took place before (and after) illness provided an occasion, a bracket within her life world, for the media program to be a treat. Yet the story conveys something ritualistic about the event, which happened "only when" and "normally". The cold was "annual", but she could not predict its arrival. The interplay of expectations and surprise shifted her consciousness, making her body the center of attention and eligible for special treatment, including a shift in watching television to "the middle of the day".

In the second story of her narrative, Gahn describes herself as a "book-rat" who "was always eager to hear, read or see stories". Allowed to watch television only for a weekly series, she "sat in front of the TV with my brother and sister, and afterwards we went straight to bed". The ritual had its parallel each night when they were read a bedtime picture book or "listened to the children's radio good-night story". The contents of these media, although the focus of attention, quickly fade, and what remains is the condition that defined a routine in the life's world. Gahn later recalls getting her first magazine subscription, for *Staffette*: "I guess I liked it, although I don't remember the precise content now". The act of subscribing brings the magazine into the bracketed zone of attention, but then the magazine (as media) fades into the fringe, as a mere condition, a container for content that, in turn, she forgets except for a faint memory of good feeling.

Being pictured or named on television or in the press stands out as a signal event in many stories young adults tell of their eventual conversion into regular news consumers (Barnhurst and Wartella 1991). In his second story, Clemens Schoell describes winning a national painting contest in late childhood (pictured in the local newspaper) and getting a day off school to travel to Bonn, where he was allowed to ask then-chancellor Willy Brandt a question (filmed by a youth program). The attention of the media put an accent on the conditions surrounding and reaffirming the lived experience itself. The media heighten the form and the resulting mood, sometimes spilling over into the content of that experience, but the operations of the media usually remain in the zone of inattention, at the fringe. In his evaluation (to use Labov's term for the narrative element) of this story, Schoell remarks that being on television "was quite exciting in those days", when only the national channel was broadcasting. The power of media to confer importance Schoell already understood. The fringe condition provided a "halo of emotional values and irrational implications which themselves remain ineffable" (Schutz 1970:97).

Early in his thinking Husserl equated intuitive, unhistorical, everyday experience with the *life world,* which he later redefined as "the experience of the actually present, concrete, historical world", including its culture (quoted in Bernet, Kern and Marbach 1993:222). Through bracketing, individuals divide that world into what Schutz (1970:252–53) calls realms of experience, with distinctive provinces:

> Each province of meaning... has its particular cognitive style... characterized by a specific tension of consciousness (from the full awakeness in the reality of everyday life to sleep in the world of dreams), by a specific time-perspective, by a specific form of experiencing oneself, and, finally, by a specific form of sociality.

The participants describe the media not as a separate world but as part of the environment surrounding either personal action or witnessed content (actions by others depicted in the media). For the media aspect of their experience, the "tension of consciousness" is closer to the world of dreams, with its combination of heightened awareness and distractedness. The time perspective is the imperfect – the *always* (or *never*) in the present and the *used to* in the past. When telling stories about the media, the participants place their descriptions in the orientation (Labov's 1972 label for the setting for events) or the evaluation (for the concluding meaning) elements of the narrative structure, not in complicating actions or resolutions that occur; that is, they place media as ambiance at the margin rather than as main-event at the center of rational action.

The emergence of new mediated communication in recent decades, from cell phones that transmit television images to multiple channel satellite systems, has contributed to the general belief in a more-complicated life world for all. The younger generations, while managing these systems well, face regular accusations of giving up their agency to them, allowing games to dominate, television to take over, or both. In this view, the media fringes are moving to the center and becoming core locations for the young, as well as the channels for sending them messages about citizenship and involvement. But the relationship is not unidirectional: the media and the social in fact affect each other (see Silverstone 1997). The examples of lived experience presented here, at the level of the individual life world, are glimpses of the interactions among belief systems, the media, and behaviors, a perspective not as available in quantitative or survey studies (Livingstone 1998).

Politics as center and periphery

Like the media, politics also begins at the fringes of awareness during childhood. In his third story, Clemens Schoell narrates haltingly, conveying how unsure he is about how politics – in his case the peace movement in Germany and related media coverage – moved into conscious attention around 1980. "It is difficult to say how the media were connected to this process, but I am sure the starting point was somewhere in family discussions". Family routines consistently provide the condition that leads into attention to politics in the media, at least in Europe and the United States (Barnhurst 2000). In her third story, Ulla Gahn writes of her slowly growing awareness "mostly because my parents were involved in community and regional politics, and I just happened to be there when they discussed things". Schoell says that, during his period of political activism, the media occupied "the periphery":

> The stickers you got on the demonstrations, all the flyers, newspapers, magazines of extreme left wing groups I had never heard of before. And of course the masses on the evening news, taking visible power of our capital. And you were part of it,

all those people who entered two busses in the morning to take the long trip from our village to the capital.

Once politics entered their lives sometime in the teen years, the participants begin to relate stories that reveal a fully formed realm of experience. Entering those provinces involves awakened attention, chronological time, a heightened sense of self-at-risk, and identification with a cohesive group. Schoell reports knowing us-versus-them: "that 'we' were doing the 'right thing' while others were reading stupid teenage magazines". He exults that "we also got the girls", had interesting stories to tell, and won the opprobrium of teachers: "it's sometimes even more fun to be blamed as 'Moscow's agents' by conservative teachers than to be the good guy".

In the political world, the media also effect shifts in meaning. Schoell tells of his first speech at a public demonstration. Despite nervousness he went on stage, but the wind blew away his notes. He felt inadequate speaking without structure or facts, but then the media intervened. The local newspaper ran "a huge article on page one... including a picture of me". Not only did the coverage multiply his audience by many score, but the newspaper's description of "a spontaneous, fresh, and emotional speech" changed his judgment of the experience. When Ulla Gahn's essay turns to politics, the press likewise moves to center stage, again as the focus of correction. Her parents had often pointed out how newspapers reported "something completely different" from what actually happened. Later she and her friends wrote a letter to the editor in response to a critical review of a school concert, because "we just had to set things straight".

Despite these experiences, self-identity as citizens remains an unfocused element of the lives of participants for some time. Other recent research suggests the transitory quality of identity claims (McCrone 1998), and so the stories not only allow the observation of lived moments in transit, but also provide insights into how shifts in identification emerge from changing environments. For Gahn and Schoell, travel abroad provides the bracketing needed to find their national identities (in line with the survey claims noted in the Introduction to this volume). Gahn says she decided to finish her diploma in Canada, where she confronted life as an immigrant: "I saw how differently people get treated, just by the color of their passports and the images of their home countries". Schoell describes a trip to Cairo at age 15 as "the first time I felt 'German'". He uses quotation marks to separate out German-ness for contemplation. In both cases, travel imposed a loss of citizenship that they had previously taken for granted. Schoell writes that abroad he "experienced things like democracy, welfare-state and fair justice, and police... by their absence". The narratives sometimes foreground the media when describing political action but not when depicting political identity. Schoell says that "it is difficult to tell what role the media had in the process, because the most important for me was personal experience and personal conversation". As noted earlier, exploring difference across Europe provided the individual with a greater sense of tolerance and support for diversity, but the opportunities to experience different cultures and languages vary, given the national constraints on educational, economic, and social domains. In one European study, for example, English and Spanish respondents had less experience of languages and travel. In the United Kingdom, two thirds spoke only their native tongue, compared to localities within countries such as Austria and Germany, where 95 percent of respondents spoke another language (see van der Veen 2002).

After childhood, politics and political identity remain in the periphery until they can no longer be taken for granted. Within the political province of meaning, the media turn from fringe to focus on a fulcrum of judgment: when the media get the story wrong (for good or ill).

For those who grow up in one country but whose families came from another, identity becomes political and moves into the center of attention much earlier. A child of Korean parents born in the United States, writing at age eighteen, remembers being "bombarded with... images of what it means to be American" from her earliest years. The sources included such icons as Kentucky Fried Chicken ("the American meal for my parents and me"), the music of the Beatles (she had no idea at first that they came from Britain), Clint Eastwood films, and Marlboro cigarettes. The complication in her narrative arises because the products provided images of the culture but no interaction with its people. That isolation becomes apparent when she prepares to enter Kindergarten. In a children's book, *Morris Goes to School,* about a moose who "goes to school and gets teased", she encountered –

> images of strange coat closets, blackboards, tables and groups of children with shades of hair in multiple colors. I began to wonder why I didn't have blond hair. It even dawned on me at one point to ask why there weren't any Asian children in the book.... I remember being afraid that I would be the moose of the class. – Jennifer Y. Lee

And in fact, she does face continued loneliness and other problems, from small (being scolded for taking her shoes off when entering a room) to large (missing out on sleep-overs that conflicted with her parents' beliefs). "I excelled in school, but social acceptance was a different story", she writes. Throughout her extended meditation on the politics of American imagery, she never mentions elections, information, or political activity, until the closing evaluation, where she describes writing a college paper and then giving a speech about her immigration experi-

ences. "Finally", she writes, "some recognition". The acknowledgment itself is political and comes from herself, as well as from the school.

The American population overall is among the least traveled outside national
borders of any nation (setting aside for the moment the large internal distances
of the continent), and yet at the same time US residents hold onto a heritage as
a nation of immigrants. Research in Europe has suggested that states fostering
less travel or linguistic diversity (such as the United Kingdom and Spain) showed
less tolerance in some cases toward immigrants and ethnic minorities (see Fossum 2006; van der Veen 2002). Insights from stories beyond Europe would seem
relevant to the European experience. Local issues have universal application, as
long-serving Speaker of the House of Representatives Tip O'Neill observed: "All
politics is local".

Consider now a 22-year-old whose parents immigrated from India to France.
He considers images from when he was nine, the assassination of Indira Gandhi
impelling his "first step toward political awareness" and leading him to romanti-
cize his parents' homeland. Then, as a result of Rajiv Gandhi's murder, he began
to feel antagonistic:

> I was embarrassed to be Indian. I was ashamed at their inability to clean up their
> politics.... the concept of nationalism appalled me, and I began to look at India
> more critically, never losing my interest for this country but feeling less a citizen
> of it than I had been before. – Shayan Sanyal

After each event, writing a paper for school brought politics out of the fringes and
into rational awareness. Then he confronted difference directly, in France when
skinheads attacked and beat him up as he returned from his high school home-
coming dance, and in the United Kingdom when he began to use internet news
groups to raise objections to the "racist and fascistic platform" of the French party,
Front National. "I am French", he writes. "Well, that's what my passport says. I
don't really think I am. What I mean to say is that I don't really feel French". He
later adds: "No, I am not European.... Furthermore, I am not a world citizen and
don't aspire to be". Through the internet, he says, he has found others who –

> are as "citizen-less" as I am; I guess that together we form some sort of commu-
> nity,... a virtual community; a community that has allowed me to express and
> keep track of political issues relating to two countries that I will always be invari-
> ably attached to but will never be a full-fledged citizen of, in either the ethnic or
> political sense.

He does hold legal citizenship in France, but his experiences with racism, like those
of Lee, have taught him a distinction. Lee says her family began to feel American once they achieved economic success: "We obtained it", she writes: "The nice

house, the cars and the backyard (but no picket fence)". The image comes close to the ideal, with one gap, the lack of a protective barrier of whiteness. Although they confront the political world much younger, the children of immigrants share with others a common definition of politics as an image infused with identity and emotion. In Weber's words, "a nation is a community of sentiment" (1958: 176). That emotional dimension of their experiences is just what critics since the Progressive Era have decried as they defined citizenship as a rational and purposive activity.

Emotional politics

One's legal citizenship does not spring from reason but from an accident of birth. A child enters not a life world of instrumental action but a political realm of someone else's choosing, which becomes a source of attachment, fondness, and, later, identity. In her life history, a young adult from the Midwest expresses nostalgia over the "simple and happy" time growing up in the United States. The mind may *conceive* of others' citizenship in the abstract but *remembers* one's own, as James (1890: 239) suggested: "Remembrance is like direct feeling; its object is suffused with a warmth and intimacy to which no object of mere conception ever attains". A 26-year-old from the countryside in Denmark describes her small village as the center of the world, that is, until about age ten when she discovered it "was far away from everything", from "the queen, the national Museum, the Royal Ballet, and the Tivoli" as well as from "the rest of the world".

Her life world then filled with inexplicable juxtapositions. Her parents read the newspaper and watched the evening news regularly, and the distant yet powerful world invaded her cozy surroundings.

> The contrast between my "cocoon world" and then the world as I saw it through the media every day was difficult for me to comprehend. I often remember being terrified after watching the news, and in fact, some of the most vivid and scary memories from my childhood were caused by confusion and by the way I mixed up... the two worlds. – Trine Vrang Laursen

Under the care of parents, she encountered a political realm of presumed safety that eventually fell under a shadow. The media revealed the contradiction. A Canadian, 28, recalls watching documentaries that depicted "a paradise for a young kid", but "one day I turned the channel and saw what is now etched in my mind for good" – the slaughter of bottle-nose dolphins off the coast of Japan.

> The bay ran red with blood, crested with salt foam whipped up by the thrashing tails of the panicking dolphins. This struck me as odd. After the initial revulsion dissipated, I was confused over how television could, on a "Nature" episode, portray dolphins as intelligent, highly developed beings and then, rather coolly in a newscast, simply report this "occurrence" and show ten seconds from some outraged "activist"... – John Lironi

Despite being "confused", his judgment of the event clearly takes a stand against the cool brevity of the news report. Feeling preceded reason. Husserl (1981:23) defined feeling as a mode of valuing and said, "Through reflection, instead of grasping [those values] simply,... we grasp the corresponding subjective experiences". A 27-year-old from Bulgaria, recalling the death of Leonid Breshnev, describes how feeling entered in:

> we were flooded with mourning music... and people paying their last respects and his funeral and how the Soviet people grieved for him.... Then I became extremely sad also — I was in fourth or fifth grade.... I was absolutely carried away with the emotions of these foreign people, I was crying in front of the television, experiencing a great loss of I-don't-know-what.... My parents were cool about this whole tragic event. I even thought, "Oh, how insensitive and cold the adult people are". – Daniela Petlekova

The essay by a 22-year-old from Lithuania also describes Breshnev's death, remarking on how "very strange" it seemed. In such cases, the "material sensations actually present may have a weaker influence... than ideas of remoter facts" (James 1902:61). Laursen recounts her earliest memory of the funeral of Egyptian President Sadat, which she found "mysterious and absolutely horrifying". Sanyal, the 22-year-old from France, recalls the assassination of Indira Gandhi: "the episode marked me", he writes. "I can still remember my parents dropping their cutlery on their plates, a clang that resonated in the silence".

In life history essays, the political realm forces itself into the peaceful life world of childhood with the shock of death or tragedy witnessed through the media (Barnhurst 1998). Usually the events involve national figures, although some bring private lives into the public eye, such as the accidents recounted by two women, 25 and 21, from Norway and the Americas, whose kinsmen came into the news. A Puerto Rican, 24, starts her essay with the police murder in the Cerro Maravilla of two students affiliated with the cause of national independence, which shocked her into awareness of politics and death and then reverberated through later experiences when her family got tied in government documents to the independence movement.

Faced with the absurd juxtaposition of an encompassing state that can sustain life and yet rests on the power to destroy life (see Weber 1958) and of a media environment in which the capacity to show the wonders of the world rests on the power to shock, the narrators of these life stories often express fear. A 23-year-old from Italy refers repeatedly to "institutionalized murder".

Laursen's life history, after contrasting the "cocoon world" with the assassination of Sadat, tells five stories about her encounters with fear. Because of his rhetoric of evil empire, she became terrified of President Reagan, pictured in the Danish newspapers "as a lunatic with a wild expression in his eyes and 'pet-rockets' sticking out of his pockets". Her parents' calming argument "that he would not press 'the big red button', because naturally he did not want to die himself" backfired after Reagan remarked in a news conference "that some would survive and that it might be necessary to sacrifice the rest". Laursen could no longer sleep at night and for months found herself arrested by fear "every time I heard a plane approach the nearby airport, because I was certain that they would drop the bomb on Denmark". Later, because of the Chernobyl accident, she "wondered if it was safe every time I ate a sandwich". Then the campaign against AIDS began, and she says of her friends, "we all acted really cool.... But really we were petrified". Soon after came the Gulf conflict, when she felt "tense and restless" and needed to monitor the hostilities on CNN.

These fears eventually led her to obey the requirements of informed citizenship. She signed a petition demanding the closure of a Swedish nuclear plant, followed political news, debated issues with classmates, joined a political party, and attended its meetings. As Weber (1958: 79) asserts, "in reality, obedience is determined by highly robust motives of fear and hope".

Flashes of defiance

The life histories highlight a common response to the frightening political realm: an effort to assert one's free agency. For the participants from newly independent states, the lack of political freedom parallels the need for (and growth of) personal independence. At age eight, the Lithuanian spent a summer in her ancestral village and came upon her grandfather listening to the radio alone late at night. "His face was very strange, very serious", she writes. Ordered to bed, she stayed behind the door and overheard words such as *White House* and *Washington*. He was listening, she later learned, to the Voice of America.

After recalling the rise of Mikhail Gorbachev and expectations for change, she describes witnessing the re-establishment of an independent state as "one of the most memorable events in all my life". When the Soviet army intervened, she joined her countrymen in public demonstrations.

> All that night, warming ourselves near the fires and drinking hot tea, we listened to the Voice of America, Radio Free Europe, and other Western radio stations (all our national stations were closed by the Soviets).... thousands of Lithuanians, gathering at the parliament, government, and other important sites... resolved to defend their freedom... – Laura Gvozdaite

Her narrative thus closes the circle, from her grandfather's (illicit) to her own (open) defiance. Several of the life histories form similar chiasms. Bulgarian Daniela Petlekova, who mourned Breshnev's death in childhood, next recalls –

> high school and the forbidden voices of Radio Free Europe and the BBC.... The secrecy of the action and the danger of being discovered (we were threatened with being expelled from school and turned in to the police) made the most extensive listeners heroes. Nevertheless,... we were not so much listening... as talking about the listening itself.

She, too, witnessed the Communist breakdown and arrival of free elections, with the inevitable backlash. Her narrative culminates with a return to radio, but this time as a worker on the production staff of Reuters, trying to form an independent view of the violent demonstrations at the parliament in Sofia.

Even among the survivors of national crises, focused attention on politics comes intermittently, never in constant, sustained fashion as envisioned for the rational-active citizenry. As Dewey (1927: 123) asked rhetorically, Does the public "come into being only in periods of marked social transition when crucial alternative issues stand out...?" Schutz (1970) used Kierkegaard's term *leap* to characterize the transitions in the intentional life from one province of meaning to another. The leaps into the political realm came less often for those in stable democracies, and their periods of inattention lasted longer. Dewey (1927: 137) observed that the history of local politics "shows in most cases a flare-up of intense interest followed by a period of indifference". Laursen finishes her narrative of fearful memories with a story of living in Britain and sharing a flat with coworkers whose television agenda ran from "Eastenders" to "Noel's House Party". "I was absolutely amazed when I went home for Christmas to find out that the USSR had been dissolved in the meantime. I did not know".

The looking-glass reflection of sporadic flares in the political landscape occurs when the life histories describe personal appearances in the news. At the end of his narrative, Canadian Lironi recounts one such moment, when he joined protesters blockading the Clayquot Sound near Vancouver Island:

> I was not a "protester tourist" or a life-long city dweller. I have worked, lived, and played in these forests since I was born. My home town was... a lumber town of a few thousand, only 80 kilometers away....

> On the day of my arrest, my face was beamed... around the province.... The cop
> was my age and shaking just as hard as I was. After I was processed and released
> by the Royal Canadian Mounted Police, I went to a hotel... and decided to watch
> some TV. There I was, in full frame among other protesters.... "Radical anti-log-
> ging protesters", "urban dwellers dictating to country folk", "destroyers of the pro-
> vincial economy".... people I worked with, other students, neighbors, my parents'
> neighbors — all they saw was a young guy with long hair defying authority. Prob-
> ably on drugs, probably with a criminal record.

Once again the news got the story wrong, but the attention ends quickly, and soon
Lironi returns to inattention: "Since then, I have to admit", he writes, "I have mel-
lowed out a bit". The defiance that characterizes the political realm often involves
resisting political news itself in the narratives. A young adult from Italy recalls his
mother listening to the morning news on Radio Radicale. Sometimes when he
asked for music instead, she would put a tape on the radio-cassette player:

> The Doors was more like me. It was something I could relate to easier than the
> news.... I could not understand the meaning but I could really feel something.
> Whereas the buzz of the news was nothing else, just buzz at that moment. –
> Emanuele Salerno

Choosing music not only felt better but also represented autonomy, which he as-
sociates explicitly with acquiring his own radio-cassette. He writes that the radio
"transfers information, energy to you, which then has an emotional effect". Weber
(1958: 62) called such choices, which relate ideas to the material world, "elective
affinity".

Only later, after studying English and receiving a book of lyrics, could Salerno
"understand better the liberationist and alternative goals touched in the songs"
of Jim Morrison and the Doors. He returns to the theme with a story about his
grandfather's radio and another program with a different buzz he couldn't understand. He made sense of the politics later, and he uses the word "*sense*, meaning
emotionally connected". In the coda to his narrative, he concludes: "Probably all
that I have experienced drove me now to consider the freedom in thinking – in
word and expression". One's affinity – the passions and intuitions springing from
the fringe – anticipates and fixes the operations of reason, James (1902: 475) said:
"It finds arguments for our conviction; for indeed it *has* to find them. It ampli-
fies..., defines..., dignifies it and lends it... plausibility".

A sense of the loss of one's freedom can provide the most sustained engagement with the political sphere. Dewey (1927: 168) noted that "sometimes the
sense of external oppression, as by censorship... arouses intellectual energy and
excites courage" (see also the discursus on the conditions of freedom in Weber

1958:70–74). A 24-year-old from Belgium structures his entire narrative on the assertion of autonomy:

> I remember being in first grade. My teacher punished me for talking with a friend by covering my mouth with a sticker. I had to keep this terrible thing on my mouth the entire day. – Martijn Bakx

He concludes that the event, which colors the remainder of his life narrative, "introduced me to the principle of politics". In each succeeding story, he recalls other events that reinforced his commitment to equal and free expression, from trivial fights with his brother over the remote control, through song lyrics he loved during high school, to the rights he learned from American films. When South Africa won the world rugby championship, he saw Nelson Mandela "cheering like a little child". He imagined himself, "a real sports addict", in jail for decades unable to cheer with others, and "it made me feel one with Nelson for a moment". Freedom of expression bred unity, and that led him to see himself as "a citizen of the world". It is this sense of unity that, despite the negative course of their conception of citizenship, the Progressives saw as the ultimate ideal. Royce (1969) called it The Hope of the Great Community (in an essay under that title).

In life history accounts, the sense of unified community marks the high points in experiences with the political world through the media (Barnhurst and Wartella 1991, 1998; Barnhurst 1998, 2000). A young adult from the Netherlands, despite her lack of interest in politics, describes herself watching news dutifully with her father and seeing the observance of two minutes of silence, when the nation pauses each year to remember those fallen during World War II and the Queen places flowers on the grave of –

> the unknown soldier, but as a little girl I wasn't sure how to think about him, because I didn't know what he looked like. I also remember getting mad at the cars I heard driving down the street. How dare they...? – Charlotte Alofs

She recalls her grandmother's stories of the Dutch resistance and of a brother who died in the German concentration camp in Holland. Her grandmother showed her several documents, including a woman's account of a conversation with a prisoner the day before his execution. "She asked him if he was scared and he replied that he wasn't, because it was an honor to die for his country. This prisoner was my grandmother's brother. He was eighteen".

Her grandmother also showed her his last letter, written with calm formality. Alofs remembers "being amazed" at such fortitude in the face of death. "It made me feel proud to be a part of that family, and it made me feel proud to be Dutch", she writes. "It gave me a sense of *us,* meaning my people". Weber (1958:27) says that "it is immensely moving" when a person of any age "really feels such responsibility with heart and soul" and continues –

> somewhere he reaches the point where he says, "Here I stand; I can do no other". That is something genuinely human and moving. And every one of us who is not spiritually dead must realize the possibility of finding himself at some time in that position.

Alofs herself wondered if she "would have felt the same way if I had been in that position. Would I have joined the resistance, would I have thought it an honor to die for my country? Would any of my friends think that?" She then recalls visiting the Anne Frank House and being struck by the physical presence of the bookcase entrance to the hiding place and overwhelmed by photographs of concentration camps. "I could barely look at the pictures", she writes, expressing surprise that she still remembers them exactly, "and I don't think I will ever forget".

Her own encounter with war occurred during the 1990s Gulf conflict, watching CNN coverage that "gave me a sense of us, the 'good guys', against them". She felt "almost glad" that Holland sent a ship, and she writes, "I think I was proud as a person from a very small country to belong with a superpower like America.... 'So this is what war is like in the nineties,' I remember thinking to myself". The violence of the Gulf conflict filtered through only later, and then only because she saw visual images of a hostage soldier being released. The overwhelming presence of the United States, which a 24-year-old from Canada, for example, calls "the real measure of status and power" in his consciousness as a citizen, underscores the interplay of defiance and unity in the essays.

Alofs returns at last to unity, concluding her narrative with the moving story of her first commemoration day after arriving in Amsterdam to study. "So there I was together with thousands of other people being silent for two minutes", she writes. She describes the incredible stillness, the diversity of the people, their unity of purpose, and the preponderance of youth, despite how long ago the events transpired. "It didn't matter, we still cared and we were not going to let this be forgotten". Like others of her generation, she experienced community despite her professed lack of interest in politics and failure to take measurable action herself.

Old ideas, new experiences

Most theory in media studies proposes a rational relationship between users, media forms, and content: the media disseminating and the audience responding, all to accomplish economic, political, or cultural ends. The experiences participants described here have another quality; their practice differs from theory. In night vision, the more the eyes focus on an object, the less visible it becomes; only by avoiding a steady gaze directly at an object can the eyes detect it. In reading the life history documents, I found those most focused on citizenship less informative about their subject but full of intriguing insights about the media operating in the periphery of politics. Likewise those focused most directly on the media contained the most penetrating image of the fringe experience of political life.

Considered schematically, the life histories present the media as a background for personal identity, citizenship, and politics (see Figure 2). Identity for these young adults plays out more or less engulfed by the media. Politics exists as a kind of media genre, largely divorced from personal experiences associated with the participants' identities. Citizenship is also more or less disconnected from personal experiences, although it can be the link between identity and politics existing at a remove from the life world. What political experiences the participants described took place within the zone at least influenced by media, and the media came into focus usually as objects of politics.

Findings from cross-European survey research on the political participation of youth (the EUYOUPART project 2003–2005) confirm the importance of the media as a source of information about politics and reveal national differences. Respondents in all countries prefer television as a medium, but those in Finland and Estonia use the internet more often as a source of political information. Radio still plays a key role in Austria and Germany (Muxel 2005).

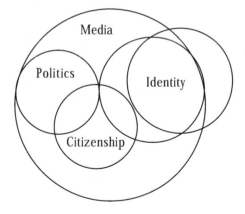

The experience of citizenship as a marginal aspect of identity among the young adults, who feel more or less surrounded by the media but distanced from politics

Figure 2. Citizenship as experienced

What the life histories show, however, is that long after the contents of the media are lost, the surrounding conditions remain, bearing just a trace of residual feeling. The events that manage to survive tend to have (or to take on) visual form in the participants' memories and continue to exert an influence as an ideal (or counter-ideal) image, not as a set of logical arguments. The life histories present a picture of citizenship, while defining self-identity as another, largely separate image. The picture of political life that emerges from the fringes is full of clashes and empty argument, stubborn in the face of competing values. Emotion precedes reason, fear and hope in some cases goading the narrators into actions aligned with ideal citizenship (but usually not). The leaps from one realm to another accommodate long periods of quiescence, interrupted by moments of defiance that allow for the dialectic of autonomy and (comm)unity.

The analysis required a constant sense of the whole (of, for example, the media surround, rather than a focus on one particular medium or category of content). It inspired not a search for stasis but for patterns in the continual changes and ongoing adjustments. In short, the life histories suggest not an instrumental use of media for gratification or maintenance of community (although these functions exist) but a sort of media environment, a space where a set of dynamic systems operate. Like any natural system, the media environment deserves closer attention, demands appreciation and respect, and merits conservation. Scholars and activists who examine the media and citizenship have an impact on that environment, even when doing primarily theoretical work.

The social thinkers I read from a century ago held in common a view of citizenship. They did not envision social life, politics, or the media operating primarily at the fringes of consciousness, except in cases worthy of censure. Schutz, for example, described the ideal type of well-informed citizen. Unlike the man on the street, who "accepts his sentiments and passions as guides", the citizen-type was fully capable to "decide who *is* a competent expert" and "make up his mind after having listened to opposing expert opinions" (1970: 239–41). Although James (1890: 247, footnote) argued that "we cognize through feeling", the legacy of the reforms that culminated in the Progressive Era moved politics away from emotion. At a time when many American workers preferred a corrupt politician, whom they could chase out of office, to an expert mandarin, who would look down on them and whom they could not remove (see Weber 1958: 18), reformers championed the ideal of merit-based civil service, which placed a premium on objective measures and expertise. (Perhaps the American workers had it right.) Another Progressive reform, the secret or so-called *Australian* ballot, hid the emotional foundations of citizenship behind the curtains of the polling booth, concealed in the interior of the individual (Schudson 1998).

Regarding the media as a social institution, Dewey (1927: 180) decried –

> the triviality and "sensational" quality of so much of what passes as news... crime, accident, family rows, personal clashes and conflicts are... breaches of continuity; they supply the element of shock which is the strictest meaning of sensation; they are the *new* par excellence.

And he worried that the individual had become inured to "this method of collecting, recording, and presenting social changes" (1927: 180). Weber (1958: 96–97) noted that the "conditions that accompany journalistic work... produce those results which have conditioned the public to regard the press with a mixture of disdain and pitiful cowardice" and went on to observe that "our great capitalist newspaper concerns... have been regularly and typically the breeders of political indifference", which accompanies fear and paralyzes thought. Among the reformers, Godkin (1898) noted that newspapers failed to convey public opinion for several reasons. Advertisers, who paid an increasing share of publishing costs, had wrested the attention of newspaper conductors away from readers. The heavy investment in industrial plant (required to establish and operate a press) focused newspaper conductors on the interests of capital (which required high-volume, high-speed production) rather than of citizens. Readers devolved into an audience of buyers, whose opinions were valued as consumers, not as citizens.

The Progressive movement proposed several reforms for the media. Godkin (1896, 1898) more than once pressed the need to create a means other than newspapers to measure public opinion, and he pointed to science as an alternative avenue for discovering how the public formed opinions on new subjects. Others in the movement (e.g., Beard and Beard 1931) echoed his solution, and Lippmann (1922) proposed the creation of scientific intelligence bureaus independent of the press to gauge public opinion. As a further reform, Godkin (1898) recommended higher standards of news gathering and presentation. He criticized newspapers for publishing a multitude of disconnected items, reminiscent of a marketplace that had to move a mass of products quickly. Public opinion forms slowly through prolonged discussion and extended reading, he argued, and to remedy the problems created when democracy expanded to include many new, uninformed voters, journalists needed to present events in priority based on professional judgment.

Like their other projects, Progressive reforms of the media were largely put into place. Over the course of the last century, an extensive industry of survey research firms emerged, dedicated to the measurement of public opinion (Herbst 1994). Some are now affiliated with news businesses, but others are free-standing or based in non-partisan institutions such as universities. At the same time, journalism modernized and its workers professionalized along the lines Progressives recommended. In their presentation of events, newspapers shifted away from the coverage of many, unrelated events (Barnhurst and Mutz 1997), and they began to map the social world according to priorities (Nerone and Barnhurst 1995). The redefinition of journalism to fit the Progressive prescription later spread to broadcast news (Steele and Barnhurst 1996). Other Progressive reforms, such as the abolition of child labor, required legislation or direct government intervention, but the definition of news did not. National policy rarely regulates directly what passes for news.

Among the citizens who wrote life histories examined here, these reforms have done little to move their lives closer to the ideal. Dewey diagnosed the source of the problem: the fitting of new citizens into old conceptions of citizenship. At the time he was writing, scale seemed the principal difference. "We have inherited, in short, local town-meeting practice and ideas. But we live and act and have our being in a continental national state" (1927:111). Outdated political institutions had an impact on individuals: when "the needs of the newly forming public" encounter old, established, and incompatible forms, "there is increasing... apathy, neglect, and contempt" (1927:31). He concluded that apathy results whenever the discrepancy grows "between actual practice and traditional machinery" of politics, making "thousands feel their hollowness even if they cannot make their feeling articulate" (1927:134–135).

The life history narratives echo Dewey's analysis and also indicate a clear discomfort with received forms. A young adult from the United States, for example, describes the world as "so spread apart". A 28-year-old from Canada writes, "I find *citizenship* an outdated, anachronistic ideal". After a century of complaints about the failures of citizens, the current generation responds to citizenship as one would to a chronic grumbler, by dismissing the importance of the complainer and the reality of the complaint, for which Weber coined the appropriate term: "political hypochondria" (1956:62). Dewey listed the symptoms: querulousness, impotent drifting, uneasy snatching at distractions, idealization of old ways, facile optimism, and the intimidation of dissenters (1927:170). As the 24-year-old Canadian concludes, "I feel that blissful acceptance of scathing cynicism is the root of this story, and I suspect this is not the case for myself alone".

What can be done? If the news media create and sustain environments, then there must be room for a symbolic breed of environmentalism. Environmental movements raise consciousness of problems, envision a different world, and then call for action to move from old to new. Much more research is needed to explore both the theory of citizenship and the experiences of citizens in different parts of the world. The analysis presented here has attempted to raise awareness of the conflict between citizenship-as-idealized and the examples of citizenship-as-lived. It is too soon to call for specific actions, but the experiences reported here do make it possible to speculate about how to re-envision citizenship.

Dewey proposed "a subtle, delicate, vivid, and responsive art of communication" in order to "take possession of the physical machinery of transmission and circulation and breathe life into it". He argued, "Artists have always been the real purveyors of news, for it is not the outward happening in itself which is new, but the kindling by it of emotion, perception and appreciation". He then concluded: "Democracy... will have its consummation when free social inquiry is indissolubly wedded to the art of full and moving communication" (1927:184). Although he was critical of publicity for its "extraordinary facility in enlisting" what he called the "emotional partisanship of the masses" (1927:169), he missed a basic distinction, damning the means along with the dishonest ends of those "who have something at stake in having a lie believed" (1927:177). Clearly the essential element Dewey identified is also what young adults today miss: the wedding of political news with the emotional life, which was lost when citizenship was redefined a century ago. Dewey (1927:182) did recognize that "judgments popularly formed on political matters are so important... that there is an enormous premium upon all methods which affect their formation". He hoped that new modes of presentation, springing out of art, would touch a deeper level of people's lives.

Institutional reform could then follow. "The problem", he suggested, "is in the first instance an intellectual [one]: the search for conditions.... When these conditions are brought into being they will make their own forms. Until they come about, it is somewhat futile to consider what political machinery will suit them" (1927:146). Dewey identifies several steps leading eventually to institutional reform: to reevaluate the old and accept new images of citizenship, to create conditions that foster new citizens, and to let institutions move toward the new picture of citizenship. This essay seeks to contribute to the first step by critiquing the old and pointing to some elements of a new model of citizenship.

Re-envisioning citizenship has precedent in theory. Weber (1958:64) suggested the notion of "world images", the ways that specific strata envision social conditions. Schutz (1970:246) observed that the order of things "reveals itself merely in images by analogical apprehending. But the images, once constituted, are taken for granted". Those old images may be replaced. Through something akin to what James (1902:83) called the "ontological imagination", previously "unpicturable beings are realized". Weber's observations seem especially pertinent. He visited America to see the connections between membership in a religious denomination and civic and economic life. He found that what he called church-mindedness was "rapidly dying out" at the beginning of the 20th century (1958:306). As it became irrelevant, membership in voluntary associations replaced it, in "a process of secularization" (1958: 311) that has continued with the decline of association involvement a century later. A new image of citizenship must now take its place.

That new image might place emphasis on the emotional experience of identity. As shown schematically (see Figure 3), the image might acknowledge how the participants understand the media and politics as elements in the fringe. Citizenship might be enlarged to include the many ways individuals resist by, for example, not voting, the ways they withdraw during varying periods between their flashes of engagement, and the ways they feel membership in many levels of community. In some ways, the EUYOUPART project, mentioned earlier, considered idealism and disillusionment in relation to politics, as well as questions of belonging at local, national and supranational levels. European youth generally had low interest in politics and participation in activist groups, but most had an idealistic concept of politics as a means of solving problems. Their disillusionment grew out of the actual practice of politics in concrete situations. Feelings of belonging varied across countries, although the respondents generally ranked a strong sense of affiliation with family the highest and supranational identities (European, world citizen) the lowest. In the United Kingdom and France, youth expressed a stronger sense of affiliation with nation than with town or region, but belonging to town, region and nation were more or less equally important in Italy.

Following Dewey's steps toward reform, what next requires attention is which conditions encourage citizens in that new model. The experiences examined here can suggest a few conditions. First, activities that encourage bringing media and politics out of the fringes and into focused attention caused a shift in the life histories (as in previous studies, see Barnhurst and Wartella 1991, 1998). Several essays, for example, mention school work that invited reflection on politics and the

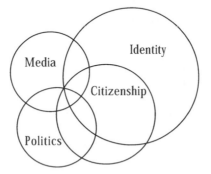

The possibility of citizenship as important to identity, with both less dependent on politics, and the media playing a minor role.

Figure 3. Citizenship as Reimagined

media, and further study could explore how such assignments help make a life project of citizenship. Second, free and open distribution of political ideas and events also had an impact (again as in previous studies). The 26-year-old from Spain became a regular reader after receiving copies of newspapers with parents on an airplane, where attendants distribute the day's edition for free. Shayan Sanyal found the bridge between his childhood in France, his heritage in India, and his life in the United Kingdom through the free access to the internet he received while in college. In each case, news of politics stood outside the usual business of buying and selling, even if only briefly. Although the condition may seem difficult to sustain, political communication requires some insulation from the market, and further study might explore how to make such experiences more widespread. To promote political participation, the EUYOUPART project recommends school activities, which foster political engagement outside of school, and recommends wider use of media that require active reception (such as newspapers and the internet), which help strengthen political involvement (Muxel 2005). Third, the essays point to benefits from the presentation of clear political options (a finding supported in previous cross-national comparisons, Barnhurst 2000). Those who lived through national crises had the clearest sense of their own autonomy, but others also benefited when the media presented more than one ideological option. Further research is again in order, but these three conditions might begin the discussion of how to renew citizenship. Dewey (1927: 200–201) hoped that "Every care would be taken to surround the young with the physical and social conditions which best conduce to release of personal potentialities".

Instead of the logical-rational citizen of Progressive thought, perhaps citizens today *imagine* choices and take *symbolic* actions, within what Husserl called quotation marks. The new political realm might resemble the world of fantasy that Schutz (1970: 257–258) described:

> We have no longer to master the outer world and to overcome the resistance of its objects. We are free from the pragmatic motive..., free also from the bondage of "inter-objective" space and inter-subjective standard time. No longer are we confined within the limits of our actual restorable, or attainable reach.... there are no "possible accomplishments".

In the context of citizenship beyond the end of the twentieth century, Schutz might have been describing activism on the internet. If Dewey had it right, institutional forms, whether through the internet or by some other means, will eventually follow the kinds of citizenship the new generation imagines. Once the image takes shape, perhaps from this and other research on young adults, the institutional logic can follow. As James (1902: 31) argued, "the essence of 'government' " might include a range of things, "one of which is more important at one moment and others at another". It is apparent that the rational side of citizenship is not the most important in young adults' experience. Rather than continue stifling citizens with that ideal, the time has come to set them free.

References

Almond, Gabriel A., and Verba, Sidney. 1963. *The Civic Culture: Political Attitudes and Democracy in Five Nations*. Princeton, NJ: Princeton University Press.

Barnhurst, Kevin G. 2000. *Political Engagement and the Audience for News: Lessons from Spain* [Journalism and Communication Monographs 2.1]. Columbia, SC: AEJMC.

Barnhurst, Kevin G. 1998. "Politics in the fine meshes: Youth, power and media". *Media, Culture and Society 20*(2): 201–218.

Barnhurst, Kevin G., and Mutz, Diana. 1997. "American journalism and the decline of event-centered reporting". *Journal of Communication 47*(4): 27–53.

Barnhurst, Kevin G., and Wartella, Ellen. 1998. "Young citizens, American TV newscasts, and the collective memory". *Critical Studies in Mass Communication 15*(3): 279–305.

Barnhurst, Kevin G., and Wartella, Ellen. 1991. "Newspapers and citizenship: Young adults' subjective experience of newspapers". *Critical Studies in Mass Communication 8*(2): 195–209.

Beard, Charles A. 1949. *American Government and Politics*. 1910. New York: Macmillan.

Beard, Charles A., and Beard, William. 1931. *The American Leviathan: The Republic in the Machine Age*. New York: Macmillan.

Berelson, Bernard R., Lazarsfeld, Paul F., and McPhee, William N. 1954. *Voting: A Study of Opinion Formation in a Presidential Campaign*. Chicago: University of Chicago Press.

Berlant, Lauren. 1996. "The theory of infantile citizenship". In *Becoming National: A Reader,* G. Eley and R. G. Suny (eds.), 494–508. New York: Oxford University Press.

Bernet, Rudolf, Kern, Iso, and Marbach, Eduard. 1993. *An Introduction to Husserlian Phenomenology*. Evanston, IL: Northwestern University Press.

Blumer, Herbert. 1933. *Movies and Conduct*. New York: Macmillan.

Bogart, Leo. 1989. *Press and Public,* 2nd edition. Hillsdale, NJ: Lawrence Erlbaum.

Campbell, Angus, et al. 1976. *The American Voter.* 1960 Chicago: University of Chicago Press, 1976.

Conover, Pamela Johnston, and Searing, Donald D. 1994. "Democracy, citizenship and the study of political socialization". In *Developing Democracy,* I. Budge and D. McKay (eds.), 24–55. London: Sage Publications.

Converse, Philip, et al. 1972. *1965 Canadian National Election Study.* Ann Arbor, MI: Inter-University Consortium for Political Research.

Craig, Stephen C., and Bennett, Stephen E., eds. 1997. *After the Boom: The Politics of Generation X.* Lanham, MD: Rowan and Littlefield.

Dewey, John. 1927. *The Public and Its Problems.* New York: Henry Holt and Company.

Delgado-Moreira, Juan M. 2000. *Mulitcultural Citizenship and the European Union.* Aldershot: Ashgate.

Dell'Olio, Fiorella. 2005. *The Europeanisation of Citizenship. Between the Ideology of Nationality, Immigration, and European Identity.* Aldershot: Ashgate.

Eliasoph, Nina. 1998. *Avoiding Politics: How Americans Produce Apathy in Everyday Life.* Cambridge: Cambridge University Press.

EUYOUPART 2003–2005. Available at <http://www.sora.at/de/start.asp?b=14>. Accessed 8 January 2007.

Fossum, Jon Erik. 2006. Arena Working Papers. WP 01/17. pp. 1–30. Available at <http://www.arena.uio.no/publications/wp01_17.htm>. Accessed 8 January 2007.

Godkin, Edwin Lawrence. 1896. *Problems of Modern Democracy: Political and Economic Essays,* M. Keller (ed.). Cambridge, MA: Harvard University Press.

Godkin, Edwin Lawrence. 1898. *Unforeseen Tendencies of Democracy.* Boston: Houghton, Mifflin and Company.

Herbst, Susan. 1993. *Numbered Voices: How Opinion Polling Has Shaped American Politics.* Chicago: University of Chicago Press.

Husserl, Edmund. 1981. *Shorter Works,* P. McCormick and F. A. Elliston (eds.). Notre Dame, IN: University of Notre Dame Press.

Husserl, Edmund. 1927. Phenomenology. *Encyclopaedia Britannica 17*(946): 699–702.

James, William. 1890. *The Principles of Psychology,* Vol. 1. New York: Dover, 1950.

James, William. 1902. *The Varieties of Religious Experience: A Study in Human Nature.* New York: Modern Library, 1999.

Jamieson, Lynn (Project Coordinator) 2005. "Final report: Orientations of young men and women to citizenship and European identity". Project no. SERD-2000-00260. Available at <http://www.sociology.ed.ac.uk/youth/>. Accessed 8 January 2007.

Labov, William. 1972. *Language in the Inner City.* Philadelphia: University of Pennsylvania Press.

Lerner, Daniel. 1966. "Some comments on center–periphery relations". In *Comparing Nations: The Use of Quantitative Data in Cross-National Research,* R. L. Merritt and S. Rokkan (eds.), 259–66. New Haven, CT: Yale University Press.

Livingstone, Sonia. 1998. "Mediated childhoods: A comparative approach to the lifeworld of young people in a changing media environment". *European Journal of Communication 13*(2): 435–456.

Lippmann, Walter. 1922. *Public Opinion.* New York: Free Press, 1965.

McCrone, David. 1998. *The Sociology of Nationalism.* London: Routledge.

Milbrath, Lester W. 1965. *Political Participation: How and Why Do People Get Involved in Politics?* Chicago: Rand McNally.

Muxel, Anne. 2005. "Which factors can motivate youth participation in democracy". Available at <http://www.sora.at/images/doku/fnsp_motivating_factors_for_participation.pdf>. Accessed 8 January 2007.

Nerone, John C., and Barnhurst, Kevin G. 1995. "Visual mapping and cultural authority: Design change in US newspapers, 1920–1940". *Journal of Communication 45*(2): 9–43.

Newman, W. Russell, Just, Marion R., and Crigler, Ann N. 1992. *Common Knowledge: News and the Construction of Political Meaning.* Chicago: University of Chicago Press.

Nie, Norman H., Verba, Sidney, and Petrocik, John R. 1979. *The Changing American Voter.* Cambridge, MA: Harvard University Press.

Putnam, Robert D. 1995. "Bowling alone: America's declining social capital". *Journal of Democracy 6*(1): 65–78.

Reissman, Catherine Kohler. 1993. *Narrative Analysis* [Qualitative Research Methods 30]. Newbury Park, CA: Sage Publications.

Royce, Josiah. 1969. *The Basic Writings of Josiah Royce,* Vol. 2., J. J. McDermott (ed.). Chicago: University of Chicago Press.

Rushkoff, Douglas, ed. 1994. *GenX Reader.* New York: Ballantine.

Schudson, Michael. 1998. *The Good Citizen: A History of American Civic Life.* New York: Martin Kessler Books.

Schutz, Alfred. 1970. *On Phenomenology and Social Relations: Selected Writings,* H. R. Wagner (ed.). Chicago: University of Chicago Press.

Silverstone, Roger S. 1997. "New media in European households". In U. T. Lange and K. Goldhammer (eds), *Exploring the Limits: Europe's Changing Communication Environment,* pp. 113–34. Berlin: Springer-Verlag.

Steele, Catherine A., and Barnhurst, Kevin G. 1996. "The journalism of opinion: Network coverage in US presidential campaigns, 1968–1988". *Critical Studies in Mass Communication 13* (3): 187–209.

Van der Veen, Maurits, A. 2002. "Determinants of European identity: A preliminary investigation using Eurobarometer data". Available at <http://www.isanet.org/noarchive/vanderveen.html>. Accessed 8 January 2007.

Weber, Max. 1958. *From Max Weber: Essays in Sociology,* H. H. Gerth and C. W. Mills (ed. and trans.) New York: Oxford.

Wilshire, Bruce. 1968. *William James and Phenomenology: A Study of* The Principles of Psychology. Bloomington, IN: Indiana University Press.

Wilson, Woodrow. 1961. *Constitutional Government in the United States.* 1908. New York: Columbia University Press.

The narrative bias

Political marketing on the world wide web

Michela Cortini and Amelia Manuti
University of Bari

Introduction

Within the psychological domain, the Internet and its manifold implications are rapidly becoming one of the most interesting topics of research. Most studies focus attention on the possibilities granted by this new medium, both as a support for scientific investigation and as a useful resource for collecting data. Nevertheless, this research perspective fails to value the growing importance played by the Internet as an object of research *per se*, that is to say as a new social mass medium (Jacobelli 1998; Morris & Ogan 1996; Reips & Bosnjak 2001).

This research tries to overcome such shortcomings by adopting the perspective of virtual ethnography (Boudourides 2001; Jonas, Breuer, Schauenburg & Boos 2001), collecting rich, descriptive and contextually situated data and interpreting the embedded practices derived from the use of the Internet. The focus of the contribution is on a particular example of asynchronous computer-mediated communication – websites – and on a specific communicative genre, that is political discourse.

According to the critical perspective (Fairclough 1993; Fairclough & Wodak 1997; Van Dijk 1993; 1998), discourse is considered not simply as a vehicle to spread ideologies and world views, but rather as a form of social practice with a very pragmatic function, as it concretely shapes reality and thus personal and social identities (Mininni 2000). Indeed, each communicative event has both a 'presentation' (the pure informative function) and an 'orientation' aspect (a more directive function), which becomes more evident within political communication, meant as a communicative format which directly invests in the interests of public opinion (Gerstlé 1992; Lemke 1995). By such a policy, language becomes a language of action as it has a prescriptive function: it pushes people to behave in a way that is consistent with the sake of the collective.

Therefore the aim of this contribution is to investigate the dynamics through which such 'language of action' is actually structured within political discourse, arguing that the peculiar features of the new medium may have transformed the traditional format of political communication (Newhagen & Rafaeli 1996; Singh & Dalal 1999; Tumber & Bromley 1998). Particular reference will be made to the Linguistic Intergroup Bias Model (LIB), which describes a systematic bias in language use that may contribute to the perpetuation of stereotypes in intergroup relationships (Maass, Salvi, Arcuri & Semin 1989). More specifically, the Linguistic Intergroup Bias Model deserves attention, since its functioning is mainly based on the process of self-categorization, leading us to understand that the language we use shapes the way we think about and categorize ourselves. In such a sense, political identity could be meant as one of the several levels of the self-categorization system, which range from political thought to geographical belonging. From a European perspective then, the process of political identification could be both a strategy to share ideas and behaviour and also to differentiate the self, when for example national identity becomes more salient than political.

The changing nature of political communication in the age of the Internet

The support of new media to the process of political participation has transformed what has been traditionally called the "parties' democracy" into a "public democracy" (Manin 1990: 42). Indeed, the nature of new media offers to all potential voters exploring the Internet, the possibility of having access to political knowledge and information in real time and with fewer cultural and economic restrictions (Axford & Huggins 2000; Barnett 1997; Hacker & van Dijk 2000; Street 1997).

The features and the communicative modalities of computer-mediated communication allow a political party to establish a more direct, interactive and somehow critical kind of relationship with its voter. The web differs from television or the press in that political content on the web is communicated directly without any physical mediation, such as the host in political broadcasting programs or the editor in newspapers. This allows for a more personal kind of participation, since the potential voter is able to choose his/her personal route of navigation, using those instruments for different purposes (Galimberti & Riva 1997; Mantovani 1995).

However, the alteration of format and timing of political communication does not change the fact that argumentation still forms the greater part of this kind of discourse, an indispensable device for fostering a successful public image. Being a persuasive kind of discourse, the analysis of political communication should focus on discursive strategies, since it is common knowledge that the more favourably a politician is presented and 'narrated', the greater his or her chance of appealing to the electorate (Mininni 1992).

By adopting a narrative approach (Bruner 1991; Gergen & Gergen 1988) to investigate political argumentation, politics can be viewed both as a self and a collective narrative. Indeed, politics can be conceived as a fact, as topical news in the public agenda (McCombs & Shaw 1993), and as a narrative, which, by reporting the story of the party, mirrors the story of its voters.

As with every other kind of story, politics too has its plot, its characters, its narrative stages and its discursive genre (Greimas 1979; Morin 1976; Propp 1966). The most evident feature of the political narrative is thus the constant competition between the protagonist and the antagonist (i.e. the political parties), who both perform an action, using their skills to manipulate each other and to profit from the situation. They fight for the possession of a desired and valuable object (i.e. a vote) until the conclusion (e.g. after the election), when one of them succeeds in obtaining their desired goal.

Being a narrative, politics contains also fictional elements. Hence, all the parties tell their story, often lying and masking reality in the process. They highlight their personal features and merits while discrediting the other's image. As noted by Goffman (1959), all the political leaders play a role, as in theatre, trying to fit as much as possible within the schema of the perfect politician, i.e. democratic, tolerant, sensitive to the needs of the electorate, and so on.

But, as already stressed, political communication is not only a self narrative (Bruner 1991; Gergen & Gergen 1988; Trzebinski 1995) which is focused on the description of the political leader and of his/her personal features. In self-presenting, the parties tell something about themselves, their story, their values and aims, but at the same time their discourses reflect social and collective expectations and thus group values (Turner 1975; Tajfel 1981; Tajfel & Turner 1986). A party is, in fact, more than ideology to its voter; it identifies a set of social norms and values which could contribute to strengthening the voter's positive self image, thus also explaining the causal attribution and the perceptive gap between in- and out-group, as we will see later in testing the LIB model hypothesis.

In other words, the narratives displayed by the political parties are argumentative in nature as through these they play for what Ghiglione (1988:8), in his contractual theory of communication, terms the "*enjeu*" ('stake') implied by each communicative event. According to this perspective, meaning is negotiated in/by communicative interaction: it is the outcome of a co-construction which continuously leaves markers in a system of negotiated references. Hence, the '*enjeu*' could be seen as the result of both the affordances which characterize the enunciative situation and the interpretative schemata activated by the personal aims, needs and interests of the interlocutors. In this chapter, the *'enjeu'* is represented by the political campaign, which of course assumes different value connotations according to the different interlocutors involved.

Between politicians' language and intertising: From commercial to political marketing

As for the type of language used by the parties to introduce themselves on the Internet, this can be regarded as an original fusion of what is generally referred to as "politicians' language" (Mey 1985), that is the conventional set of argumentations and behaviour used by politicians in order to persuade and attract the audience, and "intertising" (De Martini 1996), a neologism blending the concepts of interactivity and advertising.

It should not be forgotten that the parties' web pages represent a particular kind of political advertising. Indeed, the expression of ideology in discourse is usually more than just an explicit or concealed display of a person's beliefs, but mostly shares the persuasive function of traditional advertising: speakers want to change the mind of the recipient in a way that is consistent with their beliefs, intentions and goals. As with commercial advertising, political advertising aims at promoting and selling items, highlighting their pluses and their benefits, but, unlike commercial advertising, it promotes persons and ideologies instead of objects. Thus, its main goal is to gain more votes. Moreover, its persuasive effects could be more powerful and prolonged as compared with those generated by commercial advertising. The pluses implied by political advertising are ideas and political programs, while the benefits derive from the membership of the social group which is perceived as stronger and having power. This finds amplification in the use of the interactive medium. As already mentioned, computer-mediated communication conjugates the advantages of ease and rapidity granted by the traditional old media (television, radio, press) to the possibility of coming directly into contact with the source, expressing almost in real time personal opinions, taking part in the 'Show of Politics' (Thompson 1995).

Political competition in action: Self vs. others' presentation. The linguistic intergroup bias model

As the discursive and argumentative structures of political communication on the web are the focus of this study, the Linguistic Intergroup Bias (LIB) Model (Arcuri, Maass & Portelli 1993; Maass 1999; Maass & Arcuri 1992; Maass, Ceccarelli & Arcuri 1996; Maass, Milesi, Zabbini & Stahlberg 1995; Maass, Salvi, Arcuri & Semin; 1989) has been adopted to investigate bias in language use. The rationale of this model comes from a well-known notion in social psychology, the ingroup bias, which is particularly evident when people are called to judge others' behaviour in competitive contexts, such as in the political arena (see Figure 1).

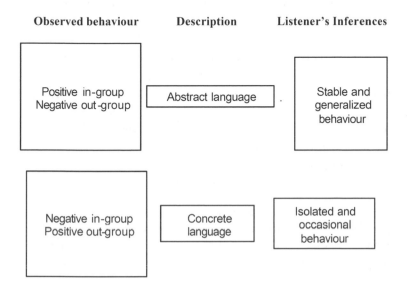

Figure 1. The LIB model (adapted from Maass 1999: 91)

By the process of intergroup comparison, individuals tend to establish a difference which is in favour of their own group (ingroup favouritism). In other words, after having defined themselves in terms of group belonging, individuals seek to achieve positive self-esteem by positively differentiating their ingroup from the outgroup on some valued dimension. This quest for distinctiveness means that when people's sense of who they are is defined in terms of 'we' rather than 'I', they want to see 'us' as differentiated and better than 'them', in order to feel good about who and what they are. Actually, belonging to a positive social group means perceiving the self as a member of that group in positive terms. This is why people are daily engaged in protecting their self-image and in confronting this positive image with the negative image of other groups.

Social identity (Deschamps 1988; Tajfel 1981; Tajfel & Turner 1986; Turner 1975) is thus based on two assumptions: cognitive and motivational. It is cognitive insofar as the categorization process leads the subjects to overrate intergroup differences and to undervalue ingroup differences. It is motivational as what motivates discrimination is the need for self-esteem. One of the most effective modalities through which this comparison process is run, is the discursive manipulation of the locus of control in attributional processes (Heider 1958). Research on systematic ingroup favouritism reveals that generally people attribute the success of ingroup behaviour to internal causes more often than they do when judging outgroup behaviour. The opposite can be said for unsuccessful behaviour, which is justified with internal causes for the outgroup and external for the ingroup, in consonance with Maass, Salvi, Arcuri and Semin's (1989) model. This asymmetry could be manipulated by the use of abstract or concrete terms, which show significant influence on the interpretation process and on the kind of inferences made about the actors' behaviour; the linguistic bias that a transmitter displays is shown to influence the type of inferences that recipients make (Wigboldus, Semin & Spears 2000).

Thus, language is considered as the main vehicle through which stereotypes and prejudices are communicated and perpetuated. This is why Maas (1999) believes that this attributional bias becomes more evident in the use of particular discursive structures as summed up by her main hypothesis:

> A *positive behaviour* displayed by an *ingroup member* will be described in relatively *abstract terms*, whereas the same behaviour shown by an *outgroup member* will be described in relatively *concrete terms*. On the contrary, *negative behaviour* will be described in *concrete terms* when displayed by an *ingroup member*, but in *abstract terms* when displayed by an *outgroup member* (Maass 1999: 80).

This concept of language abstraction has been adopted from Semin and Fiedler's Linguistic Category Model (1988; 1992), which distinguishes between four levels of abstraction, through which an episode could be described, having thus significant effects on the listener's inferential process. The first level is characterized by the so-called Descriptive Action Verbs (DAV). This is the most concrete level of expression, as it makes direct reference to observable behaviour. For example, the verb 'to phone' is a descriptive verb as the interlocutor can understand and interpret this action unambiguously. The second level is the one of Interpretative Action Verbs (IAV), which refer to some generic behaviour and which are very difficult to interpret univocally. An example is the verb 'to help', as people have different interpretations of what helpful behaviour could be (i.e. physical help in doing something or psychological support). At the third level, State Verbs (SV) are to be found, that is those verbs which make reference to psychological states of the interlocutor, such as 'to hate' or 'to wish', and which do not have any connection with the concrete episodes described. The last level is represented by Adjectives (ADJ), which constitute the most abstract level of language as they emphasize stable and foreseeable features of the actors (Maasss & Arcuri 1992; Maass, Salvi, Arcuri, & Semin 1989; Semin & Fiedler 1988).

Using this continuum, Semin and Fiedler (1988) have shown that the use of abstract linguistic formula play a strategic role in influencing the listener's point of view about the episode as they suggest inferences which could be stable in time and particularly informative about the actor's personal features. On the other hand, the use of a concrete term or verb suggests that the behavioural episode is an isolated event, not necessarily linked to the actor's stable characteristics, thus resulting in a restrictive effect, if put in relation with negative ingroup and positive outgroup features. The statement "A is aggressive" sounds very different in comparison to "A hits B". Moreover, this statement has different implications depending if A is an ingroup or outgroup member. The aggressive character of A could be then differently exploited as a stable and typical feature of all outgroup members or as an isolated episode due to contextual variables.

Aims and methodology

The corpus of data of the present study is made up of web pages drawn from the sites of the most famous Italian political parties on two important political occasions: the regional elections in April 2000 and the general election in May 2001. The aim is to test the LIB hypothesis, that is to analyse the discursive strategies adopted by the parties to describe themselves and their competitors, with particular reference to the level of language abstraction. Besides content analysis (Kelle 1995), a critical approach to discourse analysis (Fairclough 1993; Fairclough & Wodak 1997; Richardson 1996; Van Dijk 1993; 1998) has been adopted as a theoretical and methodological frame, so as to better investigate the ideological structures hidden within political discourse.

With the aid of the software *NUD*IST*[1] (Richards & Richards 1994; Richards & Richards 1996), a hierarchical categorization tree has been created (Araujo 1995) which is made up of 5 main nodes (parent nodes) and several subnodes (child nodes) for each (see Figure 2):

---

1. NUD*IST, or Non Numerical Unstructured Data Indexing Searching and Theorizing, is computer software developed to aid users in handling non numerical unstructured data in qualitative analysis, by supporting processes of coding data in an index system, formulating patterns of coding and thus theorizing about the results obtained. For more information on the software NUD*IST see http://www. qsr.com.au/software/n4/n4.htm

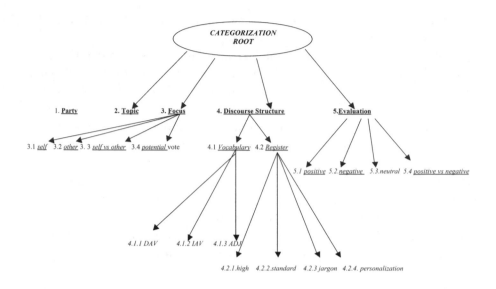

Figure 2. The main part of the categorization system

- Party, with child nodes *Democratici della Sinistra, Verdi, Rifondazione Comunista, Lega Nord, Alleanza Nazionale, Forza Italia, Lista Bonino, Centro Cristiano Democratico*;
- Topic, with child nodes family, economy, health, farming, school, immigration, nature, animals, etc.;
- Focus of discourse, with child nodes self, other, self versus other, potential voter;
- Discourse structure, with child nodes vocabulary, divided into descriptive and interpretative verbs and adjectives, and register divided into high, standard, jargon and personalization;
- Evaluation, with child nodes positive, neutral, negative, positive versus negative.

Each political website (*Forza Italia, Alleanza Nazionale, CCD, Lega Nord, Lista Bonino, Democratici di Sinistra, Verdi, Rifondazione Comunista*) has been analysed in detail with special attention to the links "Who are we" (self presentation) and "What do we want" (aims and goals). In addition, the selected extracts have been categorized, focusing on the topics which mirror more vividly the political competition (i.e. Politics, Economy, Religion, Nature, etc.) (Denzin & Lincoln 1994). The category 'topic' has been intersected with the category 'party' in order to investigate their different argumentative techniques. More specifically, special attention has been dedicated to the intersection of the categories 'focus of discourse' (on the party itself, on the potential voter, on the other party) with 'evaluation' (positive, negative, positive vs negative, neutral). Secondly, the category 'discourse structure', which accounts for the self and others' presentation strategies, has been examined both to see how the political leaders actually 'sell' themselves and to test the LIB hypothesis, thus arguing for a correlation between discourse style and positive ingroup description. A further analysis has been focused on the categories 'topic' and 'discourse structure' in order to reveal the ways in which the political parties promote their opinions, giving an Italian echo of previous political communication research elsewhere (Castel 1995).

The strategies of political marketing: How the parties sell themselves on the web

The analysis of the first corpus (regional elections 2000) follows a complex categorization, but in the second corpus (general election 2001) attention was focused on a recurrent narrative device found within the first study, that is on the competitive narrative. Unlike the first study, where the websites of 8 different Italian parties were separately coded, the second study put all the parties into a single category (parent node) called 'political array', which was divided into three subnodes: *Casa delle Libertà* (right-moderate wing), *Ulivo* (left-moderate wing) and *Independent* (political minorities which do not identify in any array). This strategy is justified by the fact that, during the 2001 political campaign, most parties' websites were linked to each other and referred to the political leader of the array they sided with. As for the other nodes (topic, focus of discourse, discourse structure and evaluation), they have remained the same as in the first study.

Most of the sites changed little in their graphical layout and the organization of main contents, but what attracts attention is the political programmes of each array. These programmes are all examples of the competitive narrative encountered within the first study, as each proposal is emphasized by the reference to rivals. This has presented an interesting opportunity to analyse the LIB hypothesis and to test if the different nature of political competition (regional versus national) would change the discursive strategies of the parties involved.

Study 1: Regional elections 2000

The first finding concerns the testing of the LIB model hypothesis. Parties describing themselves in positive terms use descriptive action verbs in 87.5% of cases (with an agreement rate of 71.4% among three researchers who have separately coded all the units of analysis). This contradicts the LIB model, which states that positive behaviour displayed by an ingroup member will be described in relatively abstract terms. Consider the following webpages (Figures 3 and 4), drawn from the *Verdi* and *Forza Italia* parties. Here the political programme of each is stressed in very concrete and clearly positive terms and the so-called 'moral values' which distinguish each party are depicted curiously in descriptive terms.

ELEZIONI REGIONALI

SCEGLI UN BUON MOTIVO PER CAMBIARE

E' tempo di puntare davvero a una vita di qualità per tutti. Noi Verdi vogliamo un futuro ecologicamente sostenibile, una società della convivenza pacifica e solidale, della legalità e della tutela dei diritti individuali, più libera da burocrazia e soprusi, rispettosa dei diritti di tutti gli esseri viventi. Per questo noi, con voi, vogliamo dare forma alle Regioni dei cittadini, dell'ambiente e della solidarietà.

PER UN CIBO DAVVERO SANO E UNA AGRICOLTURA PULITA

Noi Verdi consideriamo l'**agricoltura** un'attività fondamentale per l'uomo e per l'ambiente. Va però garantito il rispetto della Natura, dei suoi cicli naturali e delle sue risorse. E ogni cittadino deve essere certo della genuinità di ciò che mangia. Le proposte dei Verdi sono:

* istituire "mense biologiche" nelle scuole per difendere la salute dei bambini e dei ragazzi

* salvaguardare le specie animali e vegetali in via di estinzione

* recuperare le terre di collina e di montagna, rimboscarle o renderle più fertili con nuove pratiche agricole

* considerare l'agricoltore come un custode del territorio e riconoscergli un ruolo vitale nella difesa dell'ambiente

* combattere l'inaridimento del suolo

Noi Verdi ci batteremo perché ogni Regione vieti la coltivazione e la vendita di **cibo geneticamente modificato** e per garantire a ogni cittadino il diritto di sapere ciò che mangia.

PER TANTI NUOVI POSTI DI LAVORO "VERDI"

Figure 3. Web page from *Verdi*

The strategy chosen by the *Verdi* to introduce themselves to the voter is noteworthy. The party mixes concrete and abstract levels of self-description, obviously making use of positive terms. More specifically, the appeal to the voters is evident by the concrete slogan "*Dai un sorriso al futuro. Scegli i Verdi*" ("Give a smile to the future. Choose Verdi"), which is enhanced by the descriptive verbs *dare* (to give) and *scegliere* (to choose). The description of the main aims of the party in the first paragraph are also introduced by the concrete verb *volere* (to want), although they are further stressed by more abstract adjectives *pacifico* (peaceful), *solidale* (in agreement with), *individuale* (individual), *libero* (free), *rispettoso* (respectful).

This mixed strategy could have been adopted for two reasons. The party aims to build a positive self-image, both as concretely effective (use of descriptive action terms) and as stable and coherent across time (use of adjectives). Moreover, at the end of the first paragraph, we find another concrete sentence emphasised by the descriptive action verbal phrase *vogliamo dare* (we want to give). It is no accident that concrete expressions are used in addressing the voter directly as a sort of memorandum for the political date to come.

Similarly, the analysis of the *Forza Italia* party web page reveals a concrete discursive strategy. The beginning of the sentence is always stressed by the descriptive *vogliamo* (we want), followed by a list of concrete expressions such as "*vogliamo* un paese dove lo stato sia al servizio del cittadino e che si *astenga* da tutte quelle attività che possono essere *affidate* alla libera iniziativa dei privati che di solito *le fanno* meglio e a minor costo" (*we want* a country where the State would be to the citizens' service and would *abstain* from all those activities which could be *delegated to* the free initiative of private companies, which usually *do them* better and at a lower cost).

When parties talk about their competitors, the results fit with the LIB model as shown in the following example, where a negative behaviour displayed by the outgroup is described in abstract terms:

(1)   *I poli sono uno contro l'altro solo in televisione. Sono sempre uniti quando si tratta di dividersi la torta del potere politico*
      'The poles are one against the other only in television. They are always united when the cake of political power is to be divided' (*Lista Bonino*)

Although the analysis of political discourses highlights a notable difference when parties talk about the self in terms of descriptive rather than interpretative strategy (see Figure 5), it leads us to the conclusion that political communication cannot be schematised or reduced to any specific model as this type of communication needs to be considered differently according to the style, aim and context of discourse.

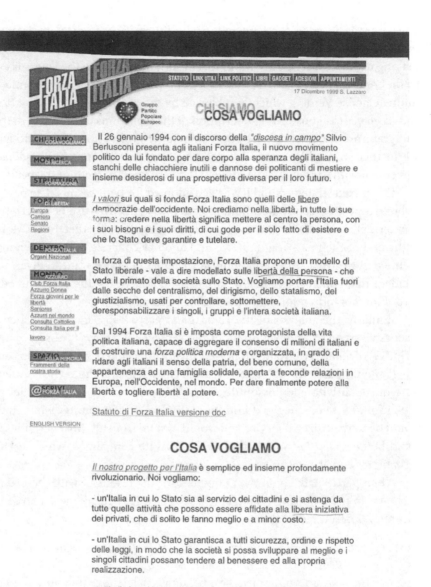

Figure 4. Web page from *Forza Italia*

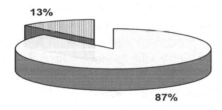

Figure 5. Parties showing themselves in positive terms

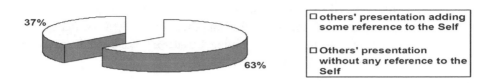

Figure 6. Parties talking about their competitors

Actually, an additional, interesting result, which would require verification by further studies, concerns the intersection of two specific categories, 'focus' and its subcategory 'self versus other', and 'evaluation' and its subcategory 'positive versus negative'. In short, when a party talks about its rivals, it does not limit itself to depicting the other, but it adds some references to the self (63 %), comparing its positive features with their negative ones (see Figure 6).

This kind of discourse has been termed "competitive narrative" (Cortini & Manuti 2002: 144), since it shows political communication as a fighting field, where the final prize is the voter. In the following, we will discuss five examples which illustrate this type of narrative.

In example (2) below, the self-presentation strategy displayed by the *Lista Bonino* party is based on the negative description of Emma Bonino's political competitors (Berlusconi and D'Alema) to which she makes explicit reference. To support this, descriptive concrete verbs with a negative evaluation, such as *non erano consapevoli* (were unaware of), are used in reference to outgroup behaviour while descriptive concrete verbs with a positive evaluation are used to refer to what the radicals have done (*costruivano* (built) and *sperimentavano* (experimented with)).

(2)   *Finchè i partiti di regime non erano ancora consapevoli neppure di ciò che fosse Internet e la new economy sono potuti crescere in Italia nonostante i monopoli i costi stratosferici delle infrastrutture telefoniche la rigidità del lavoro e i mille*

> *ostacoli alla libera iniziativa imprenditoriale. I radicali intanto grazie alla agorà da dieci anni costruivano una delle aziende italiane più innovative e avanzate del mondo delle tematica e sperimentavano nuove forme di partecipazione democratica attraverso Internet. Come le sanguisughe i due poli e i loro quaranta subpartiti Berlusconi e D'Alema in testa pretendono adesso di mettere le mani anche su questa fetta dell'Italia libera e produttiva.*
> 'Whilst the regime parties were unaware of what the Internet and the new economy were, in Italy they have gradually grown, despite monopolies, high prices of telephone infrastructures and all the obstacles to free initiative. In the meantime, over 10 years the radical party built, thanks to Agorà, one of the most innovative and advanced Italian firms within the worldwide web and experimented with new forms of democratic participation through the Internet. Like leeches, the two "poles" and their forty subparties, Berlusconi and D'Alema first of all, are now claiming this slice of the cake of the new free and productive Italy' (*Lista Bonino*).

The narrative structure is also very rich in adverbs such as 'while' and 'in the meantime', creating a sort of dialectic opposition between the ingroup and the outgroup, which leads the reader to acknowledge quite automatically the merits of the former in contrast with the latter.

In example (3) the same narrative modality is adopted through the almost obsessive repetition of the word 'thanks' in reference to the social conquest of divorce, which the radicals have obtained and to whom their rivals should be grateful.

(3)   *Sfaciafamiglie! Il CCD ha criticato Emma Bonino. La verità comunque è che tutti i leader politici del polo hanno una nuova famiglia grazie alle nostre battaglie, grazie ai nostri successi e grazie al divorzio così come quasi un milione di famiglie italiane. La critica nei confronti dei radicali è dunque particolarmente scorretta da parte loro.*
'You let the families fall apart! The CCD has criticized Emma Bonino. The truth however is that all the political leaders of the pole have a new family thanks to our battles, thanks to our successes and thanks to divorce as well as almost a million Italian families. This criticism of the radicals is thus particularly unfair of them' (*Lista Bonino*).

Figure 7, drawn from the *Lista Bonino* party, shows the explicit opposition between the self and the other expressed by the words:

(4)   *ATTENTO! Sembra incredibile ma tutti gli altri partiti e tutte le altre liste sono contrari a queste riforme. Tutti vogliono avere più potere e più denaro ai*

*danni tuoi, dei cittadini, delle donne e degli uomini con i loro problemi, le loro
speranze, le loro disperazioni. Perché credono nel potere e non in altro.*
'Pay attention! It seems unbelievable but all the other parties and all the other
allies are against these reforms. All other parties want more power and more
money, at your own expense, at the citizens' expense. Because they believe in
power and nothing else'. (*Lista Bonino*)

In example (4) it is particularly interesting to highlight how the opposition is
repeatedly referred to using the word 'other', first to stress that an outgroup exists
(*gli altri partiti* (the other parties)) and secondly to emphasize that the outgroup
wants different things from the ingroup (*le altre liste sono contrarie a queste riforme*
(the other alliances are against these reforms)). In addition, the use of the imperative is particularly interesting. Generally, political marketing does not often use
this mode, since there is the risk of presenting the self in a negative way (Petitjean
1999), which is inconvenient in terms of persuasion (Petty & Cacioppo 1986).
Imperatives used in politics may be divided into two types: metadiscursive and
injunctive (Petitjean 1995; 1999). Metadiscursive imperatives are generally used
at the beginning of the discourse in order to catch the interlocutor's attention and
to mark what follows. Injunctive imperatives represent a form of psychological
influence on the interlocutor and may be divided into three types: injunctive-re-
quest, a direct appeal, generally within the semantic field of 'to vote'; injunctive-
authority, which tries to gain the other's consent assuming a specific competence
of the interlocutor; injunctive-slogan, ritual sentences, anchored to specific analo-
gies or interpretative repertoires, which characterize the whole political campaign
(Potter & Wetherell 1987; Wetherell & Potter 1992).

The injunctive request imperative form (*attento*) used by Emma Bonino in
example (4) is metadiscursive only on the surface. Indeed, the interlocutor is explicitly invited to pay attention not only to what follows from a discursive point
of view but, in addition, to the wider political arena. He/she is alerted to be critical toward the situation, to focus on the distinction between right and wrong
and thus to avoid a biased and automatic elaboration of information (Petty &
Cacioppo 1986).

In example (5), the use of an implicit and impersonal imperative-exhortation
"They have spent money they didn't have and that you will have to pay, they are irresponsible and dangerous. *This is the right time to stop them and send them home*"
seems to anchor the request to some external and non-biased evidence according
to which the electorate has to make some inferences from the other parties' behaviour. In such a way, the *Lista Bonino* moves the competitive narrative from the
level of ingroup-outgroup opposition to the level of outgroup-voter relationship.

(5)   *Hanno speso soldi che non avevano e che avrebbero dovuto restituire, sono irresponsabili e pericolosi. Questo è il momento giusto per fermarli e mandarli a casa. Tu puoi farlo con il tuo voto.*

'They have spent money they didn't have and that you will have to pay back, they are irresponsible and dangerous. This is the right time to stop them and send them home. You can do it with your vote *(Lista Bonino)*.

Libertà di lavoro e d'impresa

Lavorare, guadagnare e restare onesti: chiedete, chiediamo troppo?

Com'è possibile andare avanti con un fisco che rapina più della metà del reddito, con leggi assurde che ci proibiscono di scegliere gli orari e i luoghi di lavoro, che costringono ad essere evasori, imprenditori "clandestini", lavoratori in nero?
Essere onesti significa spesso uscire dal mercato, divenire imprenditori falliti e lavoratori disoccupati.
E infatti siamo il paese in Europa dove le donne e i giovani non solo trovano meno lavoro, ma sono rassegnati a non trovarlo, spesso non ci provano nemmeno più; dove le persone, se non sono protette da qualcuno, non se la sentono di "rischiare", di investire alcunché.
Chi ci rende impossibile la

Perché l'Italia colga le occasioni di crescita economica e di occupazione offerte dalla new economy di Internet, occorrono regole nuove, poche e e liberali.
I nostri referendum vogliono riformare un mercato del lavoro che penalizza i giovani e le donne e rende meno competitive le imprese italiane. Con le nuove forme di lavoro, quelle che i sindacati vogliono vietare, negli Stati Uniti -ma anche in Olanda ed in Gran Bretagna- milioni di disoccupati, in particolare fra le donne, hanno trovato un'occupazione regolare, magari a part-time.
Per questo, ci vuole il coraggio di sfidare i pregiudizi e gli interessi di chi non vuole cambiare nulla: noi abbiamo dimostrato di avere sia il coraggio che la forza politica per modernizzare l'Italia. I giovani, le donne, i disoccupati, gli imprenditori che affrontano la competizione internazionale non vogliono andare "a destra" o "a sinistra", vogliono andare avanti! Anche noi!

ATTENTO! Sembra incredibile, ma tutti gli altri partiti e tutte le altre liste sono contrari a questa Riforme. Tutti vogliono avere più potere e più denaro, ai danni tuoi, dei cittadini, delle donne e degli uomini con i loro problemi, le loro speranze, le loro disperazioni. Perché credono nel potere, non in altro.

http://www.radicali.it/2000/lavoro.html   05/04/00

Figure 7. Web page from *Lista Bonino*.

This strategy has two main effects on the political audience, itself strategically constructed as the ingroup. First of all, the process of political identification between the party and its voters is strengthened, as the outgroup is seen as an enemy to be fought against together for the sake of society. Furthermore, in both examples this discursive modality shows the advantages of giving the voter a more active role as a consumer of politics rather than a passive member of the audience. His/her vote acquires a more factual than ideological value, as the political choice could contribute to actively change the situation. In this way, political marketing seems to be definitively caught in the web of "wooden language" (Slama Cazacu 1997: 285), which is actually a kind of void communication, which conveys no message. In order to obtain the voter's consensus, the voter is made the protagonist, and politics, in some sense, lets the voters talk in order to ensure the identification between electorate and party (Habib 1992).

In the last example below, from the *Centro Cristiano Democratico* party, the opposition between the self and the other is evoked, very significantly, by the rhetorical use of personalization, as it recalls explicitly the names of political enemies and stresses the relevance of the discursive category 'us' (CCD). Moreover, according to Perdue, Dovidio, Gurtman and Tyler (1990) the simple use of ingroup-belonging discourse markers (i.e. pronouns such as 'we') gives positive connotations to the discourse, eliciting a positive predisposition in the voter. Indeed, the political battlefield described is made up of two strongly opposed positions, which forces the reader to take part in at least one of them.

(6) *Non abbiamo bisogno di molte parole per ricordare agli elettori che cos'è il*
     CCD. Chi ha la passione per la politica conosce le nostre battaglie parlamentari.
     Quelle in favore del pluralismo scolastico, contro la rigidità burocratica di cui il
     ministro Berlinguer ha rappresentato l'esempio più tipico.
     'We do not need too many words to recall the CCD to the voters. Whoever has
     passion for politics knows our political battles. Those in favour of a scholastic
     pluralism, against bureaucratic stiffness, of which Minister Berlinguer has
     been the most typical example' (*Centro Cristiano Democratico*).

Study 2: General election 2001

The second study reveals results which are consistent with the first one. Nonetheless, the focus of discourse here seems to be on the *ingroup*. Thus, a higher percentage of references to the ingroup and its behaviour (20%) rather than to the outgroup (0.82%) was found in comparison with the first study. This could be due to the different nature of the political competition, which is now focused on the leaders and their concrete proposals rather than on the competition between the parties. Another feature which emerges in this corpus is a greater recurrent use of the pronoun 'we'. The *ingroup* is identified with an inclusive 'we', which refers to the Italian people, so that the daily demands of the common man correspond to those that the political leaders wish to solve urgently (as in examples (7) and (8)).

(7)   *Vogliamo dare a tutti i cittadini del 2006 un paese rinnovato, disegnato non soltanto da noi ma dalle parole, dalle idee e dai gesti di tutti, poichè ne siamo tutti parte.*
        'We want to give to all the citizens of 2006 a renewed country, designed not only by us but by the words, by the ideas and the gestures of all, as we are all part of it' (*Ulivo*).

(8)   *Sta a voi decidere di dare il vostro voto alla forza politica, che attraverso il referendum e l'azione non violenta vi ha dato la possibilità concreta di riformare il vostro paese anche contro il volere del governo.*
        'It's up to you to decide to give your vote to the political force, which through the referendum and non violent action has given you the concrete possibility to reform your country even against the government's will' (*Lista Bonino*).

This corpus too is rich in *competitive narrative*, that is a narrative which focuses positively on the ingroup's successes and negatively on the outgroup's failures (10.3%), although the modalities through which this narrative is expressed are slightly different.

The independent array directly appeals to the voter (*Sta a voi* – it's up to you), emphasizing the responsibility he/she has in the political decision-making. However, there is also evidence of a more impersonal style, which aims at conveying the sense of participation to the shared demands for political renewal (*Vogliamo dare a tutti i cittadini del 2006 un paese rinnovato* (We want to give to all the citizens of 2006 a renewed country)).

Furthermore, although the independent array makes reference to an homogeneous outgroup, i.e. the *Lista Bonino* party introduces itself as an alternative voice above all political distinctions, the other two arrays *Casa delle Libertà* and *Ulivo* make direct reference to the categories of right and left, often in negative terms, as in example (9).

(9)   *Vogliamo qualcosa di diverso dal solito luogo comune caro alla destra*
        'We want something different from the old common place darling to the right' (*Ulivo*).

Examples (10) and (11) illustrate competitive narrative drawn from the independent and the left-wing, *Ulivo* arrays, where this discursive strategy is present in

25% and in 13% of cases, respectively. In contrast, the corpus of the *Casa delle Libertà* array prefers narrative strategies based on the description of the party's successes; competitive narrative is not present at all.

(10) *Quando la destra Italiana fa appello allo stato assistenziale e centralista fa riferimento ad una vecchia immagine della nazione che le riforme degli ultimi cinque anni hanno definitivamente cancellato.*

'When the Italian right wing appeals to the charitable and centralist State it makes reference to an old image of the country which the reforms of the last five years have finally erased' (*Ulivo* array).

(11) *Contrariamente agli altri partiti che si presentano all'elettorato con lunghi programmi politici, pieni di promesse e posizioni su differenti questioni, la Lista Bonino presenta soltanto un riassunto delle battaglie politiche che il movimento radicale ha portato avanti negli ultimi dieci anni.*

'Contrary to other parties which introduce themselves to the electorate with long political programs, full of promises and positions on different issues, the Lista Bonino presents simply an abstract of the political battles the radical movement has run within the last decade' (*Independent* array).

As for the distribution of narrative strategies within the arrays, the independent pole (made up of political minorities which do not identify in any array, as for example the Lista Bonino Party) seems to prefer a self-presentation, which mostly uses positive, descriptive, concrete terms (see Figure 8). This partly contradicts the LIB model hypothesis, which suggests that a concrete description usually leads us to consider the episode or the behaviour observed as isolated and casual. Nonetheless, these concrete references by Emma Bonino to the referendum or to all the political battles of the *Lista Bonino* Party could be interpreted as a discursive strategy that she is using to emphasise the gap between her party, which is concrete and effective through time, and the slogans of the other arrays, which according to her are useless 'words'.

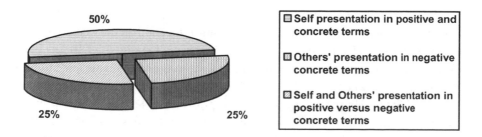

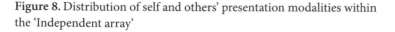

Figure 8. Distribution of self and others' presentation modalities within the 'Independent array'

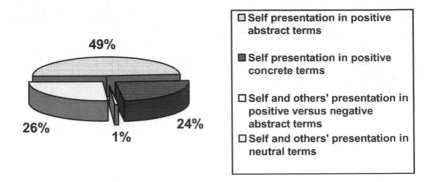

Figure 9. Distribution of self and others' presentation modalities within the array 'Casa delle libertà'

In contrast, the array *Casa delle Libertà* chooses an abstract self-presentation (see Figure 9). The leader, Silvio Berlusconi, enthusiastically cites the great political deeds of his party and his proposals, but gives no concrete reference either to the contents or to the context of his intervention. Moreover, the corpus of this array confirms the hypothesis of the LIB Model, as the use of abstract terms is supposed to lead the voter to stable inferences about actions and behaviour of the party involved, as shown in example below.

(12)   *Se vogliamo una Italia prospera e competitiva nel mondo della new economy dobbiamo investire nella cultura e nell'istruzione.*
'If we want Italy to be wealthy and competitive within the new economy context we should invest in culture and education' (Forza Italia).

Discussion: The voter caught in the web of the parties

The data from this pilot research suggests that the LIB model does not fit every kind of discourse, and in particular political communication on the web, conceived here as self and collective narrative. Since the original study, the LIB has been tested in over 30 experiments conducted in a wide range of linguistic and cultural contexts, obtaining language biases consistent with the model, i.e. party affiliation (Karpinski & von Hippel 1996), competing sport teams (Franco & Maass 1996), Northern versus Southern Italians, (Maass, Milesi, Zabbini & Sahlberg 1995) or women against men (Fiedler, Semin & Finkenauer 1993; Guerin 1994). However, this is the first study applied to a political campaign on the web, that is to say to political communication with very peculiar features, due both to the context (the elections) and the medium (computer-mediated communication).

The study reveals results which are only in part consistent with the LIB model, showing that when interpretative verbs are used to describe positive features of the self, the narrative continues with very concrete and descriptive sentences, in particular verbs, to re-affirm their actual political identity and programs as shown in example (13):

(13)   *I radicali sono stati l'unica forza politica che è riuscita a rompere questo equilibrio con l'arma costituzionale del referendum.*
'The radicals have been the only political force to succeed in breaking this balance, with the constitutional tool of referendum' (*Lista Bonino*).

This orientation toward concreteness could be connected with a common sense belief widespread in Italy according to which politics has lost its ideological importance, becoming a show focused on characters more than on ideas. Indeed, similar results have also been found in the French political context (Ghiglione 1989; Ghiglione & Bromberg 1998). Furthermore, probably because of the constant growth of new parties, Italian politicians need to be very concrete in order to combat and overthrow this universal social representation of politics.

Moreover, what should not be forgotten is the relevant role played, in this case, by the context of discourse, that is the electoral campaign. It should be remembered that the discourses presented here were produced the week before the regional elections. So the imminent competition forced the political leaders to be more clear and concrete and as rhetorically effective as possible so as to have a better chance of winning against their rivals.

A strategy used by all the web pages is to give the voters the chance to express their opinions. Some links, for instance *Lista Bonino*'s 'Join the banner campaign' ask voters to judge the banner of the party and to show their affiliation by publishing the banner on their personal websites in order to contribute to the popularity of the party itself. This seems to create a sort of invisible contract between the party and the voter, a sort of '*do ut des*', that is a mutual exchange between party and voter, where the voter can give his opinion but in turn shall communicate the campaign by being a sort of *trait d' union* (Branca, Rosoff & Marinelli 1994). Furthermore, to strengthen this public image as a democratic and available interlocutor, the party publishes some voter comments and the politicians answer voters' questions to stimulate the exchange.

Similar tactics can be observed on the *Forza Italia* website. For instance, the column *Scrivi sul muro* (Write on the wall) (see Figure 10) publishes online messages which comment on the political situation and which obviously side with the ingroup against the outgroup (e.g. *Ci vuole una rivoluzione per mandare a casa*

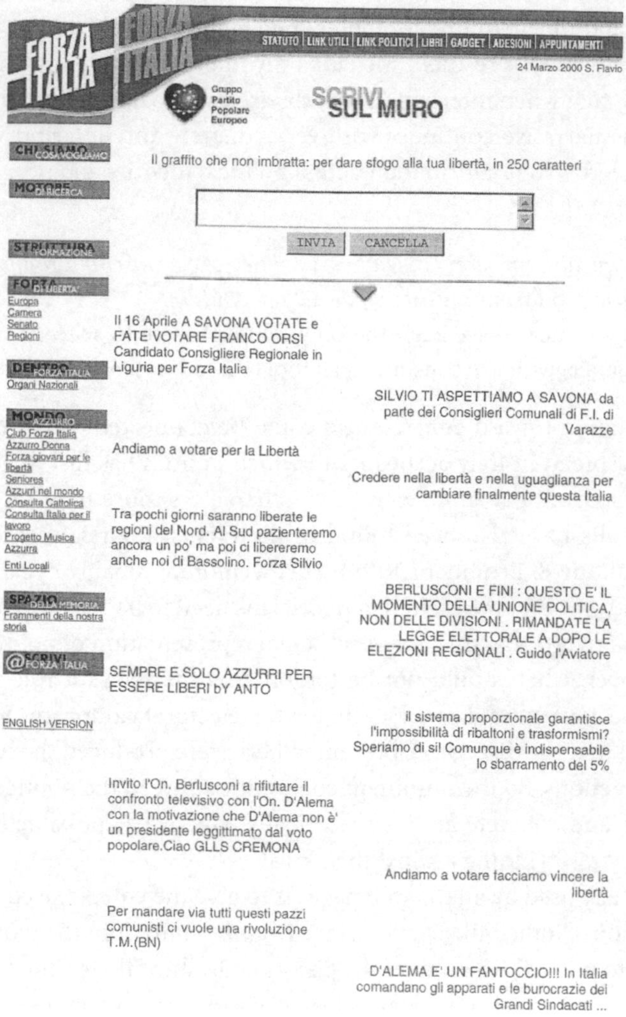

Figure 10. A page from the *Forza Italia* website I

tutti questi pazzi comunisti ("A revolution is needed to send home all these mad communists") or *D'ALEMA E' UN FANTOCCIO* ("D'ALEMA IS A PUPPET!!")).

Moreover, the link *Scegli il tuo governatore ideale* (Choose your ideal governor) (see Figure 11) stresses the (strategic) availability of the party to hear the needs of common people, as it dedicates a page to them where they can express themselves freely. The identikit (as it is termed on the site) of the ideal governor – as emphasised also by the percentage of popular consent – seems obviously to be focused on the values (family, care for elderly people, youth employment etc.),

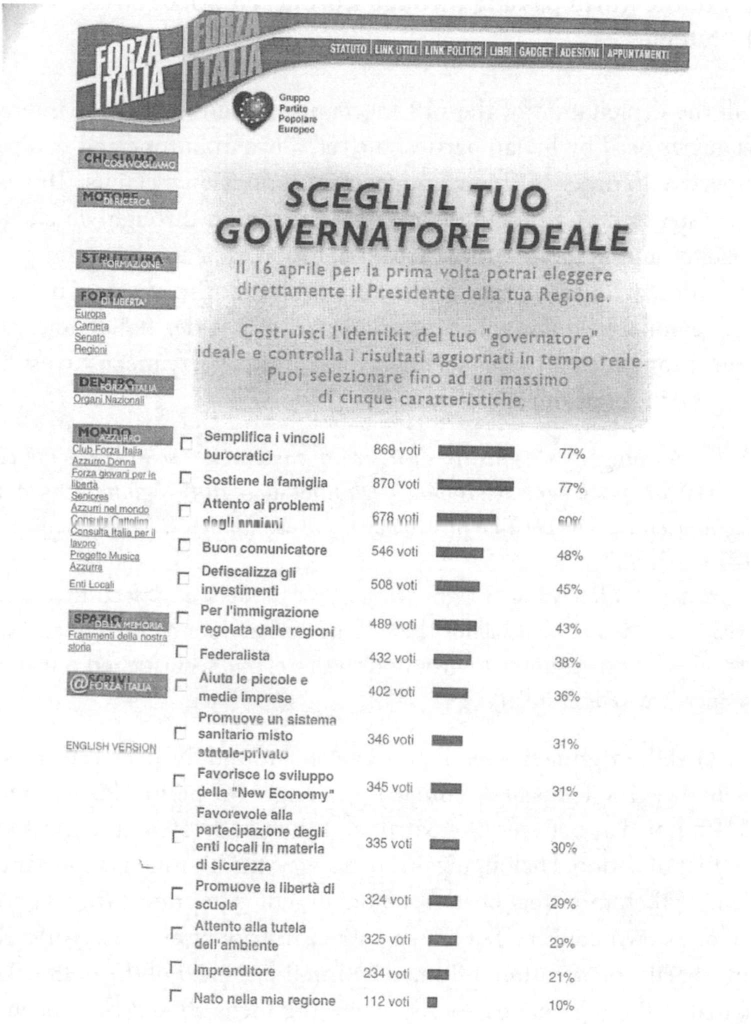

Figure 11. A page from the *Forza Italia* website II

on the political proposals (to simplify bureaucracy, to develop small and medium size firms, to renew the health system etc.) and on the personal features (businessman, talkative, attractive, always smiling etc.) of Silvio Berlusconi and his party, as if to highlight that there is no valid opponent to him within the political scenario. This strategy, in addition, is a way to let someone else (the potential voter, or, let's say, the common man) talk in positive terms about the candidate.

From Italy to the world passing through Europe: New narrative political strategies

Along with the exploitation of the LIB mechanism, there is another interesting rhetorical device used by Italian parties: the reference to Europe and to a world-wide perspective in order to frame and legitimize one's own claims. This is discursively constructed as a process of over-categorization through which, sometimes explicitly and sometimes implicitly, the invitation to share the political programme presented leads the interlocutors to think of themselves not simply in terms of regional belonging, but rather as part of a wider Italian and, consequently, European project. In this sense, voting for that party means to espouse a more far-sighted European view of politics.

> (14)   *Non è un progetto di sinistra, di destra o moderato: è semplicemente ciò che occorre fare per il bene dell'Italia e degli Italiani, se tutti vogliamo che la nostra nazione cresca, che cresca il nostro benessere economico, la nostra sicurezza e la nostra libertà.*
> 'This is not a left-wing, a right-wing nor a moderate project: this is simply what is needed to be done for the sake of Italy and for all the Italians' sake, if we all want our country to grow, our welfare, our security and our freedom to increase' (*Forza Italia*).

In example (14) the argumentation is constructed around the over-categorization of Italian identity. The focus of discourse is no longer the political battle between right and left, nor that between the North and the South. Here, the most salient category is that of national belonging: in such a way, the ingroup is represented by Italian identity, therefore what becomes more urgent is to protect the welfare and security of one's own country. Such a narrative strategy of over-categorization is particularly worthy of attention if framed within the context of the political event analysed, that is the regional elections, where the focus should have been most probably on regional affairs. This use of what we may call a *rhetoric about Italy* becomes also a marketing communication device by which the actual outgroup is represented by those who struggle for local interests instead of being concentrated on national welfare.

A similar process of over-categorization is to be found in relation to the general election, where communication very often orientates towards European affairs, instead of being anchored exclusively in Italian issues. This strategy works rather implicitly within discourse as showed by example (15), taken from the *Ulivo* array.

(15) *A partire dalle nostre grandi radici – l'antifascismo il patriottismo costituzi-*
onale la cultura cristiana-intendiamo costruire una società protesa in avanti che
sappia tutelare e sviluppare i grandi valori di pace libertà democrazia e giustizia
sociale propri del riformismo italiano ed europeo.
'Starting from our great roots – the antifascism, the constitutional patriotism,
the Christian culture – we aim at building a society which is oriented toward
the future, which is able to defend and to develop the great values of peace,
freedom, democracy and social equality, those values that belong to Italian
and European reformism' *(Ulivo* array).

In this example, the reference to Europe is generally rather implicit. It is hinted at
through the claim about the Christian origins of Italy, which the Italian press has
often linked to the discussion about the European Constitution (i.e. whether explicit reference to Christianity should or should not be made in such a document).
At the end of the sentence, however, the reference to Europe becomes explicit,
where Italian reformism is seen as part of the more general European movement.
This permits a more transparent process of over-categorization, which, in a sense,
seems to transcend Europe when the party talks of *a society*, intended to have not
geo-political borders but rather invisible borders, characterized by shared values.

Reference to Europe may also function as a way to gain credibility with the
electorate, as is illustrated by example (16).

(16) *In tutto il mondo è stata considerata la migliore commissaria europea, il miglior*
ministro in tanti anni.
'All over the world she has been considered the best EU commissioner, the
best governor and EU minister for many years' *(Lista Bonino* Party).

This exemplifies elliptic comparison, since Emma Bonino is presented as the best
politician in absolute terms, thus neglecting any reference to her concrete acts
as well as those of her rivals. The *Lista Bonino* Party reinforces its claim by using
Europe as a marketing strategy to catch the voter's attention and to give authority
and credibility to the candidate's public reputation in a context beyond Italy.

Conclusions: From the language of action to a European rhetoric

The typology of the web pages analysed mixes features of advertising style (objective versus subjective) with the reception modalities. In other words, on almost
every site the objectivity of the political proposal introduced to the voters is linked
and mixed with the subjective needs of the electorate, particularly by the repeated
use of the 2nd person pronoun 'your', which helps to create and maintain the di-

rect contact between the party's offer and the voter's request. In this way everyone is satisfied: the voter perceives his/her opinions to be important to the party, while the party obtains popularity and political consent.

As for the LIB hypothesis, the examples drawn from both political campaigns show that political communication shares only in part the features of the model. Indeed, by focusing on concrete features while describing the self, political communication confirms its concrete finality, that is to say it is a language of action.

Related to the LIB hypothesis is the use of what might be called a *European Rhetoric*, that is the process of over-categorization switched to by the political parties when presenting themselves as involved with Italian and European (if not universal) interests and welfare rather than with specifically local interests. This is a strategy to stress the difference between the ingroup and the outgroup, since the ingroup is depicted as the only party able to guarantee such universal interests to the voters, relying once more on what we have called elsewhere (Cortini & Manuti 2002) a *competitive narrative*.

References

Araujo, Lourdes. 1995. "Designing and refining hierarchical coding frames". In *Computer-Aided Qualitative Data Analysis,* U. Kelle (ed), 96–104. London: Sage.

Arcuri, Luciano, Maass, Anne and Portelli, Giovanna. 1993. "Linguistic intergroup bias and implicit attributions". *British Journal of Social Psychology* 32: 277–285.

Axford, Barrie and Huggins, Richard. 2000. *New Media and Politics.* London: Sage.

Barnett, Steven. 1997. "New media, old problems: New technology and the political process". *European Journal of Communication* 12(2): 193–218.

Boudourides, Moses. 2001. "New directions of Internet research". In *Perspectives on Internet Research: Concepts and Methods,* J. Kai, P. Breuer, B. Schauenburg and M. Boos. (eds). Available at < http://www.psych.uni-goettingen.de/congress/gor-2001/contrib/articles.html />. Accessed 23 February 2007.

Branca-Rosoff, Sonia and Marinelli, Cécile. 1994. "Faire entendre sa voix. Le courrier des lecteurs dans les trois quotidiens marseillais". *Mots. Le Langage du Politique* 4: 25–39.

Bruner, Jerome. 1991. "The narrative construction of reality". *Critical Inquiry* 18:1–21.

Castel, Philippe. 1995. "Les formulations du référent-noyau comme trace de positions idéologiques". *Bulletin de Psychologie* 48: 681–686.

Cortini, Michela and Manuti, Amelia. 2002. "Il Marketing Politico sul WEB: Strategie discorsive di auto-presentazione dei partiti Italiani". In *Virtuale. Com. La Parola Spiazzata,* G. Mininni (ed), 123–155. Napoli: Idelson-Gnocchi.

De Martini, Alberto. 1996. *Pubblicità sull'Internet.* Milano: Lupetti.

Denzin, Norman K. and Lincoln, Yvonna S. 1994. *Handbook of Qualitative Research.* Thousand Oaks: Sage.

Deschamps, Jean Claude. 1988. "Social identity and relations of power between groups". *Advances in Social Psychology* 21: 85–98.

Fairclough, Norman. 1993. "Critical discourse analysis and the marketization of public discourse. The universities". *Discourse & Society* 4: 133–168.

Fairclough, Norman and Wodak, Ruth. 1997. "Critical discourse analysis". In *Discourse as Social Interaction*, T. A. van Dijk (ed), 258–284. London: Sage.

Fiedler, Klaus, Semin, Gun and Finkenauer, Catrin. 1993. "The battle of words between gender groups. A language biased approach to intergroup processes". *Human Communication Research* 19: 409–441.

Franco, Fabia and Maass, Anne. 1996. "Implicit vs. explicit strategies of outgroup discrimination: The role of intentional control in biased language use and reward allocation". *Journal of Language and Social Psychology* 15: 335–359.

Galimberti, Carlo and Riva, Giuseppe. 1997. *La Comunicazione Virtuale*. Milano: Guerini.

Gergen, Kenneth J. and Gergen, Mary M. 1988. "Narrative and the self as relationship". *Advances in Social Psychology* 21: 17–55.

Gerstlé, Jacques. 1992. *La Communication Politique*. Paris: PUF.

Ghiglione, Rodolphe. 1988. *La Comunicazione è un Contratto*. Napoli: Liguori.

Ghiglione, Rodolphe. 1989. *Je Vous Ai Compris ou l'Analyse des Discours Politiques*. Paris: Dunot.

Ghiglione, Rodolphe and Bromberg, Marcel. 1998. *Discours Politique et Télévision*. Paris: Presses Universitaires de France.

Greimas, Algirdas J. 1979. *Semiotique. Dictionnaire Raisonné de la Theorie du Language*. Paris: Hachette.

Goffman, Erving. 1959. *The Presentation of the Self in Everyday Life*. New York: Doubleday.

Guerin, Bernard. 1994. "Gender bias in the abstractness of verbs and adjectives". *Journal of Social Psychology* 134: 421–428.

Habib, Laurent. 1992. "La Communication électorale: Quelles difficultés?" *Pouvoirs* 63: 91–101.

Hacker, Kenneth L. and van Dijk, Jan. 2000. *Digital Democracy: Issues of Theory and Practice*. London: Sage.

Heider, Fritz. 1958. *The Psychology of Intergroup Relations*. New York: Wiley.

Jacobelli, Jader. 1998. *La Realtà del Virtuale*. Bari-Roma: Laterza.

Jonas, Kai J., Breuer, Peter, Schauenburg, B., and Boos, Margarete. 2001. *Perspectives on Internet Research: Concepts and Methods*. Available at < http://www.psych.uni-goettingen.de/congress/gor-2001/contrib/articles.html />. Accessed 23 February 2007.

Karpinski, Andy and von Hippel, William. 1996. "The role of linguistic intergroup bias in expectancy maintenance". *Social Cognition* 14: 141–163.

Kelle, Udo. 1995. *Computer-Aided Qualitative Data Analysis*. London: Sage.

Lemke, Jay L. 1995 *Textual Politics: Discourse and Social Dynamics*. London: Taylor & Francis.

Maass, Anne. 1999. "Linguistic intergroup bias: Stereotype perpetuation through language". *Advances in Experimental Social Psychology* 31: 79–121.

Maass, Anne and Arcuri, Luciano. 1992. "The role of language in the persistence of stereotypes". In *Language, Interaction and Social Cognition*, G. R. Semin and K. Fiedler (eds.), 58–78, Newbury Park: Sage.

Maass, Anne, Ceccarelli, R. and Arcuri, Luciano. 1996. "Linguistic intergroup bias: Evidence for intergroup protective motivation". *Journal of Personality and Social Psychology* 71: 512–526.

Maass, Anne, Milesi, A., Zabbini, S. and Stahlberg, Dagmar. 1995. "The linguistic intergroup bias: Differential expectancies or ingroup protection?" *Journal of Personality and Social Psychology* 68:116–126.

Maass, Anne, Salvi, D., Arcuri, Luciano, and Semin, Gun. 1989. "Language use in intergroup context: The linguistic intergroup bias". *Journal of Personality and Social Psychology* 57: 981–993.

Manin, Bernard. 1990. *Métamorphoses du Gouvernement Représentatif.* Rapport CNRS 9017 A.

Mantovani, Giuseppe. 1995. *Comunicazione ed Identità: Dalle Situazioni Quotidiane agli Ambienti Virtuali.* Bologna: Il Mulino.

McCombs, Maxwell and Shaw, David L. 1993. "The agenda setting function of mass media". *Public Opinion Quarterly* 36:176–185.

Mey, Jacob. 1985. *Whose Language: A Study of Linguistic Pragmatics.* Amsterdam: John Benjamins Publications.

Mininni, Giuseppe. 1992 *Diatesti. Per una Psicosemiotica del Discorso Sociale.* Napoli: Liguori.

Mininni, Giuseppe. 2000. *Psicologia del Parlare Comune.* Bologna: Grasso.

Morin, Viviane. 1976. *Rhétorique de l'Ambivalence.* Paris: Hachette.

Morris, Merrill and Ogan, Christine. 1996. "The Internet as mass medium". *Journal of Communication* 46(1): 39–50.

Newhagen, John E., and Rafaeli, Sheizaf. 1996. "Why communication researchers should study the Internet: A dialogue". *Journal of Communication* 46(1):4–13.

Perdue, Craig, Dovidio, John F., Gurtman, Michael B. and Tyler, R.B. 1990. "Us and them: Social categorization and the process of intergroup bias". *Journal of Personality and Social Psychology* 59:475–486.

Petitjean, Luce. 1995. "L'impératif dans le discours politique". *Mots. Le Langage du Politique* 43: 22–36.

Petitjean, Luce. 1999. "Des présidentiables à l'impératif". In *L'Image Candidate à l'Election Présidentielle de 1995,* Groupe Saint-Cloud (ed), 171–182. Paris: L'Harmattan.

Petty, Richard E. and Cacioppo, John T. 1986. *Communication and Persuasion: Central and Peripheral Routes to Attitude Change.* New York: Springer Verlag.

Potter, Jonathan and Wetherell, Margaret. 1987. *Discourse and Social Psychology: Beyong Attitudes and Behaviour.* London: Sage.

Propp, Vladimir J. 1966. *Morfologia della Fiaba.* Torino: Einaudi.

Reips, Ulf D. and Bosnjak, Michael. 2001. *Dimensions of Internet Science.* Lengerich: Pabst Science Publishers.

Richards, Tom J. and Richards, Lyn. 1994. "Using computers in qualitative research". In *Handbook of Qualitative Research,* N.K. Denzin and Y. S. Lincoln (eds), 445–462. Thousand Oaks: Sage.

Richards, Tom J. and Richards, Lyn. 1996. *QSR NUD*IST 4 User Guide.* Melbourne: QSR.

Richardson, John T.E. 1996. *Handbook of Qualitative Research Methods for Psychology and the Social Sciences.* Leicester: BPS Books.

Semin, Gun and Fiedler, Klaus. 1988. "The cognitive functions of linguistic categories in describing persons: Social cognition and language". *Journal of Personality and Social Psychology* 54(4):558–568.

Semin, Gun and Fiedler, Klaus. 1992. "The inferential properties of interpersonal verbs". In *Language, Interaction and Social Cognition,* G. R. Semin and K. Fiedler (eds.), 58–78. Newbury Park: Sage.

Singh, Surendra N., and Dalal, Nikunj P. 1999. "Web home pages as advertisements". *Communications of the ACM* 42(8): 91–98.

Slama Cazacu, Tatiana. 1997. "Manipulating by words". *International Journal of Psycholinguistics* 13(3): 285–296.

Street, John. 1997. "Remote control? Politics, technology and electronic democracy". *European Journal of Communication* 12(1): 27–42.

Tajfel, Henri. 1981. *Human Groups and Social Categories: Studies in Social Psychology.* Cambridge: Cambridge University Press.

Tajfel, Henri and Turner, John. 1986. "The social identity theory of intergroup behaviour". In *Psychology of Intergroup Relations*, S. Worchel and W.G. Austin (eds), 7–24. Chicago: Nelson.

Thompson, John B. 1995. *The Media and the Modernity. A Social Theory of the Media.* Cambridge: Polity Press.

Tumber, Howard and Bromley, Michael. 1998. "Virtual soundbites: Political communication in cyberspace". *Media, Culture & Society* 20: 159–167.

Turner, John. 1975. "Social comparison and social identity: Some prospects for intergroup behaviour". *European Journal of Social Psychology* 5: 5–34.

Trzebinski, Jerzy. 1995. "Il sé narrativo". In *Il Sé Come Testo*, A. Smorti (ed), 60–81. Milano: Giunti.

Van Dijk, Teun A. 1993. "Principles of critical discourse analysis". *Discourse and Society* 3(1): 87–108.

Van Dijk, Teun A. 1998. *Ideology. A Multidisciplinary Approach.* London: Sage Publications.

Wetherell, Margaret and Potter, Jonathan. 1992. *Mapping the Language of Racism. Discourse and the Legitimation of Exploitation.* London: Harvester Whearsheaf.

Wigboldus, Daniel H.J., Semin, Gun R. and Spears, Russell.2000. "How do we communicate stereotypes? Linguistic biases and inferential consequences". *Journal of Personality and Social Psychology* 78(1): 5–18.

Are Brummies developing narratives of European identity?

Michael Toolan
University of Birmingham, UK

Introduction

In this paper I am interested in the European identity – if any – of Brummies (the latter is the colloquial name for 'ordinary' people born and bred in Birmingham cf. Geordie for natives of the city of Newcastle). I want to probe the extent to which ordinary people in an ordinary part of Britain – Birmingham – may be developing some slight, but at any rate growing, sense of themselves as Europeans. If they are, I argue, this must entail some shift (again, no doubt slight at first) in their sense of self and identity, and some change in the personal narratives they will tell. For a person's European-ness (or race, or gender, etc.) to be demonstrably part of their identity, it is not necessary for their narratives ever to be *about* Europe, explicitly; but I would argue that Europe must at least be in the background of some of those narratives, or be part of what Bhaya Nair has called the 'impli-culture' (Bhaya Nair 2002: 179–188, 224–234), or treated as in defining contrast with something within the narratives. Conversely, if all of a person's narratives make sense and have interactional value without any mention or presupposing of or opposing of Europe, then the latter has no more role in their identity than the Antarctic or Atlantis have.

The issues involved are complex and interrelated, but an appropriate place to begin is with the very idea of Europe. I won't dwell long on the 'What *is* Europe?' question. Depending on whether you use political association, economic ties, geographical connection, defence ties, linguistic commonalities, shared recent history, ethnic similarity, and so on indefinitely, we can identify many different Europes, and these are neither all based on a common core nor without Europe-internal 'non-European' patches. The Europe of the twenty-seven EU states is but one of many Europes. But like others, it has a strong family resemblance with received ideas of Europe, and I think we must take it as common ground that such ideas are real and powerful.

Self and identity

A useful starting-point for brief notes on the nature of self and identity in the postmodern world are these remarks from Giddens (1991: 53, 54):

> self-identity …is not a set of traits or observable characteristics. It is a person's own reflexive understanding of their biography. self-identity has continuity- that is, it cannot easily be completely changed at will – but that continuity is only a product of the person's reflexive beliefs about their own biography…. A person's identity is not to be found in behaviour, nor – important though this is – in the reactions of others, but in the capacity *to keep a particular narrative going.*

The reference to the sustaining of a narrative at this quotation's close is importantly contrastive with the 'set of traits' standard, in its implicitly social and discoursal frame. A narrative cannot be judged to have been 'kept going' except by means of ratification by others, an audience or co-narrators, with whom the narrating self shares a context of situation. So to Giddens's characterizing of self-identity must be added the point that identity is crucially a process with a recipient design or dialogical element. That is to say, the various means by which a person projects their narrative of personal identity (above all through discursive choices – and within discourse, above all in talk – but also by means of choices of dress, food, religion, leisure activity, ethnic affiliation, sexual orientation, home and furniture preferences, etc.) are not merely expressive of self but also responsive to other (the response may constitute solidary assent to, or a warding off of that other, or fall somewhere in between). The way that identity is multiple, performed, and impermanent has been well captured by Lemke (2002: 72):

> What else is an identity but the performance, verbally and nonverbally, of a possible constellation of attitudes, beliefs, and values that has a recognizable coherence by the criteria of some community?

Identity has arguably never been more transient, less compulsorily stable and permanent than it is in the west today (giving rise to the concept of the 'liquid individual' who in time changes career, partner, country of residence, etc.). Identity assignment is also often a resource by means of which individuals, institutions and states seek to stabilize and 'discipline' the potential fluidity of human roles and relations, for a multiplicity of social purposes, including equity of treatment. As an impermanent phenomenon, identity is something continuously to be performed, by all the semiotic means available, including multi-modally. Thus, besides an individual's verbal 'witness' (their conversational style, accent, dialect, their oral and written narratives, and so on), identity can be expressed by (or inferred from) a person's choices in dress, food, leisure pursuits, work habits, and elsewhere.

Do people in Birmingham have a sense of European identity? Birmingham's official tourist literature trumpets that the city has more canals than Venice, and more trees than Paris, which reflect a kind of Europe-mindedness. But otherwise, and notwithstanding various twinned-city arrangements, Birmingham might be felt to have only a limited sense of its 'membership' of the European cultural framework. And yet how would one begin to prove or disprove such a claim, moving beyond the anecdotal (e.g., my Greek Ph.D. student who complains that there are 'too many Greek' people in the city) or the statistical (e.g., the extent of use of European languages here, the availability of European commodities)? Do Brummies even think that Birmingham is in Europe? Do they affiliate with distinctively European forms of life, for example in ways of playing sport, in diet and cuisine, in religious practices, in legal arrangements, in employment and industrial practices, in education, in language? Are there moments in the rich flow of their everyday lives when Birmingham people can be heard saying 'Oh but we Europeans tend to X....'? Or, 'In Europe, we....'? Or '(You) non-Europeans habitually X...'? Or, if they are not heard *saying* any of these, are they at least tacitly *implying* them, by means of other of their sayings and doings? Identity entails discrimination. Are there then any situations of *discrimination* in favour of or against Brummies, on the grounds that they are Europeans? (In such cases, it will not be criterial that the person is a Brummie – they should be equally able to be Madrilenos or Athenians – but that they are European.) If identity requires discrimination and contrast (with *something*) we must nevertheless beware of pre-judging what that contrast will be. Recent research in political science, for example, suggests that with the exception of extreme right-wing voters, most Europeans find no clash between a national and a European identity; in fact there is a positive correlation: the more a person feels Irish, the more likely they are to feel European (Bruter 2005). So the 'other' of European-ness seems not to be nation (but there must be an other).

If the answer to these questions tends to be 'No', the short explanation I believe lies in the fact that we in Europe are pulled in two different directions: globalization and localism. The old bumper sticker said *Act locally, think globally*, and made no mention of anything in between. Similarly, everywhere you look in Europe you see harmonizing forces at work: financial, economic, legal, educational and perhaps linguistic arrangements which strive to be applicable throughout Europe and even beyond. Partly in reaction to this – as a recuperative or compensatory response that gives renewed recognition to particularity of place, circumstances, history, acknowledging what is democratic in fostering devolution and subsidiarity – localism in many forms has been revalued (this remains so even though this antonymic pair exercise a pull which is opposite but not equal). In brief, everywhere in Europe we see signs of global identity, and in many places we also see signs of local identity; what we do not see, arguably, are signs of *European* identity. For that matter, we may ask how many distinctively European visual icons are there, that might be set beside such British signs as the Queen's head in profile as on the postage stamps, the bulldog, the lion, the Union flag, representations of Big Ben, the Houses of Parliament, Beefeater guards, bewigged English judges, the flat-cap-wearing Northerner, and so on? The only *European* visual sign that immediately comes to mind is the ring of golden stars – so established an emblem of Europeanness that in the UK anti-EU campaigners have a bumper sticker which has this ring of stars with a diagonal red line running across it.

I am not sure that there are established contrastive moments, sites or signs of Europeanness within popular Birmingham culture, and as a result it is a moot point whether ordinary Birmingham people have a sense of European identity. But in saying it is a *moot* point, I don't intend to declare, without further discussion, that it is an *untenable* point. If it *is* a tenable claim that Brummies have some European identity, it will be so only if this identity does not involve much in the way of overt exclusionary (and inclusive) discourses, behaviours, and so on. And that is where we get to the late modern or post-modern crux: can you have a particular identity or affiliation without display/adherence/upholding of various discriminatory markers of inclusion and exclusion? This for me is a question with no simple answer.

It also needs to be acknowledged that the socio-political world has moved on a considerable distance since the research for this paper was done; in particular, in the wake of the 11 September 2001 atrocities, a mythical Manichean world of black and white, Al Qaeda vs. America, global terrorism vs. globalized democracy has been projected by powerful political and media interests. In everyday lives in Birmingham like everywhere else, allegiances and identities are inevitably immensely more subtle and complex. But with, in the background, the non-Islamic West's anxieties about engaging with so-called Islamic states, a current uncertainty centres on how soon, and under what conditions, will Turkey be permitted to join the EU. This political question is also one of identity: is Turkey, a predominantly Muslim country in contrast with the historically Christian traditions of all 27 current EU countries, sufficiently compatible with these latter (not just in religion but in political and legal arrangements) for the act of identity that EU membership constitutes to take place? As we know, some EU members like France are tending to answer No, not yet. On the other hand one notices also a parallel between a local polity like Birmingham, where Muslims are a significant minority in a historically white and Christian city, and an EU enlarged to include Turkey.

Another phenomenon that has perhaps become more palpable over the last decade or so is the particularly prominent role played by two distinct age-groups of middle-class Europeans in the practical performative achievement of European identity: educated, dependentless young adults, and the active economically-comfortable retired. These groups more than others, and in large numbers, are seizing the opportunity to study and work, or live and play, respectively, in whichever part of Europe is congenial to them. All this is facilitated by new provisions and arrangements, cultural and practical as well as legal and technical, to say nothing of the comparative ease and cheapness of travel. With the coming of the euro, exchange rates are in many situations a thing of the past; but the rate of *cultural* and *interpersonal* exchange, e.g. between Brummies and other Europeans, has never operated in such large volume.

Monitoring the narrative performance of European identity

The 'direct method' of probing the Europeanness of Birmingham people, by simply going up to them and asking, is fraught with obvious unreliabilities, which stem from the well-known divergence between what people *say* they believe, and what their behaviour suggests they believe. Oral narratives of personal experience are an invaluable mediation here because, despite being verbal, they are as much a behaviour as a saying. After Lakoff and others (e.g., Lakoff and Johnson 1980), cognitive and social linguists are used to talking about the conceptual metaphors we live by. In somewhat parallel fashion, I wanted to determine whether there are certain identifiable local narratives by which people in communities or sub-communities live by. It seemed to me that one way of uncovering ordinary people's sustaining narratives would be by analysing a representative sample of talk from a series of local-radio phone-in discussion programmes, which are ostensibly on the tellable ups and downs of everyday life in Birmingham. I have proceeded on the assumption that something might be revealed about ordinary people's sense of themselves, and of their relation to Europe and their ideas of Europe – the stories they tell themselves about Europe – by scrutiny of the way they talk about Europe in a relatively random sample of phone-in local radio programs broadcast in the Birmingham conurbation (aka the West Midlands), by the BBC local radio station Radio WM.

There are many kinds of phone-in radio shows. Those that I particularly monitored turned out to have less of the broad opinion-airing and 'village-pump' function, than I had imagined they would, where the radio phone-in facilitates a kind of live and unscripted and unmanaged political meeting. But in the phone-in shows I monitored, hosted by local celebrities Ed Doolan, Carl Chinn or similar trusted figures (both shows have a strong local following), I expected to hear numerous stories about 'Birmingham yesterday and today'. On occasion, people do phone in to such programmes on the grounds, roughly, that they want to resolve or simply discuss a topic in the public domain, that extends beyond their own local social network of family and friends, about which they care a good deal. But on the days I monitored, calls that raised issues of broad community concern were rare at most. Rather the focus was on personal difficulties securing entitlements, home-repairs, and the like: or callers wanted practical help with practical difficulties. Callers are often retirees, or out of work, or housebound; they seem to be predominantly white (less true of Chinn's afternoon programme), roughly equally of either sex and tend to be middle-aged or older. Doolan's participants seem to be overwhelmingly working-class, Chinn's more mixed; Doolan's participants in effect consult him as if – as is probably true – they lack easy access to professional advice from a bank manager, lawyer, accountant, etc.

In the course of telling their implicit stories of personal difficulty, frustration, and very occasionally of success, I expected a macro-narrative about 'Birmingham past and present' to emerge. And in the course of that more intermittent macro-narrative, I wanted to see whether these phone-in tellers and chroniclers also indirectly told a story (or stories) about other things: the second World War, 'loss of jobs to Europe', being a part of Europe or being different from it, and so on and so forth. I hoped that, spontaneously and in this relatively unconscious way, they would in some small way 'narratively perform' whatever European identity they might tacitly lay claim to.

In reality, the task proved to lie somewhere between difficult and impossible. Over several weeks in April 2000, I monitored many hours of local talk-radio involving the two cited broadcasters, who pilot two- to three-hour long programmes in the mid-morning and afternoon slots on Radio WM respectively. (Radio WM is the BBC local radio station, WM standing for West Midlands: the principal audiences are people in Birmingham, Coventry and Wolverhampton.) Somewhat to my surprise, I have not heard even oblique mentions of Europe in either the presenter's bully-pulpit pronouncements or in the callers' requests, complaints, observations, etc. Discoursal absence or silence can undoubtedly be salient in certain contexts, as Ruth Wodak has shown (Wodak 1991; 1995) in drawing our attention to the silence in the Austrian New Freedom Party's declarations about the Nazi period, concerning the Nazi genocidal destruction of Jewish people. But what to make of the local talk radio silence with respect to Europe is a different issue, with a different significance.

Here, for example, is a list of the topics raised by a sequence of calls on Ed Doolan's programme, on one Monday morning:

> Carol in Oldbury phones in to thank the local St John's Ambulance volunteers for their generous participation in a local fundraising event;
>
> Julie H., visiting the West Midlands from Australia, phones in with names of relatives she is trying to trace, who 25 years ago were living in Nuneaton...
>
> Arthur G. is recently back from a week-long holiday in Blackpool (120 miles to the North-West); he travelled both ways by National Express coach, and the driver got lost both ways; the return journey took 8 hours, and Arthur wants an explanation (and compensation perhaps?)
>
> Peggy in Castle Bromwich has a grown-up daughter who wants to get a dog, but one that she'll be given instructions on how to care for it.
>
> Rina phones in with details of a dog she has found, which she wants to re-unite with its owner.
>
> Anne in Rubery phones in, in need of a plumber and a plasterer--the previous plumber has abandoned the job, leaving an entire bathroom suite laid out in pieces in her front room...
>
> Elderly man whose wife has recently died is trying to get rid of a car passenger-side swivel seat, for easy entry/exit by a disabled person...
>
> Presenter, Ed Doolan, interpolates a rambling spot about uncovering and playing one of his first on-air tapes which, egotist that he is, he found both excruciating but worth talking about on-air now for about 10 minutes.
>
> Bob G. phones in from Streetly about the leaking roof in his apartment block, on a run-down estate, which turns out not to be council-owned but in private hands, and how can the landlord be pressed to do the repairs...

And so on. My thesis is that, for ordinary Midlands people like Carol, Julie, Arthur and so on (who are of course only a small segment of the full spectrum), a part of the macro-narratives of their lives and identities can be extrapolated or inferred from the seemingly random 'encyclopedia' of facts and values and concerns on display in their phone-in talk. This won't be the full macro-narrative: given the nature of the particular radio show, and certain taboos and conventions, their sexual and religious identities, for example, may not be performed here (but other phone-in programmes do enable such airings). But a kind of underlying coherence can be postulated of this partial macro-narrative, a coherence affirmed by the fact that this diversity of voices and contributions are all to the same programme, to the same ultimate addressees (the listening audience) and to the same immediate addressee, the radio host, with their rights to speak and to silence – that is, to add some shape and structure to callers' contributions.

There are many valuable commentaries on the place of narratives in our sense of our selves and our identities, from the broadly cultural (Antaki and Widdicombe 1998; and Georgakopoulou 2006, who emphasizes the importance of 'small' narratives), to the social psychological (Polkinghorne 1988) to the constructionist (Bruner 1991 and, more socio-politically-oriented, Somers 1994 and Hearn 2002) to the educational-linguistic (Michaels 1981), the social-autobiographical (Brockmeier and Carbaugh 2001; De Fina 2003) and the health-oriented. Schiffrin (1996) is particularly germane, if not uncannily applicable. It takes as foundational the assumption that the narratives we tell each other *verbalize* and *situate* experience as text, and that in so doing, such narrative texts provide "a resource for the display of self and identity" (1996: 167). There is an interesting continuity between the self-portraiture that Schiffrin's article charted, at the intimate level of mother-in-law/daughter-in-law relations, and the kind of Europeanness disclosures or enactments that I was looking for. For example, the first of the two personal narratives Shiffrin analyses (172–180) is on the topic of Jewish-Gentile intermarriage in American society, and on the ways in which a young woman's mother subtly *performs* her sense of her distinctive Jewish identity in the course of recounting certain conversational episodes with her daughter. One such is:

Mother: You're goin' out with a <u>Gentile</u> boy?
Daughter: Well <u>Daddy</u> knows his father.
Mother: <u>I</u> don't care. [sc. that you are going out with a Gentile: MT]
(Schiffrin 1996: 175)

Schiffrin notes that the mother seems to see intermarriage "as a threat to the continuation of a thriving Jewish tradition in America" (172); and the mother elsewhere remarks of Gentiles that "they're different" (174), and also reports her daughter finding that dating a non-Jew is unsatisfactory since "It's not what I'm used to" (174). In the second story that Schiffrin analyses (180–190), a daughter-in-law is uncomfortable addressing her mother-in-law as Mom, and this is represented as 'a sore spot' by that mother-in-law. After a heated discussion, the mother-in-law suggests that as a fall-back option she should address her by her first name, but: "She still can't bring herself to say Zelda, so she calls me nothing!" (180).

Schiffrin comments that the daughter-in-law's resistance over naming is "the threat posed by someone who has already become an 'insider' ... but refuses [in naming behaviour] to act like one." (181) Furthermore, in calling her mother-in-law by no name, the daughter creates what Schiffrin calls "a symbolic vacuum" (190). Again, both these characteristics I suggest may have their analogues in local discourses about Europe. That is, Birmingham people might be found speaking about Europe in ways characteristic of 'the resistant insider', leaving or creating symbolic vacuums. But as I have already indicated, really not enough spontaneous evidence has arisen to confirm or disconfirm these possibilities.

But there is a fundamental methodological difference between Schiffrin's approach and what I attempted. Whereas I have sought to garner evidence of European mindedness by means of lurking and observing, invisibly as it were, Schiffrin set about creating the materials that she would then use as data: she organized discursive interviews with subjects, retaining considerable control of topic. This makes sense since her aim was to show how, in the course of their personal narratives, people construct self-portraits: the focus is on the sociolinguistic resources used, rather than the particular identity that is projected. But where one wants to describe and understand European identity, it is controversial whether it is sensible for the analyst to ask selected people what they think of Europe and Europeans, hoping for the narratives to spill out. More effective might be the consulting of two or three people, preferably ones who know each other, and asking them about their sense of Englishness, or of West Midland-ness, or indeed their sense of being a 'world citizen' – i.e., orienting informants and potential narrative -tellers to one of the categories that relatively straightforwardly contrasts with 'Europeanness'.

In light of this, I want to know if the same principle applies to what we might here call 'European narrativizing'. That is, are Europeans an ethnic group, and do their stories differ from those of non-Europeans in demonstrable ways? From one perspective the idea seems bizarre, profoundly different from the everyday idea of what an ethnic group is. On the other hand it was perhaps implicit, all those years ago, in Whorf's postulation of Standard Average European as a single normative set of language cryptotypes associatable with a particular unified mindset. I particularly want to know if Europeans are, at some level of analysis, *one* ethnic group, because if they are not, and if it is further felt that they can never become one, then, arguably, my entire enquiry would be mistaken.

Are Europeans an ethnic group?

The question now raised, then, is what counts as an ethnic group. Before the law, in England and Wales, recent cases where prosecution under the Race Relations Act has been attempted have led senior law lords to rule (in *Mandla v Dowell Lee* 1983) that an ethnic group (in the terms of the act) will be characterized by a long shared history and shared culture and customs, and that the latter will not be of an exclusively religious nature; at slight variance with these criteria, one law lord (Templeman, in his opinion in the *Mandla* case) has added 'shared geography' as a criterion. In current practice this has meant that, in general, Jews and Sikhs are recognized as ethnic groups protected by the act, while Catholics, Muslims and Rastafarians are not (although a group of distinctively Irish Catholics or

Punjab-origin Muslims would be protected: see *Walker v Hussein* 1996). Such a complex and seemingly inconsistent position may not of course be the narrative of ethnic grouping that we live by; it has to be set alongside people's everyday ideas of belonging and affiliation, legally recognized or otherwise. And the very least that needs emphasizing is the radical break that has been effected between ethnicity and biology, race or nation; this has been eloquently reflected in the position of champions of deaf people's rights in the USA, who have campaigned for recognition of deaf people as a distinct ethnic group (with their own distinct language and culture), entitled to freedom from racial discrimination. In Toolan (2002:179) I have suggested that, following the English law lords' proscriptions as constructively as possible, it might be concluded that in English law "a group defined by ethnic origins" reduces essentially to the following: "A self-identified and other-recognized group with a long and distinct culture, where that culture entails significantly more than purely religious observances".

In current English law, then – and even with the bolstering of the Race Relations Act by the equal treatment provisions of the Human Rights Act 2000 – whether any group with an identifiably distinct culture counts as an ethnic group becomes a matter of largely subjective determination. In *Dawkins v. Dept. of the Environment* (1993) Lord Neil decided that the sixty years since the founding of Rastafarianism was "not long enough" to count as a long history, and this alone seems to have been the basis on which the appeal failed. As for Europe, or more specifically the European Union, would the Lord Neils of this world perhaps say that, like Rastafarianism, it was developing into a group defined by ethnic origins by virtue of its developing distinct culture, and only lacked longevity?

Turning back to allusions or 'implicultural' invocations of Europe and European-ness in the local Birmingham media, it is perhaps worth noting that Europe is somewhat more prominent in the print media, such as the daily newspaper the *Birmingham Post*, than on local radio. There are many reasons for this contrast, to do with audience and function, too numerous to discuss here. Suffice to say that a number of leitmotivs of UK-European relations are sounded in various subsections of the newspaper (including stories about 'those crazy continentals' and 'those corrupt Eurocrats'), reflecting a predominant hostility to stronger ties with Europe. The data or story-making is not all one way: in the issues of if that I examined, the newspaper was addressing and construing the fact that Birmingham's own cultural icon, Sir Simon Rattle, had moved on to become principal conductor of the Berlin Philharmonic with whom he had produced enthusiastically-received concerts in Vienna. It is hard for any Birmingham news outlet to report these developments without at least a grudging acknowledgement of Anglo-German common ground: Sir Simon's move forces Birmingham to 'share' him with Berlin. In any event, outside the letters page (itself vulnerable to selective editing), a newspaper such as the Birmingham Post is not a forum for ordinary people, in which they can perform their own narratives of identity. To a much greater extent, local phone-in radio shows are.

EU says

I want to end with the radio phone-in programmes, which in general carried the disappointing message that Europe plays at best a slender role in the stories and identities of (some) ordinary Birmingham people. Because – a light at the end of the Channel tunnel, perhaps—there occurred, on the last day of my process of monitoring, one call that mentioned Europe, and was in fact the only call that made the slightest mention of Europe or the EU. I call it 'Harry and the Water Meter', but I have an alternative title for it which I will come to later. Below I reproduce a transcript of the relevant part of Harry's on-air exchange with the host of the show, Ed Doolan (designated as H and ED, respectively, in the transcript).

Harry and the Water Meter
[Ed Doolan Show, radio WM, am, 4 May 2000]

H: Exactly. Anyway what I've phoned for is to er be of help I hope to er a lot of people who're in the same position as meself, living alone, and er, seventy-three years it's took me to find that there is such a thing as a free meal

ED: Ooh tell me

H: Now, I listen to er radio 4 every morning and a couple of months ago they announced that the EU says Water Board has got to fit water meters free of charge

ED: Yes, that's right

H: So I waited, and I applied, they came last week, before they did any thing I said I wanted to know how much... Not a penny

ED: that's right

H: I said fair enough. Secondly, am I going to save money. Definitely. If you live on your own

ED: Yes

H: It's gonna be about eighty quid savings

ED: Yes

H: So I said OK go ahead. Within an hour it was all done, they cleaned up they was smashing. Right? Now, this is what I say about a free meal

ED: Now this is true. This is very true Harry and we've been talking about

H: Anybody anybody living on their own,

ED: Yep

H: You see my water bill was about two hundred and twenty quid

ED: Mm

H: A year.

ED: Mm

H: Well, eighty quid, we moan about the seventy-five pence ro-raise, but there's about one pound fifty, goin' beggin', a week.

ED: I say this to anybody living on their own, if you aren't on a water meter you should be

H: That's right, that's right

ED: And, the water companies will actually send you a little a little er formula so you can work out yourself

H: Yep

ED: Whether you're better off, but if you're living on your own you are better off, I'm telling you

H: When I, when I phoned them up to to make enquiries and they said some-body would come they asked me for a er password, so that er you know I wouldn't let anybody in who wasn't er official

ED: Which water company, Harry?

H: It was, erm, South Staffs

ED: Very good, very good [loud inbreath] well done well that's good Harry that's good news

Harry clearly selects the message that 'there is such a thing as a free meal' as his story's moral. But from a different perspective, this narrative's moral might have been that EU directives can be a good thing. Hence my alternative title for the story of Harry and the Water Meter is 'God Bless the EU!' (or, to be really provoc-ative, 'God Bless Our Gracious EU'!). After all, the EU encouragement to people to meter their water, hence record and think about how much of this precious commodity they use, and the EU's further provision that retired homeowners be entitled to have a meter fitted free of charge, means, as Harry well knows, that he will save £1.50 per week henceforward. And this is double the niggardly and widely-criticized 75 pence increase that the government had recently made to the state pension. For Harry, at the time he tells his story, the EU has been twice as good to him as the British government; in light of which, at the time of his call, with which of these – the UK or the EU – might Harry's loyalties lie?

One could also say 'God Bless the Water authority', but it is clear that they are only doing what the 'EU says'. At the same time, Harry's account is one with recur-sive embedding of 'problem-helper-solution' narratives of a loosely Greimassian kind (Greimas 1966). If the EU fills the Helper role in the superordinate narrative, South Staffs water board employees are the Helper in the immediately embedded narrative, and adjoined to these is a third narrative where Harry himself is Helper, alerting all other seniors to this 'free lunch' in the form of a free, bill-reducing water meter.

It would be tempting to see the role of the EU in Harry's everyday story of Brummie folk as symptomatic of a growing significance of Europe and European-ness in the life-stories of ordinary Birmingham people. "EU says", Harry says, and one can easily imagine further narratives, identity-statements, in which the EU says or does or is spoken of or done to; and similarly, for other identifiably European phenomena. But clearly this is not guaranteed, such is current local and national ambivalence about Europe, however the latter is defined. What does however seem beyond question is that much the better way to uncover folk iden-tifications is by 'bottom-up' research strategies, rather than 'top-down' scrutiny of, for example, the national media which can all too easily manufacture narratives and identities just as they do consent.

This is why local talk radio *ought* to be one good place (by far from the only place) to gather everyday self-representations, including stories, of ordinary lo-cally-affiliated people. Focussing on local radio phone-in shows, with an over-whelmingly locally-minded and working-class audience and participation group, I attempted to eavesdrop on narrativizations of Europeanness (or non-European-ness). The eavesdropping or overhearing strategy seems to me often to be more reliable than more participatory or interventionist methods, where, for example, one induces interactants to talk about their holidays, or travel, or working abroad, or what people think about Americans, and trawls 'the product' for construals of Europeanness. And yet the latter, arguably, is less artificial and more authen-tic than any questionnaire approach. Nevertheless, the 'overhearing' technique, with the given body of unwitting informants, yielded little in the way of reliable evidence – unless one is to draw the conclusion that these ordinary Brummie folk, within the context of the radio phone-in programme, were not in the least oriented to any putative European-ness. Rather, they were fully taken up with get-ting someone to fix their bathroom, or leaking roof, or getting some tax refund, or complaining about local council services, and so on. Their selves, identities, and personal narratives were, in this partial and limited and unrepresentative sample, almost entirely invested elsewhere than in or in relation to Europe – with the one interesting exception of Harry. It is likely that there would have been more of the same if a larger sample of talk radio shows, across a longer span of time, had been monitored, but the methodology itself seems to me defensible; and it might well be that a second sampling now, or in the near future, might reveal a gradual iden-tity shift, towards or away from European-ness (here in Birmingham or indeed anywhere else in Europe).

One objection to this scrutiny of local talk radio is simply to attribute the absence of mentions of Europe to the host and the callers' judgement that Europe is not discursively relevant to the kinds of issues that these programmes should cover. By the same token, do people in Lyons or Lisbon, for example orient explicitly to European identity in local radio phone-ins? To respond to the second point first, this rhetorical question awaits an empirical answer, but my expectation could be summed up, as found in the Birmingham case, as "only slightly". Thus my speculative conclusion is not that Birmingham people identify less with 'Europe' than residents of other European cities, but that for all kinds of Europeans, other, mainly more localized kinds of identification make the pan-regional sense of identity remain deep in the discursive background. But this returns us to the first objection: perhaps to look in local talk radio for acts of European identity is simply to look in the wrong place. As I have tried to argue above, I believe non-political, non-current affairs, local talk radio is a 'site of special discursive interest', particularly for the voices of the ordinary woman or man, *despite* the fact that various kinds of topic (religion, party politics, sex) are not ratified topics and may even be kept off the programme by producers or other gatekeepers. Certain kinds of identity will out, are displayed, around the edges or in the interstices of the on-air conversation about parking spaces for people with a disability or the unreliable bus service from Northfield to the city centre. Every time someone phones in to air a complaint that unironically begins "My wife and I were shopping at Sainsbury's the other day" they are performing a heterosexual identity, asserting they are economically active, indicating 'loyalty' to one of the few-remaining and controversially powerful supermarket companies, and aligning with standard English dialect (Cf. "Me and the wife were shopping…"). In the same way, I believe, European identity needs to be performed in some way, however obliquely, off the record, or accidentally, if it can be said to exist; a 'use it or lose it' principle applies, at least as far as the social or public domain is concerned. If you never say, do, dress, eat, spend, etc. like an Aston Villa fan, to what extent are you one? Now it would be perfectly possible to argue for the (growing) European identity of Brummies by other means: for instance, if statistics show a massive increase in the volume of visits to Europe from Birmingham in recent years, or disproportionate growth in the Birmingham consumption of 'European' food, goods and services, or growth in the numbers of marriages between Brummies and nationals of other European states; and so on. But these are all aggregative; only in situated discourse can we examine particular acts of identity: particular Brummies talking about their European partner, or the Serrano ham they brought back from Spain, or how their company brochures are printed in Bratislava. Those kinds of stories can crop up in informal social settings – pubs, clubs, kitchens and living-rooms. But they involve the further difficulties that they require assiduous overhearing with some means of recording the activity; and where not actively elicited, they are usually aimed at a tiny domestic audience. In talk radio ordinary peoples' stories are volunteered, certainly not elicited by the discourse analyst, and knowingly and consequentially directed to a large and largely anonymous audience.

One final thought I would emphasize is that identity (and the narratives it fosters) can often be thought of as both serious and fun at the same time, like a game or sport. The 'performance' aspect of identity helps to justify one in saying that it is recreational, and good exercise: it keeps you alert. Like most games, identity performance requires that there be opposing teams, and winners and losers. It is only when some group imagines that they are winners all round (have the best in every category: children, food, countryside, language, army, constitution, artists, scientists, etc.) that the game is no fun.

References

Antaki, Charles, & Widdicombe, Sue, eds. 1998. *Identities in Talk*. London: Sage.
Bhaya Nair, Rukmini. 2002. *Narrative Gravity: Conversation, Cognition, Culture*. Delhi: Oxford University Press.
Brockmeier, Jens, and Donal Carbaugh, ed. 2001. *Narrative and Identity: Studies in Autobiography, Self and Culture*. New York: John Benjamins.
Bruner, Jerome. 1991. "The narrative construction of reality". *Critical Inquiry*, 18(1):1–21.
Bruter, Michael. 2005. *Citizens of Europe? The Emergence of a Mass European Identity*. Basingstoke: Palgrave-MacMillan
Dawkins v Dept of the Environment. Court of Appeal [1993] IRLR 284
De Fina, Anna. 2003. *Identity in Narrative: A Study of Immigrant Discourse*. Amsterdam/Philadelphia: John Benjamins Publishing Company.
Georgakopoulou, Alexandra. 2006. "Small and large identities in narrative (inter)-action". In *Discourse and Identity*, A. De Fina, D. Schiffrin, and M. Bamberg, (eds.), 83–101. Cambridge: Cambridge University Press.
Giddens, Anthony. 1991. *Modernity and Self-identity: Self and Society in the Late Modern Age*. London: Polity.
Greimas, Algirdas-Julien. 1966. *Sémantique Structurale*, Paris: Larousse.
Hearn, Jonathan. 2002. "Narrative, agency, and mood: On the social construction of national history in Scotland". *Comparative Studies in Society and History* 44(4): 745–769.
Lakoff, George, and Mark Johnson. 1980. *Metaphors We Live By*. Chicago: University of Chicago Press.
Lemke, Jay. 2002. "Language development and identity: Multiple timescales in the social ecology of learning". In *Language Acquisition and Language Socialization*, C. Kramsch (ed.), 68–87. London: Continuum.
Mandla v Dowell Lee. House of Lords [1983] IRLR 209 and [1983] 2 AC, 562.
Michaels, Sarah 1981. ""Sharing time": Children's narrative styles and differential access to literacy". *Language in Society* 10: 423–442.
Polkinghorne, Donald E. 1988. *Narrative Knowing and the Human Sciences*. Albany: State University of New York Press.

Schiffrin, Deborah. 1996. "Narrative as self-portrait: Sociolinguistic constructions of identity". *Language in Society* 25(2):167–203.

Somers, Margaret R. 1994. "The narrative constitution of identity: A relational and network approach". *Theoretical Sociology* 23(5): 605–649.

Toolan, Michael. 2002. "The language myth and the law". In *The Language Myth in Western Culture*, R. Harris (ed.), 159–182. London: Routledge/Curzon.

Van Leeuwen, Theo and Wodak, Ruth. 1999. "Legitimizing immigration control: A discourse historical analysis". *Discourse Studies* 1: 83–119.

J H Walker Ltd v Hussain and others. [1996] IRLR 11 EAT

Wodak, Ruth. 1991. "Turning the tables: Anti-Semitic discourse in postwar Austria". *Discourse and Society* 2(1): 65–85.

Wodak, Ruth. 1995. "The genesis of racist discourse in Austria since 1989". In *Texts and Practices: Readings in Critical Discourse Analysis*, C.R.Caldas-Coulthard and M.Coulthard (eds.), 107–128. London: Routledge.

Rejecting an identity

Discourses of Europe in Polish border communities

Aleksandra Galasińska and Dariusz Galasiński
University of Wolverhampton

Introduction

In this chapter we shall explore discursive constructions of Europe, the European Union and the process of Poland's gaining its membership in the process of discursive constructions of identity. The data come from a major European research project within the EU's Fifth Framework Programme, which investigated the discursive construction of European identity, focusing on three-generation families living in communities on either side of the borders between the EU member-states and its ascending nations. During the life-span of three generations, these communities have undergone fundamental changes in their socio-political environment which affected the public definition of peoples' identities, such as their nationhood and their belonging to different state and social systems. While during the war and the post-war decades, the relationship between these different national entities was conflictual, since 1990 official emphasis has been on unification or collaboration and on intra-regional and trans-national harmony.

More specifically, our part of the research was carried out in the Polish border town of Zgorzelec (spring of 2000), a town created from the eastern part of the pre-war German town of Görlitz, located on both sides of the river Neisse. Up until 1970, the Polish-German border, reputed to be the best-guarded border in Europe, was closed and crossing it was almost impossible. In 1970 it was opened, only to be closed again in 1981, because of the rise and crushing of the 'Solidarity' movement. Since 1989 it has been open, with free daily movement across it (see also Jajeśniak-Quast & Stokłosa 2000; Osękowski & Szczegóła 1999). Zgorzelec has belonged to the Euroregion Neisse since 1991 and together with neighbouring Görlitz became a Euro town in 1998.

Bearing in mind the town's history and location right on the then EU and Schengen border, we expected to find in the Polish data some key narratives of the new political era with regards to gradual movement toward European Union. Moreover, Zgorzelec was the only town in Poland with the status of a Euro-city. We thus expected to find traces of European identity in the narratives from this particular place. Yet, we found nothing of the sort. There is minimal evidence that any kind of European identity or Europeanness features positively as an element of the informants' identity discourse. Polish informants hardly ever mentioned the European Union without prompting, and almost never referred to Europe or European identity or community.

We shall demonstrate that the respondents rejected the European Union as a platform upon which to construct themselves in terms of transnational identities. The accession to the European Union, while seen as an opportunity to partake in a new positive economic arrangement, is never constructed as a development in social or cultural terms. On the contrary, the European Union is positioned as a threat to our informants' national way of life.

But we shall also comment upon a hint of a shift in this perception of being European in the discourses of the young generation, where we noticed instances of choosing a European identity among the youth from Zgorzelec, absent from the ideologically static narratives of the middle and old generations.

Methodology

We take a constructionist view of discourse. Our study is based on the fundamental assumption that language is a social phenomenon and as such simultaneously represents and reinforces the values and beliefs of our social environment. We share the view of critical discourse analysts that any utterance designed to represent social reality necessarily entails decisions as to which of its aspects to include or exclude, and secondly decisions as to how to arrange them. Each of the selections made in the construction of an utterance thus carries its share of values, so that the reality represented by the choices is at the same time socially constructed (Hodge & Kress 1993). Alternative representations are possible by selecting different options from the "meaning potential" (Halliday 1978: 112ff.) of a culture, but their significance changes accordingly (Fowler 1996: 4).

We think of identity as a discursive construct. There is no fixed inner sense or essence of self to be discovered, even if this is contrary to folk theories of self and identity (van Langenhove & Harré; Hall 1996). Identity is a discourse of (not) belonging, continually negotiated and renegotiated within a given, localised social context. It is, therefore, a continual process of becoming. Always provisional and subject to change, it also incorporates, however, especially at the level of conscious identification, the relatively stable narratives and images of who and what belong to 'us' (especially when it comes to such constructs as nation) and who and what belongs to the domain of other (for a recent, empirically based account of the construction of identity see Barker & Galasiński 2001 and also Wodak et al. 1999).

As a trigger for our interviews we used photographs. Instead of asking several questions, we showed pictures of the town to our informants and we asked them to comment upon the photos. By allowing our interviewees to choose their own topics in their own words, we minimalised interfering with the lexico-semantic rendering of their accounts with our own language. Towards the end of the interview, however, we also asked a number of specific questions which were of interest to us. (For a detailed account of the interview procedure see Meinhof & Galasiński 2000 and also Meinhof 2002). One such question was a direct query regarding the significance of the process of extension of the EU. Importantly, much of the data we quote below comes from that part of the interview and was not selected by the informants in the open-ended part.

In ceding the interview agenda to the interviewee, we also assumed that the symbolically charged images of their domicile would trigger narratives which would not only describe the places represented, but would serve as a spring board for narratives in which the informants would position themselves, both explicitly and implicitly with regard to the realities shown. We also assumed that the question-answer session would engender narratives in which the speakers would 'perform belonging' or indeed 'not belonging'. Indeed, the interviewees' accounts were also constructions of their experiences of the realities surrounding them, and as such, they were positioning them as social actors operating in their realities. It is these positionings that we focus upon here.

Social and political processes

The chapter draws upon lived experiences of the most significant changes in Europe of the 20th century: post-communist transition and the EU enlargement. The end of communism in Central and Eastern European countries has marked revolutionary changes in the lives of their citizens, changes which only a few years before were even hard to think of, let alone predict (see Holmes 1997; Sakwa 1999; Verdery 1996). But the dramatic changes in public and private freedoms also meant that the comfortable official and private certainties and ideologies of the Cold War were called into question. The 'return' to Europe has proved much more difficult and painful than anyone expected, as the relative security of guaranteed employment vanished almost overnight (Burawoy & Verdery 1999; Wedel 1992).

The social, political and economic changes in Central and Eastern Europe have been accompanied by radical changes in the public and private discourses in the countries. A new 'more European' style of political discourse had to be invented, new history, new textbooks, new laws, new constitutions had to be written to both reflect and construct the new realities. Simultaneously Western Europe has also undergone major social and political changes mainly (but not only) resulting from the expansion of the European Union, reported in depth in several discourse analytic studies (e.g. Busch and Krzyżanowski 2007; Krzyżanowski and Oberhuber 2007; Muntigl, Weiss and Wodak 2000). Our text will discursively analyse individual social actors' accounts of the social and political processes mentioned above. In the process we shall demonstrate that there is a dialectic relationship between the post-communist transition and the recent political transformations in Western Europe.

Rejection

The most characteristic feature of the Polish data is that the informants draw a clear distinction between their own identity (mainly constructed in terms of Polishness) and what might be seen as the idea of Europeanness or European identity. There is an opposition between *us, our nation, our nation state, our country, our interests (matter, business) Poles, Poland, here* and *Europe, this Europe, this Union (EU), there*. This opposition is clear both in the case of being in favour of joining the EU and in the case of having doubts about it, as well as when the informant is right against the idea. As we indicated, our respondents rejected the European Union as a platform for the construction of transnational identities. This rejection has two dimensions: political and civilisational. Politically, the EU is represented in terms similar to the domination of the Soviet Union in Poland, with Germany taking over the role of the USSR. The official attempts at constructing an inter-regional, bi-national, or European level suggesting the existence of Euro-region Neisse or Euro-city Zgorzelec-Görlitz, are consistently made sense of in terms of the nation-state. At the civilisational level, the European Union is juxtaposed with the construction of Polishness (or even Eastern Europeanness). Even though represented mainly in negative terms, the latter successfully competes with the perceived western character of any possible 'European identity'.

Political rejection

Witness the following example, when a member of the oldest generation comments upon the expansion of the EU:

(1)   RF, female, old generation

RF: *ja nie: coś coś mi się to: ja nie: wie:m może dlatego że
człowiek stary inaczej jest. ale to mi się to zjednoczenie
JA NIE WIErzę że to będzie dobrze*

I: *nie wierzy pani?*

RF: *NIE.*

I: *a czemu?*

RF: *dlatego że – wie pani. może dlatego że mnie to: ci
sowieci tak to wszystko -- że KO:MUŚ będzie podlegać –
Polska. ja: ja nie rozumiem tego. może żeby KTOŚ MI
PORZĄDNIE WYTŁUMACZYŁ*

I: *rozumiem*

RF: *ale tak to mówię pani że NIE. nie wie:rzę NIE WIERZE że
będzie tam że będzie dobrze.*

I: *nie wierzy pani?*

RF: *NIE.*

I: *to myśli pani że: to niedobrze że Polska chce wstąpić do
Unii czy chciałaby pani=*

RF: *=przecie PCHA:JĄ się tak NA CHAMA JE:ZU kochany jakby w
Polsce – w Polsce niech się wezmą wszyscy do pracy to Polska
będzie bogatsza jeszcze jak i te Stany.*

(RF: I don't, I kind of, I don't know, perhaps it's because one is old, it's
different. But I don't this unification. I don't believe it's going to be
good.

I: you don't believe.

RF: No.

I: why not?

RF: because – you know – perhaps it's because the Soviets have. all this.
That it will be dependent from someone. Poland. I don't understand
this. Perhaps someone could explain it to me well.

I: I see.

RF: but I'm telling you that not. I don't believe. I don't believe that it's
going to be good in there.

I: you don't believe.

RF: no.

> I: so you think it's not good that Poland wants to join the Union,
>   would you want
> RF: but they are forcing themselves in. Jesus, as if in Poland, may they
>   all get to work, then Poland will be richer than the States).

The informant starts by expressing her doubts about the whole process of joining the EU. Clearly she has a problem with naming the EU. She uses terms like
zjednoczenie ('unification') and even after the interviewer's help with finding a
proper name at the end of the quoted extract, she uses the term *Stany* (states).
This is how the informant makes sense of the nature of this political process. She
constructs it in national terms only. Poland is juxtaposed with two superpowers:
the Soviet Union – she uses the pejorative term *Sowieci* ('Soviets') and the USA.
The former is a symbol of the domination and dependence of her own country
in the past, the latter is the symbol of a wealthy and mighty superpower, which
(probably) might dominate her country in the future.

The political process is constructed in terms of political Poland's dependency
on an unnamed organisation. Thus the direct use of the verb *podlegać* ('be dependent') is supported by the reference to 'Soviets' and the noun *zjednoczenie*
('unification'). The latter might be associated with the process of the unification
of Germany. The informant, as an inhabitant of the Polish-German border land,
might be more aware of the negative experience of former GDR citizens after the
unification. Using the noun *zjednoczenie* ('unification'), she discursively constructs the possible ambivalent outcome of the event. The Polish constructed pas-
siveness and dependence upon others is also underscored by the informant's position as having no influence whatsoever on the political process she talks about.
She is forced to believe in it and she of course has doubts. She complains about
lack of understanding and wishes somebody would explain things to her. Although, we are not told who is responsible for the alleged misleading, implicitly
we learn that it is the people in power. Those who do not help her to understand
the new reality but *pchają się tak na chama* ('force themselves in') instead.

Note also the contrast between RF's references to the EU and Poland itself. It
is quite interesting that she talks about the unification and the European Union
predominantly in terms of mental processes. Thus she does not believe, she does
not understand. This changes in the last turn where, despite the question asking
about what she thinks, she chooses not to speak of herself; the reality is not filtered through her own experience. She has no doubt that the people in power are
forcing themselves in, as much as she has no doubt that if Poles work hard, Poland
will be wealthier than the US.

As we said earlier, the threat of the European Union is constructed regardless of whether accession to the European Union is viewed positively or not. Thus, while MW in Extract (2) is in favour of Poland's joining the Union, OK, in Extract (3) is against:

(2)   MW, male, oldest generation
       MW: *bo jeśli jeśli nie Unia to co?*
       I: *mchm rozumiem*
       MW: *to wrócić do tego co było czy odizolować się od*
              wszystkiego to też nie. chodzi o to żeby trzeba trzeba
              bronić naszych spraw pilnować tych spraw --- wszystkie państwa te
              które stworzą obecnie Unię one były kiedyś w
              większości w dużej części byli przeciwko temu oni byli
              przeciwko temu. nikt nie bardzo się palił do tego.
       (MW: because if there is no Union, then what?
       I: I see.
       MW: return to what used to be? Or isolate ourselves from everything,
              not either. The point is to defend our interests, guard these inter
              ests – all the countries making up the Union now, they were all
              largely against it, they were against it. No one was too enthusiastic
              for it).

(3)   OK, male, youngest generation
       I: *aha a co pan sądzi o wstąpieniu Polski do Unii*
              Europejskiej?
       OK: *ja to tak ja słucham dziennik ja to próbuję zrozumieć*
              ja tylko się boję tych naszych rolników. bo to jest – to
              jest twarda polityka do Unii. i u nas nasi rolnicy nie
              wytrzymają tego.
       I: *nie wytrzymają?*
       OK: *ja tu oglądałem to właśnie oglądam ten program jakiś tam*
              przy realizuje właśnie tam jakiś tam z Unii jakieś
              stowarzyszenie to tylko się przetrzymają jacyś rolnicy co
              mają specjalizację jedną. a nie że krowy: świnie: to i to no
              bo: nie poradzą sobie. a wiado:/ a ja mam znaczy ja mam?
              mama i tato ma rodzinę w bydgoskim dużo rolniczą i oni oni
              sobie dobrze radzą oni nie wytrzymają tego. Polak nie ma
              sza:ns gdzie z takimi kredytami z tam wszystkim.(...)
       (I: and what do you think about Poland's joining the Union?
       OK: when I listen to the news, I am trying to understand, I am just
              afraid for our farmers. Because it is a hard policy for the Union.
              And our farmers here will not cope with it.
       I: won't cope?

OK: I watched, I am watching this programme by, it is implemented by some association by the Union, only those farmers will survive who have one specialism. And not cows, pigs this and that. They won't manage. I have, I mean mum and dad have a family in the Bydgoszcz province, agricultural and they manage well, they won't survive this. A Pole has no chance with the credits like this and everything).

It seems that the difference between the two extracts is not so much the fact that the two informants perceive the union as a threat – MW by constructing Poland as having to defend its interests, OK by constructing the farmers as unlikely to survive the accession, but in the fact that MW is trying to justify, license his words about the EU. By saying that also other countries were against some unspecified things and were not enthusiastic about something also unspecified, the informant normalises his stance and thus shows himself in favour while critical in an expected manner.

In both extracts, however, Poland and the European Union seem to be adversaries. In the case of extract two, the opposition is rendered largely in militaristic terms, with defending and guarding of Polish interests, as if there was some assault possible or incoming. In OK's words, on the other hand, the Union is shown mainly as something that might blight people's lives, something one can survive or not.

Moreover, the juxtaposition of the European Union and Poland is not done at the relatively abstract level of a country and a group of countries. The nationalisation of the construction is done almost at the level of personal experience – both speakers use the pronoun *nasz* ('our'), situating themselves in opposition to whatever the EU is going to do to Poland. Whether it is 'our interests' or 'our farmers', the EU might not be constructed as a threat to the informants themselves, still, it is a threat to them as part of a larger group, people like them, Poles like them. The defence against the European Union is one that secures the informants' way of life.

Such constructions are typical. In the narratives of our informants, the European Union is never seen as a positive development, one that might offer an opportunity for something, nor a platform to identify with. It invariably means strife and slim chances of survival, never counterbalanced by the opportunities it might also offer.

Civilisation

But while the European Union is perceived as a political threat to Poland, the EU is also juxtaposed with Poland in civilisational terms. Poland is not only constructed as a weaker relative, potentially dependent upon the European Union, but it is also constructed as a country backward in relation to the EU, one which is not yet ready, in terms of its civilisation, to join in. The narrative of backward Poland is perhaps best rendered by the following extract in which the informants make a sweeping claim as to what 'we' Poles and perhaps also the country are like.

(4)   BJ, TJ, females, middle generation

    BJ: *jednak my jesteśmy jeszcze jeszcze tacy mi się wydaje troszkę jakby do tyłu*

    TJ: *do tyłu – dużo do tyłu.*

    BJ: *ja nie umiem się może wypowiedzieć ale to to jest – tak jak byśmy tak szli ale jeszcze jeszcze tak jakby=*

    TJ: *=jeszcze nie teraz nie?*

    BJ: *no niby nie dajemy się temu wszystkiemu ale: – ale jeszcze – no ale chyba do:brze że wejdzie:my? – ja wie:m?*

    (BJ: yet, we still are so, I think, a bit backward.

    TJ: backward, much backward.

    BJ: I can't express it but it's, it's as if we are going but still

    TJ: not just yet, right?

    BJ: it's as if we are holding ground with it all, but yet, but I think it's good we go in, I don't know).

Even though the extract suggests some discomfort with the way Poles or Poland are (the reference to holding ground), the informants have little doubt that Poles or Poland, the pronoun 'we' could be understood either way, are backward. The European Union is not seen here (or throughout the corpus, in fact) as an opportunity for progress, for dealing with backwardness; rather, it is an impediment which Poles must deal with on their own before attempting to join the EU.

The following two extracts also indicate Polish backwardness, but pitch this at different levels:

(5)   LK, female middle generation

    I: *tak tak tak a co pani sądzi o rozszerzeniu Unii Europejskiej o tych naszych staraniach?*

    LK: *oj – to znaczy ja ja w ogóle nasz kraj to widzę cienko w tej w tym układzie bo sama pani widzi co się dzieje.*

    I: *tak*

LK: *przede wszystkim wstyd jest a teraz nawet co to się*
        dzieje w rządzie to wstyd nawet telewizor otworzyć. i to ma
        być to okno na świat na Unię? przecież nam obywatelom jest
        wstyd właśnie za takie coś.
I: *aha aha aha a chciałaby pani żeby Polska wstąpiła do*
        Unii?
LK: *to znaczy ale żeby i Polacy się trochę zmienili.*
I: *aha rozumiem rozumiem. mchm mchm mchm*
LK: *wie pani mi o co chodzi?*
I: *tak tak tak tak*
LK: *żeby tak się z tej strony pokazali co i tam się potrafią*
        pokazać. a my gdzie? daleko daleko
I: *daleko?*
LK: *tragedia z każdej strony czy w gospodarstwie no ja mówię*
        gospodarka o rolników chodzi czy o przemysł normalny czy no
        w ogóle z każdej strony gdzie by pani nie spojrzała krachy są
        a się pchają. gdzie? -- to musi być kraj nowoczesny z resztą
        bardzo nowoczesny. – i z pieniędzmi
I: *z pieniędzmi?*
LK: *a nie z biedą. gdzie my z biedą do Unii? powódź za*
        powodzią – i nie ma kto im pomóc. dzisiaj znowuż o jak
        otworzyłam i słuchałam MA:tko święta ludzie to się w głowie
        przewraca przecież. to już chyba ja podejrzewam że prędzej
        będzie koniec świata jak my do Unii dojdziemy.
(I: so what do you think about the expansion of the European Union,
        about our attempts to join.
LK: well, I generally see our country in bleak terms, you can see yourself
        what's going on.
I: yes.
LK: first of all it's embarrassing. What's happening in the government
        it's too embarrassing to turn the TV on. And this is supposed to be
        the window to the Union. We the citizens are embarrassed because
        of such things.
I: I see. But would you like Poland to join the European Union.
LK: but I mean, but if only Poles would change a little.
I: I see.
LK: do you know what I mean?
I: yes.
LK: if only they could show themselves from the side they show them
        selves over there. And were are we? Far far away.
I: far away?

LK: disaster whichever way you look at it. be it in the farm, I mean the farmers' economy or normal industry or anything whichever way you look it's falling apart. But they still are forcing themselves in. where to? It must be a modern country, very modern, with money.

I: with money?

LK: and not with poverty. We to the Union with poverty? Flood after flood and there is no one to help. I turned it on and listened again. Mother of God it just is beyond belief. I think the end of the world will be sooner than we join the Union).

(6[1]) LS (female), TS (male), middle generation

LS: *wie pan bo to taka jest rzeczywistość i nie ma co podskakiwać na-prawdę. yyyy nieraz jak przyglądamy się karetce pogotowia nie-mieckiej jak przywożą Polaka z tamtej strony jak im to wszystko pięknie wychodzi jakie to wszystko jest przygotowane jak ta bieliz-na jest pięknie zmieniana od razu to nie jest tak że otwierają karet-kę i się sanitariusze szarpią z noszami żeby to wyciągnąć. u nich to po prostu pasuje elegancko wygląda i to jest właśnie ta Europa z której oni przyjeżdżają tutaj jeszcze do nas.=*

(LS: you know, because this is reality and there is no point in rebelling, really. We often watch a German ambulance when they bring a Pole from the other side, how it all comes off beautifully, how prepared it all is, how the bed linen is changed straight away. And it's not like they open the ambulance and the medics struggle with the stretcher to pull it out. Over there it just all fits in nicely and this is exactly this Europe they come to us from).

The denouncement of Polish civilisation is made on different levels. While LK talks about the state and its macro-economy, LS talks about the individual instances of German ambulance crews handling emergencies better than Polish medics. Despite similarities in LK's words with the extract quoted in the previous section, this time, the informant does not see the inefficiencies of Polish agriculture or industry in terms of coping with the European Union. This time, their weaknesses are constructed as not fit to join the Union. Poland is not modern enough, the political elite or the government is not up to standard (it's something to be ashamed of, as she indicates in her second move). That is underscored by the reference to disasters whichever way you turn and, finally, by the denouncement of joining 'Europe' in poverty. Incidentally, the informant identifies herself with

---

1.   This extract comes from a corpus of data collected in the Polish town of Gubin as part of an earlier research project on border identities funded by the ESRC. Gubin lies on the German-Polish border about 100km north of Zgorzelec.

her fellow citizens as unlikely to join the Union. The gap between the world of the EU and her own is so big that the end of the world is more likely to happen.

Alternatively, the general statement about 'reality' is exemplified by a reference to ambulance work. Interestingly, the comparison, obviously in favour of the Germans, is not made in terms of the people. It is not that Poles are less skilled; the point is, rather, that they have to cope with inadequate equipment. German crews have better, more modern by implication, equipment. But what is quite interesting is that the comparison is also made in aesthetic terms. The Germans' work is beautiful, the equipment and its workings are elegant. By implication, what happens on the Polish side is not so beautiful; it is ugly, quite a frequent *topos* in the comparisons between Poland and Germany, or the European Union (see e.g. Galasińska et al. 2002).

Yet the systemic, so to say, backwardness of Poland is coupled with references to Poles themselves, their working practices, their unpreparedness, or lack of maturity to join the 'better' European Union.

Consider the following extended extract from one of the informants:

(7) KG,   male, middle generation
     KG: *wie pani co (śmiech) co do jednego to my – MY MY nie*
           dorośliśmy do tego.
     I: *tak?*
     KG: *znaczy ja mówię tutaj znaczy się po Zgorzelcu i: – bo w*
           Zgorzelcu taka zbieranina tych ludzi jest.
           (...)
     KG: *no i to właśnie dlatego mówię MY? do Unii? ledwo co tam*
           w Niemczech jak ja widziałem jak tam się ro:bi:? jak tam
           pracują ludzie? a u nas no to tak dalej tak jeden stoi –
           jeden zrobi a później przestawi na to samo miejsce. nic się
           nie zmieniło. powiem pani szczerze NIE: zmieniło się nic.
     (KG: you know, for one thing, we have not grown up for it [joining the
           EU].
     I: really?
     KG: I mean I talking [looking at] Zgorzelec, in Zgorzelec there is such a
           mix [pejorative] of people.
           (…)
     KG: that's why I say. We? To the Union? Hardly, in Germany I saw how
           one works. How people work over there. And here it's still one
           stands, one does some work, then puts it back. Nothing has
           changed. I'll tell you straight, nothing has changed).

Starting by showing Poles as too immature to join the Union, the informant goes on to talk about Polish working practices. He draws upon one of the most frequent narratives of communism – extremely poorly organised work, with people being just about at the peak of inefficiency. The idea was rendered by a saying – whether you work or you lie down, you still get paid (*Czy się robi czy się leży, 2 tysiące się należy*). The 'nothing has changed' is a reference to the fact that Poland is still driven by such practices. Communism is still there.

But KG's disparaging remarks about working practices are underscored by his remarks about the nature of the town and its people whom he calls *zbieranina* ('accidental mix', normally in reference to people without a purpose, not knowing what to do with themselves). Not only are his fellow countrymen's working practices far from ideal, they themselves are the problem as well, without a clue as to what they are about, and not grown up enough.

The Polish complex?

As we said before, the European Union is neither used as a potential platform with which to form transnational identities, nor as a potential opportunity to deal with backwardness. If Poland is so behind the European Union, surely logic would suggest that Poland should join to make progress, to become less backward, to advance economically and socially. Things, however, are not that simple.

Things are not that simple firstly because of the political rejection of the Union. Despite the rhetoric of 'returning to Europe' implemented by the successive post-1989 governments in Poland, the narratives of our informants very clearly equated the EU with the USSR. Having come out from one dependency, Poland is perceived as going into another. Despite the massive governmental campaign, the result of the accession referendum held in May 2003 was not so much in doubt because of the voters' support, but because of their turnout. With some ultra-right wing parties suggesting to the voters to stay at home, only just above 56% of the voters went to cast the vote (50% was the threshold for the referendum to be valid).

Furthermore, more often than not, the European Union has been perceived not so much as a supranational organisation but, rather, as a group of countries, dominated by Germany. Indeed, whenever the threat was positioned in terms of a country, it was Germany that symbolised such a threat. With the Polish-German conflict being a major part of Polish history, the domination by Germany is an anathema.

But, as we have shown above, the problem of Polish dependency is only part of the issue. While perceiving the European Union, and particularly Germans as a threat, our informants nevertheless did suggest that Poles are able to hold their ground in the battle. Secondly, as was suggested in an earlier study (Meinhof and Galasiński 2002), the European Union was also perceived in terms of certain economic benefits. We would suggest that considerably more important are the narratives of Polish immaturity and civilisational backwardness. We would like to argue that such narratives tap into long standing myths deeply anchored in stories of Polishness (Galasińska 2006).

We see the stories of Polish unpreparedness or immaturity of Poles and Poland in the longstanding myth of Polish juniority with respect to its neighbours. Every child in Polish schools learns that the Polish state began when Emperor Otto II crowned King Bolesław the Brave. The story ends with the partitions of Poland by Russia, Prussia and Austria, resulting in the complete loss of independence in 1794. This political weakness is very much underscored by the mythology of Polish spiritual strength, very prevalent in the Polish romanticist tradition with Poland being constructed as the Messiah of nations. This tradition is still very much alive in the Polish consciousness of today (Kłoskowska 1996) and in Polish political discourse (Jaworski & Galasiński 1998). Indeed, the Polish Catholic church, when supporting the accession to the EU, talks about Poland's role as Christianising the secular Europe.

We think that the narratives of Poland's immaturity originate in such narratives of the nation. There are very few such stories which do not portray Poland as the victim of stronger, more belligerent nations. Weakness seems to be part and parcel of who Poles imagine themselves to be. This is coupled with one of the most pervasive narratives of communism in Poland, as a system which left Poland in ruins, backward in comparison to the ever coveted West. Indeed, Western Europe and the United States have always been idealised in Poles' discourses, with numerous jokes suggesting communist Poland's greyness and shabbiness as contrasted with the plush West.

So, what of the fact that the European Union is not seen as an opportunity to tackle backwardness? By implication, the European Union is a group of countries which are more developed, mature, senior. By joining the EU, Poland could be part of this seniority. And yet, the European Union is rejected. Let us quote a snippet from one interview, which, we think, renders the attitude well.

(8)   KG, male, middle generation
      KG: *(...) mówię. my chcemy do Europy wejść? do tej Unii? po: co:? – ośmieszymy się tylko.*

(KG: (...) I am saying, we want to go into Europe? What for? We'll only
        make fools of ourselves).

Poland may be the 'junior' partner in the narratives of our informants, but at the same time, it does not want to display this. Keeping up appearances and showing off oneself in style is also part of popular, Polish cultural norms: *Zastaw się a postaw się* ('Pawn yourself, but show yourself well').

The point we are arguing is that there seem to be two contradictory narratives in discourses of Polishness. On the one hand, there is one about Polish backwardness and juniority: A narrative about Poland under threat from the more powerful neighbour coupled with being in an economically and civilisationally inferior position. The other is about style, not showing one's weakness, not making a fool of oneself. The junior partner cannot become a full partner for fear of showing its juniority. To quote another saying: whatever way you turn, your back is still behind you.

In short, there seem to be no solutions, only problems in the narratives of the European Union. In a nation imagined the way Poles imagine themselves, the EU is not and cannot be an option.

Conclusions

The narratives of informants from Zgorzelec which are related to 'the European question' have two features. Firstly, they have a national dimension. Interviewees always talk about themselves as members of a nation state, a trait already noted in the case of the informants from Gubin (Meinhof & Galasiński 2005). Secondly, they are full of self-criticism. In our corpus Poles described themselves as an immature nation, not grown up enough to join the better organised Western societies, and as members of a poor, non-modern, badly ruled country, as well as a lazy and selfish society. As one of our informants put it "one needs to grow up for Europe".

This negative construction of Polishness is much more developed and complex than the notion of perceived Europeanness. The latter is mainly constructed as a positive stereotype of the better perceived group of western counties, whose epitome is often Germany. This stereotype is made up of such elements as excellent organisation, diligence and wealth.

As Polishness always clashes with the idea of being 'European', informants from Zgorzelec identify themselves as being in a different position from that of their western neighbours. The question of being European seems not to arise for our informants. The juxtaposition of two concepts of identity, always in favour of "this Union", makes the notion of European identity the object of admiration, desire and jealousy. However strong the temptation to be alike is, this goal is impossible to reach or identify with. We suggested that such a viewpoint might be the result of the metanarratives of the nation underpinning the discourses of our informants. However, we must not underestimate the particular border context in which our community lives, and which makes our informants continually negotiate their identity, more often than not in comparison and contrast with their 'more orderly and reliable' neighbours from across the river.

There is, however, a hint of a shift in this perception of being European in the case of the young generation. We noticed examples of choosing the European identity among the youth from Zgorzelec, absent from the ideologically static narratives from middle and old generations. Our two young informants who opted for the European identity gave me two different reasons for their decisions. First, and what might be an example of negative motivation – it is an attempt to escape from the negatively perceived Polishness. European identity plays the role of a refuge. It replaces the old, negative stereotype with a new one. Secondly, and more positively, Europeanness was constructed as a complement to and diversification of Polish identity, something which seems to give the informant an advantage over other young Poles who do not live on the border.

Finally, on 13 June 2004, the day of the European parliamentary elections, life wrote a postscript to the data analysed in this chapter. The record low 20% turnout in Poland and the strong electoral support of eurosceptic (or, shall we say, euro-hostile) parties are a good commentary to our analyses. While, obviously, we do not want to suggest a simple causal link between the rejection of European identities and such an electoral result, we do propose to have found one of the possible factors contributing to it. It is worth noting, incidentally, that voting patterns were similar across the post-communist world.

References

Barker, Chris and Galasiński, Dariusz. 2001. *Cultural Studies and Discourse Analysis: A Dialogue on Language and identity.* London: Sage.

Burawoy, Michael and Verdery, Katherine. 1999. *Uncertain transition: Ethnographies of change in the postsocialist world.* Lanham: Rowman & Littlefield.

Busch, Brigitta, and Krzyżanowski, Michał. 2007. "Inside/Outside the European Union: Enlargement, Migration Policy and the Search for Europe's identity". In *The Geopolitics of European Union Enlargement: The Fortress Empire*, W. Armstrong and J. Anderson, (eds.), 107–124 London: Routledge.

Fowler, Roger.1996. "On critical linguistics". In *Texts and Practices*, R. C. Caldas-Coulthard and M. Coulthard, (eds.), 3–14, London: Routledge.

Galasińska, Aleksandra. 2006. "Border Ethnography and Post-communist Discourses of Nationality in Poland". *Discourse & Society, 17*(5), 609–626.

Galasińska, Aleksandra, Rollo, Craig and Meinhof, Ulrike, H. 2002. "Urban space and the construction of identity". In *Living (with) borders identity Discourses on East-West borders in Europe,* U. H. Meinhof (ed), 119–139. Aldershot: Ashgate.

Hall, Stuart. 1996. "Who needs identity?". In *Questions of Cultural identity,* S. Hall and P. du Gay (eds.), 1–17. London: Sage.

Halliday, Michael. A. K. 1978. *Language as Social Semiotic,* London: Edward Arnold

Hodge, Robert and Kress, Gunther. 1993. *Language as Ideology,* London: Routledge.

Holmes, Lesley. 1997. *Post-Communism: An Introduction.* Durham, N.C.: Duke University Press.

Jajeśniak-Quast, Dagmara and Stokłosa, Katarzyna. 2000. *Geteilte Staedte an Oder und Neisse.* Berlin: Verlag.

Jaworski, Adam and Galasiński, Dariusz. 1998. "The last Romantic hero. Lech Wałęsa's image-building in TV presidential debates". *TEXT 18*(4), 525–544.

Kłoskowska, Antonina. 1996. *Kultury Narodowe u Korzeni.* Warszawa: Wydawnictwo Naukowe PWN.

Krzyżanowski, Michał and Oberhuber, Florian. 2007. *(Un)Doing Europe. Discourses and Practices of Negotiating the EU Constitution.* Brussels: PIE – Peter Lang.

Meinhof, Ulrike H. (ed). 2002. *Living (with) Borders. Identity Discourses on East-West borders in Europe.* Aldershot: Ashgate.

Meinhof, Ulrike. H., and Galasiński, Dariusz. 2000. "Photography, memory, and the construction of identities on the former East-West German border." *Discourse Studies 2*(3): 323–353.

Meinhof, Ulrike. H., and Galasiński, Dariusz. 2002. "Reconfiguring east-west identities: Cross-generational discourses in German and Polish border communities". *Journal of Ethnic and Migration Studies, 28*(1): 63–82.

Meinhof, Ulrike. H., and Galasiński, Dariusz. 2005. *The Language of Belonging.* Basingstoke: Palgrave.

Muntigl, Peter, Weiss, Gilbert, and Wodak Ruth. 2000. *European Union Discourses on Unemployment. An Interdisciplinary Approach to Employment Policy-Making and Organisational Change.* Amsterdam/Philadelphia: John Benjamins.

Osękowski, Czesław and Szczegóła, Hieronim. 1999. *Pogranicze Polsko-Niemieckie w Okresie Transformacji 1989–1997.* Zielona Góra: WSP.

Sakwa, Richard. 1999. *Postcommunism.* Buckingham: Open University Press.

Van Langenhove, Luk and Harré, Rom. 1993. "Positioning and autobiography: Telling your life", in *Discourse and Lifespan Identity,* N. Coupland and J. F. Nussbaum (eds), 81–99, Newbury Park: Sage.

Verdery, Katherine. 1996. *What Was Socialism and What Comes Next?.* Princeton: Princeton University Press.

Wedel, Janine. (ed). 1992. *The Unplanned Society: Poland during and after Communism.* New York: Columbia University Press.

Wodak, Ruth, de Cillia, Rudolf, Reisigl, Martin and Liebhart, Karin. 1999. *The Discursive Construction of National Identity.* Edinburgh: Edinburgh University Press.

Rhetoricians at work

Constructing the European Union in Denmark

Sharon Millar
University of Southern Denmark

Introduction

The aim of this chapter is to examine from a rhetorical perspective the argumentation strategies used by people in Denmark to construct their version of political reality in Europe, and within it their own sense of national and/or supranational identity. The context is historical in that the political reality being constructed is that of 1992 at the time of the Danish referendum on the Treaty of European Union or Maastricht treaty. This treaty, rejected by 50.7% of Danish voters, was a pivotal step on the road towards primarily Western European political, economic and cultural integration, involving areas such as foreign and defence policy, monetary union, education and culture, and European citizenship.

By the early 1990's not only was political and economic integration high on the agenda of the then EC, so was the need to further promote a European identity and consciousness, while simultaneously respecting the national identities of member states (Jacobs and Maier 1998). Identity and integration have generally been seen as inter-related by EU policy makers in that it is assumed that a greater sense of feeling 'European' among the populations of the member states will allow for further integration, an assumption that has been given some credence from research evidence. An analysis of Eurobarometer data from 1996 suggests that a sense of European identity has significant effects on support for European integration (Van der Veen 2002). From the Maastricht treaty onwards, the identity of the European Union itself has been generally based on political freedoms and rights but, as noted by Delgado-Moreira (1997), practically all forms of harmonization have been given an identity strengthening perspective by policy-makers, be this in relation to tourism or access to EU institutional libraries. What has been consistently and deliberately left unspecified by policy-makers is what is meant by "Europe" and "European", although in recent times such vagueness is coming increasingly under pressure given issues of EU enlargement and an EU constitution.

Since 1973, the health of the European construct in each member state, as seen from the perspective of public opinion, has been monitored by the European Commission via Eurobarometer surveys. These surveys give useful overviews based on aggregates, allowing for comparisons within and between member states synchronically and diachronically. Denmark has generally proved to be rather sceptical in relation to European institutions and European identity when compared to other member states; for instance in Eurobarometer 37 (1992), all countries except Denmark wanted to speed up the construction of Europe and, when asked if they often or sometimes or never thought of themselves as not only Danish but also European, Danes responded 20%, 32% and 46%, respectively, although 46% felt that in the future they could perceive themselves as Danish and European. While such statistical data is interesting, they are responses to predetermined closed questions and do not represent the voices of individuals as spoken in their own words. A different type of data is required to ascertain how individual people themselves construct the artefacts being engineered for them. In recent years, the European Commission has conducted qualitative studies regarding specific topics, but these are reported as overall summaries and not as actual discourse. Similarly, Robyn (2004) uses discourse from various sources to build various sets of statements about European identity which informants are asked to put into rank order (Q methodology), but again the discourse has been constructed by others and not the informants. In this respect, the Danish referendum on the Maastricht treaty provides invaluable material. At this time, many Danes made extensive use of a particular outlet for the public expression of personal viewpoint, namely the 'letters to the editor' section in the Danish press. Between April and May 1992, 52% of all material on EC issues in *Ekstra Bladet*, one of the country's major, national, tabloid newspapers, was in the form of readers' letters (Siune, Svensson and Tonsgaard 1992). These letters were cleverly used by the newspapers as journalistic material, often appearing with accompanying headlines and illustrations. Their often partisan use by the press aside, the letters provide a unique insight into how people were constructing through argument national and supranational institutions and structures, and their relation to them, at a significant point in the history of the European Union.

Given a referendum by default nurtures an oppositional relationship and positioning in relation to the other (yes/no; for/against), the data is well suited to rhetorical analysis, and specifically that of classical rhetoric. It is, however, important to emphasise at this point what is meant, or more especially not meant, by rhetoric. Perceptions of rhetoric as nothing more than a mechanistic, decontextualised system of dos and don'ts about how to write and give a speech, or as a taxonomy of stylistic devices are common, but they generally reflect historical developments in approaches to rhetoric, rather than the more fundamental aspects of classical rhetorical thinking itself. Certainly from this sterile perspective, rhetoric is "not adequate as an explanation of what happens as people construct discourse", as Johnstone (1996: 90) notes. Such unflattering perceptions are probably responsible in part for the relative lack of interest in rhetorical theorizing among linguists, although isolated concepts are being borrowed and adapted for use in recent, multidisciplinary approaches to discourse (for example, Van Dijk and Wodak 2000). My attraction to rhetoric lies in its holistic and multi-faceted approach to discourse, not only as a process and product, but as action. In classical times, rhetoric was concerned with public discourse and the civic arena and how this discourse created and shaped social orders, bringing about unity and cooperation through persuasive means (Lee Too 1995). Our notions of civic cooperation and types of public discourse have changed since ancient Greece, but the essential point remains: rhetoric creates, maintains and challenges social orders through the creation of persuasive argument. In a sense, rhetoric is about how people think. Staub (2001) restricts rhetoric to public thinking, "the practical thought processes common to a given civic order". Billig (1991: 1) makes the more general point that classical rhetoric saw "thinking itself" as "rhetorical and argumentative", a perspective that dovetails neatly with claims that rhetoric is an "ordinary human competence" which "manifests a primary creative impulse" (Nash 1989: ix, 218) or "a form of mental and emotional energy" (Kennedy 1998: 3).

Classical rhetoric: A brief overview

Classical rhetoric operated with five traditional canons: invention, arrangement, style, memory and delivery. These are typically dealt with separately in rhetorical theory, but they are best seen as inter-related. For present purposes, however, I will elaborate on the canon of invention only. Invention deals with the discovery of arguments; as Nash (1989: 7) puts it invention is "the capacity to find, to rummage through one's personal stock of knowledge and perception, and come up with the right connections". Hence it involves memory, not just in the sense of memories (be these individual or social), but also in the sense of memory storage and retrieval. Invention, however, should not be viewed as static, as the "recovery of already existing facts" (Scott et al. 1971: 229), but as a dynamic, creative process. Aristotlean rhetorical theory views invention as involving artistic proofs, which include three types of appeal: *ethos* – the appeal to the credibility of the character of the speaker; *pathos* – the appeal to emotions; *logos* – the appeal to reason. Within *logos* is housed inductive and deductive argument. Induction relies on the use of example or paradigm to help us move from the particular to the general; deduction uses the enthymeme, traditionally seen as a syllogism where one premise is implied rather than stated. The enthymeme is not based on fact or strict logic, but appeals to reasoned plausibility or probability. Such plausibility in turn links to the listener's system of beliefs.

Intimately linked to invention and the enthymeme are the *topoi* (topics). These are essentially "a mental store of argumentative strategies" (Covino and Joliffe 1995: 88) or as Billig (1991: 48) prefers "cognitive building-blocks". The *topoi* are often categorised into two types: 'common', that is applicable in general, or 'special/specific', that is subject/discipline-based, e.g. specific to judicial or political rhetoric. The distinction between 'common' and 'specific' is also seen in terms of form vs. propositional content; the terms will be used in this latter sense in the following.

Corbett and Connors (1999: 87) list the common topics and sub-topics (in parentheses) as follows: definition (genus, division); comparison (similarity, difference, degree); relationship (cause and effect, antecedent and consequence, contraries, contradictions); circumstance (possible and impossible, past fact and future fact); testimony (authority, testimonial, statistics, maxims, laws, precedents). Although presented here in rather taxonomic terms, these *topoi* are intended to reflect the processes typically involved in the construction of argument (opposition, analogy, definition etc.).

The specific *topoi*, interpreted here in terms of themes of common sense or values, essentially relate to social cognition and it is in this exclusive sense that the rhetorical notion of *topoi* tends to be used in the linguistic and social psychological literature (Billig 1996; Van Dijk and Wodak 2000). Rapp (2002), however, warns against a neat dichotomy between common and specific *topoi* since the distinction is far from clear-cut in Aristotelian rhetoric. From both a theoretical and descriptive perspective, it would seem truer to the original to consider the *topoi* as both form and content, working together to create argument. This will be the approach adopted in this chapter.

Given the concerns of other chapters in this volume with narrative, it is appropriate to ask how narrative fits in with a rhetorical framework, particularly as narrative has tended to be seen as something fundamentally different from argument. Bruner (1986:13), for instance, suggests that there are two distinctive modes of thought: the logico-scientific (argument) and the narrative (story). Similarly, Mumby (1993:1) argues that the "articulation of social actors as *homo narrans* provides one alternative to the model of rationality that has characterized Western thought". Classical rhetoric had generally little to say about narrative; *narratio* was part of the arrangement of an argument, but it referred to the statement of background facts or events and so was narrative in the sense of exposition rather than story-telling. Nonetheless, relating stories was viewed as a means of rhetorical proof; in his *Rhetoric*, Aristotle allows for two types of inductive reasoning, one relating past facts and the other invented for oneself, to include fables (such as Aesop's). Hellenic scholars note that many of the ancient Greek philosophers and rhetoricians, including Aristotle, used *muthos* – the imaginary, fictional tale – in the services of rational argument (*logos*). Consequently, they warn against a too easy dichotomy between 'myth' and reason in explaining the development of Greek thought. Calame (1999) takes issue with the idea that *muthos* and *logos* represented different modes of thought (cf. Bruner above), noting that *muthos* had its own logic, that of emplotment. So such narratives are more than a rhetorical proof, but may constitute an argument in their own right with their own rationality. Similarly, Hesse (1989: 106) proposes that narrative is a "form of argument", a "powerful persuasive strategy" which "derives force not from hierarchical logic, but from the emplotment of propositions". Certainly, people seem to use stories as part of argument strategies (Van Dijk 1993), suggesting that narrative is not an alternative to rationality, but helps to construct it. A number of the common *topoi,* for example, provide potential frameworks for narrating, such as antecedent and consequence (e.g. 'If I were a rich man, then …') and past fact and future fact (e.g. 'she came into work with a black eye and she said it was the door, but it's going to happen again as....').

Data

The data comes from a corpus of 279 letters and 134 snippets from letters, published during the month before the Maastricht referendum between May 1st and June 2nd 1992. The letters come from two Danish national newspapers: the tabloid *Ekstra Bladet* (153 letters, 134 snippets) and the broadsheet *Berlingske Tidende* (126 letters). The newspapers differed in attitude towards the Maastricht treaty; these were generally negative in *Ekstra Bladet*, but positive in *Berlingske Tidende*.

The holistic and inter-connected nature of rhetorical analysis favours the examination of texts as complete entities, rather than isolated fragments. For this reason, I have selected two letters from the corpus, one from a no-voter and the other from a yes-voter to allow for comparison. Other data, generally fragments from letters, will be referred to when relevant to give a cross-sectional perspective. It is to be expected that the no-vote and the yes-vote would construct the EU, Denmark, supranational and national identities differently. We might hypothesise that differing specific *topoi* would be employed, or that the same *topoi* would be used to help construct different arguments. We might also expect a stronger tendency towards *pathos* among the no-vote since themes such as patriotism and national sovereignty (and perceived threats to them) arouse deep emotions (Nash 1989). Generally, such expectations are borne out in the corpus. In contrast, we would not expect political orientation to have much influence on the strategy of argument; for instance, there is no reason to assume that no-voters would be more inclined than yes-voters to construct inductive rather than deductive arguments.

In my analysis, I will focus on three areas: the use of *topoi* in constructing arguments; the link between memory and invention; the construction of audience and identities.

The letters

Letter 1: 'no' voter
EF står for Elendigt Forbund. Siden vi blev lokket ind i EF i 1972, er arbejdsløsheden steget til uanede højder. Landmanden må ikke dyrke sine marker, men får tilskud for at lægge dem brak. Fiskerne får lov at fiske mindre og mindre og får tilskud for at hugge deres kuttere op.

Går Danmark ind i Unionen, bliver vi en tysk provins. Dannebrog vil forsvinde og blive erstattet af en fælles klud med stjerner på. Og så har vi haft vores sidste Grundlovsdag den 5. juni'91. Vores efterkommere vil stå med våben i hænderne om 60–70 år og kæmpe for et frit Danmark, nøjagtig som vi gjorde under krigen, og som kroaterne gør i øjeblikket. De vil være fri. (Ekstra Bladet 24.5.92)
(EC stands for Lousy Community. Ever since we were lured into the EC in 1972, unemployment has risen to undreamt of levels. The farmer must not cultivate his fields but gets subsidies to leave them fallow. The fishermen are allowed to fish less and less and get subsidies for scrapping their vessels.

If Denmark goes into the Union, we will become a German province. 'Dannebrog' will disappear and be replaced by a shared rag with stars on it. And so we'll have had our last Constitution Day June 5th 91. Our descendants will stand with weapons in their hands in 60–70 years, fighting for a free Denmark exactly as we did during the war, and as the Croatians are doing at the moment. They want to be free).

Letter 2: 'yes' voter
Jeg stemmer ja ved folkeafstemning den 2. juni, fordi vi derved kan styrke den nordiske opfattelse af demokrati og social bevidsthed i det samarbejdende Europa. Vi kan styrke indsatsen for en bevarelse, beskyttelse og forbedring af miljøet, f.eks. i Øster-

søen. Vi kan medvirke til at fremme en bæredygtig udvikling ikke blot i Europa, men også internationalt i samarbejde med udviklingslandene. Vi kan bekæmpe fattigdom og sygdom i udviklingslandene og medvirke til, at disse lande får en bæredygtig økonomisk og social udvikling. Vi kan udfolde vor national kultur og være med til at bevare og beskytte vor fælles europæiske kulturarv. Vi kan styrke det enkelte menneskes retsikkerhed, rettigheder og interesser i det samarbejdende Europa. For 20 år siden tog vi det første skridt ind i EF. Lad os nu fortsætte arbejdet for at sikre frihed, fred, social velfærd og en bæredygtig udvikling i et tæt europæisk samarbejde mellem selvstændige nationer. (Berlingske Tidende 20.5.92)

(I will vote yes in the referendum on June 2nd because we can in that way strengthen the Nordic perception of democracy and social awareness in the collaborating Europe. We can strengthen the contribution towards maintaining, protecting and improving the environment, e.g. in the Baltic. We can assist in promoting viable development not just in Europe, but also internationally in co-operation with the developing countries. We can fight poverty and disease in the developing countries and assist these countries in getting viable economic and social development. We can develop our national culture and be part of maintaining and protecting our common European heritage. We can strengthen the individual's public safety, rights and interests in the collaborating Europe. 20 years ago we took the first step into the EC. Let us now continue the work to secure freedom, peace, social welfare and viable development in a close, European collaboration between independent nations).

Use of topoi

In letter 1, the *topoi* of definition, comparison, relationship and circumstance have been used to construct the argument. The letter begins with a *narratio*, a statement of past, perceived facts. The opener is a form of definition, couched in an uncomplimentary word-play, which is then justified, although no explicit linguistic connective is used: the EC is lousy (because) it has brought economic problems, i.e. high unemployment, in its wake. These problems are elaborated upon, but the linguistic constructions used are non-explicit. Agentless constructions are employed, e.g. *vi blev lokket ind* ('we were lured'), *fiskerne får lov* ('the fishermen are allowed'), *landmanden... får tilskud* ('the farmer..gets subsidies'). There is no agency given to the 'we' or the occupations mentioned; they are cast in the semantic role of theme. The generic use of the definite article – *landmanden* ('the farmer'), *fiskerne* ('the fishermen') – permits generalisation; all farmers and fishermen, presumably in Denmark (as opposed to the EC generally), have got problems.

This *narratio* represents a classic rhetorical manoeuve of discrediting the opponent and sets the scene for the writer to move from past and present 'fact' to the construction of a future scenario using the *topoi* of antecedent and consequence, and comparison. This too can be seen as a form of narrative: an invented 'horror story' of sorts, but told as fact, not fiction. If Denmark goes into the Union, then Denmark will lose its status as an independent state and within a generation Danes will be fighting. This stance relies on comparison with past and present events, namely World War II and the contemporary situation in Yugoslavia. The writer is quite definite about his/her predictions; neither linguistic hedges nor mental process verbs are employed, the epistemic modal verb *vil* ('will') is used and even a specific time-frame is given: 60–70 years. What is not given is a definite specification of the enemy. The construction used is *kæmpe for* ('fight for') and the object of this phrasal verb is *et frit Danmark* ('a free Denmark'). The writer does not use a verbal construction requiring specification of the object, i.e. who one is fighting, such as *bekæmpe* ('fight') x or *kæmpe mod* ('fight against') x. The discourse focus is on what one is fighting for, namely freedom.

The common *topoi* do not stand alone, but work in conjunction with the specific *topoi* to construct arguments. One such *topos* concerns Germany and might be formulated as 'Germany dominates the Union which is bad because Germany is aggressive as history shows and aggression is bad'. This *topos* was frequently assumed in what Billig (1991:143) terms the "argumentative context" of the referendum debate. The 'no' camp referred to Germany and its militant past and present aspirations both explicitly (e.g. *Et ja vil give Tyskland magt til at videreføre Hitlers politik*. 'A yes will give Germany the power to further carry out Hitler's policies', *Ekstra Bladet* 30.5.92; *Tyskland vil være herre i Europa*. 'Germany wants to be master in Europe', *Ekstra Bladet* 24.5.92) and implicitly (e.g. *Men skal man stemme med hjertet, må det blive et klart nej til 'jawohl'*. 'If one is to vote with the heart, it must be a clear no to 'jawohl'', *Ekstra Bladet* 31.5.92; *Hvad ville de henrettede frihedskæmpere sige?* 'What would the executed freedom fighters say?', *Ekstra Bladet* 3.5.92). Some 'yes' voters also assumed the 'Germany as aggressive/militant' *topos*, but used this to construct an argument for unity so that German dominance could be curbed: *Er man ræd for tyskerne, har man på forhånd ladet sig trænge i forsvar. Det er bedre med andre små unionsmedlemmer..at føre en fælles politik*. ('If one is afraid of the Germans, one has already put oneself on the defensive. It is better along with other small union states...to conduct a shared policy', *Berlingske Tidende* 28.5.92). It should be noted that the 'Germany as aggressive/militant' *topos* was not confined to Denmark at that time, but was evident in the political and media discourse of Britain (Hardt-Mautner 1994). Galasinska and Galasinski (this volume) also note that German dominance was feared by some of their Polish informants. The extent to which this 'Germany as aggressive/militant' *topos* still survives is difficult to estimate, but it is likely to be diminishing in public thinking. As noted by Dosenrode (2002), such anti-German sentiment, despite its long history in Denmark, now tends to characterise the older generation and is in decline.

Another *topos* apparent in letter 1 is that freedom, and hence democracy, is only possible within the nation-state and may justifiably be fought for. The association between nation state and freedom was essentially about sovereignty, which was one of the main concerns of these letter-writers. This 'freedom/nation-state' *topos* aided the construction of the EU as anti-freedom and anti-democratic in Denmark (I will return to this below). It is worth noting that a Eurobarometer poll in 1999 found that Denmark, along with Sweden, were the only two member states which showed a marked difference between their levels of satisfaction with national democracy (high) and EU democracy (low) (Hug 2002).

The writer uses the *topoi* to create deductive arguments, enthymemes: If Denmark goes into the Union, we will become a German province (because Germany, an aggressor, dominates the Union); (If Denmark goes into the Union), Our descendants will stand with weapons in their hands in 60–70 years, fighting for a free Denmark exactly as we did during the war, and as the Croatians are doing at the moment (because freedom is only possible in a nation-state).

Turning to letter 2, the main formal *topos* appealed to here is cause and effect: I will vote yes because Denmark in the Union can have the following effects. Note the focus is not on the effects a Union will have on Denmark (cf. letter 1), but the effects Denmark can have in Europe and beyond. Hence Denmark ('we') has the semantic role of agent in sentences constructed in the active voice throughout. To understand the discourse structure of this letter, we again need to consider the wider argumentative context. Arguments against the treaty, such as in letter 1, typically focused on loss, be this loss of sovereignty or loss of rights, with Denmark dominated by larger countries. Letter 2 is implicitly countering that perspective and this affects the rhetorical structure: the use of the active voice, repeated syntactic parallelism (*vi kan* ('we can') + verb) and repetition of words with positive connotations (e.g *styrke* ('strengthen'), *samarbejde* ('cooperation') and its derivatives, (*beskyttelse*) 'protection' and its derivatives).

Appeal is made to a number of specific *topoi*. One is that Scandinavian notions of democracy and social awareness are different and ultimately better-developed than those of other member states, and hence the European Union as a whole. This *topos* underlies concerns expressed in other letters about, e.g. environmental issues (pollution, nuclear power), welfare benefits for the old and the sick, and equality. One no-voter (*Ekstra Bladet* 29.5.92) insists that he/she does not want anything to do with an Italy 'where the mafia and the Vatican fight for power behind an easily transparent democratic veil' (*hvor mafiaen og Vatikanet slås om magten bag et let gennemskueligt demokratisk slør*), a France that 'arrogantly explodes atom bombs on the other side of the world' (*arrogant sprænger atombomber på den anden side af jorden*), a Germany that 'just throws heavy industrial pollution all around them' (*bare vælter tung industriforurening ud i omverden*) and the English who 'still haven't understood the title system and driving on the right' (*der endnu ikke har fattet titalsystemet og højrekørsel*). This 'Scandinavian democracy is better' *topos* reminds us that the supposedly common values, such as democracy, equality etc., on which the current EU constitution is based, are themselves discursively constructed and may, thus, not be quite as "shared" as is assumed. The *topos* also explains fears expressed by some that Denmark will be overrun by immigrants from other EC/EU states seeking pensions and welfare benefits: *Med et ja til Unionen, vil alle EF-borgere frit kunne bosætte sig her i landet. De sociale ydelser er store i Danmark så vi vil blive invaderet af arbejdsløse, handicappede og pensionister.* ('By saying yes to the Union, all EC citizens will be able to freely settle in Denmark. Social payments are big in Denmark so we will be invaded by the unemployed, handicapped and pensioners', *Ekstra Bladet* 10.5.92)

Another *topos* relates to the nature of influence: it is easier to influence from within than from without. The argumentative structure of the letter ultimately relies on this: I will vote yes as this will have certain effects, effects that cannot be achieved otherwise (because it is easier to influence Europe from within a union than from outside it). This *topos* rests on another, that Denmark is a small country and small countries lack influence and are vulnerable. A fundamental and enduring *topos* of Danish public thought is that Denmark is a little country, a mentality which possibly has its roots in Denmark's relatively rapid reduction in size and influence during the 19th century with the loss of Norway and the duchies of Schleswig and Holstein. This *topos*, for instance, was very apparent in media coverage of Denmark's victory over the German national football team in the 1992 European cup final, which took place a few weeks after the Maastricht referendum. The headline in *Ekstra Bladet* (27.06.92) ran *da lille Danmark bankede Tyskland* ('when little Denmark beat Germany') and comments from people on the street included *I dag er vi blevet større. Vi er noget.* ('Today we've become bigger. We are something'). In current debates about internationalisation and globalisation, the *topos* regularly makes an appearance, e.g. a 2006 report from Denmark's 'Technology Council' is entitled *Lille land hvad nu?* ('Little country what now?').

From this 'Denmark is little' *topos*, derive two conflicting notions of influence: the one above (as espoused by the 'yes' camp in the referendum) and the one as favoured by the 'no' camp, namely that small/weak countries get ignored by large/strong countries and so they should keep themselves out of any alliance with supranational intentions: *Hvis det bliver et ja, kan regering og folketing fly-tte ud i et forsamlingshus, for de får ikke mere at bestemme, end hvad et sogneråd i en lille landkommune vedtager.* ('If it's a yes, the government and Parliament can move out to a local hall because they won't get more to make decisions on than what a small parish committee approves', *Ekstra Bladet* 2.6.92). The fear that smaller member states will lose power in the EU was still apparent among 60% of Danes responding to a question about fear of the EU in Eurobarometer 51 (1999), where Denmark was the only country that listed this fear in their top three (al-though proportionally both Greek and Finnish respondents shared this view).

Memory and invention

My focus here is on 'social memory', a term used by Fentress and Wickham (1992) to refer to shared group memories. These are memories that have social meaning and are used to construct the present, but simultaneously can be (re)constructed by the present.

Both letters employ social memory and indeed make reference to the same memory, the vote in 1972, which saw Denmark join the EC. However, this is con-structed differently in the letters. As a no-voter with a dislike of the European integration enterprise, the writer of letter 1 negatively represents the event as the result of 'being lured', causing subsequent economic problems. The choice of lexis heightens the blame, e.g. *uanede* ('undreamt of') levels of unemployment. In letter 2, the same memory is constructed as an active choice that 'we' took as part of the first step into the EC: a beginning of the road towards something positive.

Letter 1 also makes reference to a highly significant social memory through-out Europe and beyond, World War II. Usually it was older voters who referred to this conflict and they were typically, but not always, no-voters. For this writer, clearly of the older generation, the definite form *krigen* ('the war') is an adequate referring expression. The memory is represented as Danes fighting against oc-cupation – physically struggling for a free Denmark. The inclusive pronoun 'we' is used ('just as we did during the war'), suggesting that all Danes were involved in this resistance (although in recent historical narratives, e.g. Kirchoff 2002; Poulsen 2002, matters are represented as being considerably more complex). Note too that this 'we' has ambiguous reference: a specific 'we' of my generation or a more abstract, generic 'we', such as is used elsewhere in the letter (e.g. 'we will become a German province'). This social memory of Danish resistance and free-dom-fighting influences the understanding of both the contemporary situation in Yugoslavia – a fight for freedom by Croatia – and also Denmark's future prospects in a European Union. The construction of this memory also helps sustain the *topoi* of German dominance in the Union and freedom as a characteristic of nation states.

Construction of audience and identities

· In letter 1, the writer makes no direct appeal to his/her audience – the readers of *Ekstra Bladet* – but there is frequent use of inclusive personal pronouns – *vi, vores* ('we', 'our') – which connect writer to audience. This imagined audience clearly consists of Danes – people who will understand the social memories and national symbols referred to and the specific *topoi* used. Indeed, national identity is constructed by reference to these memories and beloved national symbols – *Dannebrog*, the Danish flag, and *Grundlovsdag*, Constitution Day. Moreover, national symbols are set up against the symbols of pan-European cooperation; for instance the European flag is mocked as a 'shared rag with stars on it'. Reference to national symbols, such as the flag, the national anthem, the Queen, the currency, was made exclusively by the no-voters in the corpus. Such symbols have strong emotional appeal and endow an argument with distinct nationalistic *pathos*. Testament to the strength of these symbols was the dramatic increase in the sales of the Danish flag in the run-up to the referendum, as reported by *Berlingske Tidende* (28.5.92). It seemed the elderly in particular feared losing the national flag if Denmark went into the Union. Sales of the European flag were also up, selling primarily to corporate and public bodies rather than individuals.

The rhetorical construction of Danishness as a mutually exclusive opposite to EU/European was common among the no voters: *Stem dansk. Stem nej til Unionen* ('Vote Danish. Vote no to the Union', *Ekstra Bladet* 30.5.92); *Desværre er det ikke 'in' at være dansker men at være 'supereuropæer'* ('Unfortunately, it's not the in-thing to be a Dane, but to be a super-European', *Ekstra Bladet* 31.5.92). Given the referendum context, 'Europe/European' tended to be viewed in political rather than geographical terms, although some set up a clear relationship of opposition between the EU and Europe/European:

> *Ja, til Europa siger ja-sigerne. Selvfølgelig. Men derfor kan man det godt sige nej til Unionen. Nej til at overlade beslutningerne til et kæmpebureaukrati i Bruxelles. Jeg bor på Fyn og er europæer. Vi er da indenfor i Europa. Det har vi været i 1000 år* (*Ekstra Bladet* 24.5.92)
> (Yes to Europe say the yes-voters. Of course. But that's why one can indeed say no to the Union. No to leaving the decisions to a gigantic bureaucracy in Brussels. I live on Funen and am a European. We're surely inside Europe. We've been that for 1000 years).

Here the political entity, the European Union, is seen as a contradiction to the geographical reality of Europe and European identity. The vast majority of the letter-writers, however, constructed Europe as being equivalent to the European Community/Union. For instance, this yes-voter links being European to voting yes in the referendum: *Er man europæer og ønsker, at Danmark skal have medind-flydelse på Europas fremtidige struktur, skal man stemme ja* ('If one's a European and wants Denmark to have influence on Europe's future structure, one has to vote yes', *Berlingske Tidende* 4.5.92). This political understanding of Europe meant that 'Europe', i.e. the EU, could be constructed as a negative concept by the no-camp, with appropriate uncomplimentary referring expressions and descriptions, as evidenced in letter 1 and indeed many of the letters in the corpus, e.g. *bureaukratisk diktatur* ('bureaucratic dictatorship', *Ekstra Bladet* 15.5.92), *makværk man kalder et forenet Europa* ('botched job one calls a united Europe', *Ekstra Bladet* 10.5.92), *det militariske Europa* ('the militarist Europe', *Ekstra Bladet* 31.5.92), *Europas Forenede Stater...en kunstig skal* ('Europe's United States...an artifical shell', *Ekstra Bladet* 31.5.92); *et Europa....hvor der bag dørene i magtens kilometerlange korridorer regeres af folk uden parlamentarisk ansvar* ('A Europe.. where behind the doors on the kilometre-long corridors of power, people without parliamentary responsibility reign', *Berlingske Tidende* 14.5.92). These negative perceptions of the EU link to the 'freedom/nation-state' *topos*, where democracy is linked to the national and not the supranational, and reflect the euphemistic phrase 'democratic deficit', first coined in relation to the European institutional machinery in the 1980's.

A markedly different construction of Danish and European identity is apparent in letter 2. Here the writer makes one direct appeal to his/her audience – the collective 'we': *Lad os..* ('let us..'). This 'us' again consists of Danes, but here Danishness is characterised by the specific *topos* of shared Nordic understanding of democracy and social awareness. Europe is represented in terms of cooperation, *samarbejdende Europa* ('cooperating Europe'), between *selvstændige nationer* ('independent nations'). For this writer, national and European heritages are compatible; the former is not threatened by Europe, but can be developed within it, and the latter is shared, although what is actually shared is not elaborated on. This non-specificity of European identity was quite common and contrasted with the specificity of national identity construction, as exemplified in the following:

> *Vi skulle jo gerne blive gode europæere, men med den danske kultur i vore hjer-ter. Den nordiske mytologi, vore mange dialekter og traditioner i hverdag og fest, vores teknologiske, sociale, boligmæssige udvikling, vores natur og kunst; det er der alt sammen til belysning af det, vi danskere kalder vores.* (*Berlingske Tidende* 17.5.92).

(We shall willingly become good Europeans, but with Danish culture in our hearts. Nordic mythology, our many dialects and traditions for everyday as well as special occasions, our technological, social and housing-related development, our countryside and art; this is what together highlights that which we Danes call ours).

For this writer and the writer of letter 2, "European" would seem to equate with being Danish in a European context. There is no evidence in the letter corpus as a whole of Europe/European being defined in terms of opposition to an outside group, e.g. European vs. American. The USA was occasionally mentioned, but as a negative comparison of what the Union would become in terms of suppressed minorities, uneasy multiculturalism, violence and lack of welfare benefits. If anything, it was Europe/European that was seen as the 'other' in relation to Denmark. Interestingly, a decade after the Maastricht referendum, it was apparent that certain Danish politicians were constructing Europe/European, not in opposition to the nation-state and national identity, but in relation to a very specific outside 'other', i.e. the Islamic world. In a speech from July 2002, Peter Skaarup, the deputy leader of the Danish People's Party (*Dansk Folkeparti*), a right-wing party that was and remains anti-EU, warned of a threat to Europe, an entity constructed in terms of its Christian heritage:

> *Den alvorligste trussel mod Europa kommer fra indvandringen fra især den muslimske verden. Det er de demografiske ændringer, som er med til at ændre Europa radikalt. Og hvis de får lov at fortsætte, bliver Europa et helt andet. Skal Europa være katedralernes eller moskeernes verdensdel? Det er spørgsmålet. Hvis kontinentet Europa fortsat skal kunne karakteriseres som "europæisk" med alt det, vi forbinder med europæisk kultur, bør vi se truslerne mere kontant i øjnene.* (www.eu-oplysninger.dk/emner/fremtid/konventdokumenter/eukonvent/dk_medlemmer/doc/).
>
> (The most serious threat for Europe comes from immigration from especially the Muslim world. These are the demographic changes that are playing a part in changing Europe radically. And if they are allowed to continue, Europe will become something completely different. Is Europe to be a part of the world with cathedrals or mosques? That is the question. If the continent of Europe is to continue to be characterised as "European" with all that we associate with European culture, we ought to look at the threats directly in the eye).

Perhaps surprisingly, what we see here is the promotion of European identity, a concept that had been something of an anathema for the no-vote in 1992, by an anti-EU politician. Moreover, it is embedded within a discourse of religion. A decade previously, religion was rarely mentioned in the letter corpus as a component of national or European identity and when it was, it was articulated in terms of another age-old, binary conflict, namely Catholicism and Protestantism; the Orthodox church was not mentioned. Some feared a Catholic-dominated Europe, where, for example "Catholic-influenced laws will be passed in Brussels e.g. against free abortion" (*Katolsk prægede love vil blive vedtaget i Bruxelles, f.eks. imod fri abort, Ekstra Bladet* 29.5.92). Fears of Islam were expressed on occasion, but in relation to contemporary immigration into Denmark, not the construct of Europe itself. Paradoxically, one of the few letters dealing with what was perceived as the Islamic threat to Denmark from immigration was written by a Polish immigrant, displaced after World War II. A greater irony, given the global turmoil caused by the series of Mohammed cartoons published in the Danish broadsheet *Jyllands Posten* in September 2005, is that this letter was accompanied by a cartoon of the prophet Mohammed's beard slicing, with a sabre, the beard of the mythical Danish hero, Holger Danske (*Berlingske Tidende* 18.5.92).

The extent to which Islam is now being constructed as the 'other' to a European identity is, however, far from clear. Kølvraa (2003:29), on the basis of discursive data from young people from all over Europe involved in the 'Bridging Europe Youth Community' project, argues that what he terms the 'Arab other' is articulated in relation to national contexts and not European. It may be that the Islamic 'other' is being constructed within national frameworks as issues of immigration gain increasing significance, and then is acquiring European dimensions, as exemplified in Peter Skaarup's speech, as demands grow for a more concrete EU/European identity based on specified, delimited cultural values and more precise geographical borders.

Conclusion

The assumption in this chapter has been that the age-old concepts of classical rhetoric are still able to give insights into the strategies of argument in contemporary public discourse and, hence, insights into the processes of public thinking, that create and change political and social orders. Combining issues of cognition with structural, linguistic concerns, rhetoric permits a more holistic view of discourse production. Using two letters as examples, it is clear that the rhetorical strategies systematised within classical thinking are used by ordinary Danish citizens for the purposes of argument. Regardless of their viewpoint, they weave together *topoi,* enthymeme and memories to create not only the fabric of an argument, but their vision of political reality. Depending on their viewpoint, this vision resembles a horror story with an undemocratic, militaristic Europe absorbing Denmark and Danishness or a Utopia where togetherness leads to social, economic and cultural advancement in Europe and beyond. In some ways, these two letters, and indeed many of the letters in the corpus, exemplify a strategy that is not well-acknowledged in the literature, namely argument producing narrative, where common and specific *topoi* are exploited to create scenarios and stories that define, in this case, the European Union, or Denmark or notions of group identity. This is not quite the same as the more well-known strategy of using stories as a type of argument or proof; for instance, one elderly letter-writer told the story of his wait to get into hospital for an operation, and, once admitted, the doctor told him the delays were due to EC regulations, and so why would anyone want to vote yes in the referendum. (Toolan's (this volume) interpretation of Harry's story about the water meter links to this use of stories as proof, in this case proof that the EU might not be all bad).

So what can be concluded about the EU and European identity on the basis of the two letters examined and the letter corpus as a whole? It would seem that in anti-EU discourse in 1992, there was a fear of German dominance and a perception of the EC/EU as undemocratic, bureaucratic and dictatorial. Pro-EU discourse did not necessarily disagree with these viewpoints, but saw union as an opportunity for improvement. The extent to which the *topoi* underlying these perceptions are still central to public thinking today can only be estimated. Fear of German dominance appears to have subsided as the EU has evolved, although notions of the EU as bureaucratic still seem to hold sway. Results from Eurobarometer 65 (2006) indicate that for 41% of Danes respondents the EU meant 'bureaucracy' for them personally, although for 36% it meant 'democracy'. Generally, however, Danish attitudes towards the EU are becoming increasingly positive, at least according to Eurobarometer data, and fears of future EU development focus more on economic and crime issues than loss of power for smaller countries and loss of national identity, although these latter two concerns remain. With regard to identity, there was little sign of an independent, well-defined European identity in the letter corpus; at best there seemed to be a realignment of national identity within the European context, at least for the yes-vote. European identity was generally non-specific and its parameter of comparison was Danish identity, positioned in a relation of mutual exclusion or inclusion. Today, while polls show an increase in attachment to Europe (EU) and European identity by Danes, there is still no specification as to what European identity might actually mean for Danes. One contender coming from certain political quarters is religion, the Christian heritage positioned in opposition to the Islamic tradition, as national concerns deepen in relation to terrorism and immigration. The fortunes of such a binary, non-secular conceptualisation of European identity remain to be seen, but as noted by the Reflection Group on The Spiritual and Cultural Dimension of Europe (2004: 8–9) Europe is not a static "fact" or "catalogue of 'European values'" but a dynamic "task and a process" meaning that questions of identity are being continuously negotiated as they are confronted with new and different contexts. Perhaps from this perspective, that people have a non-specific sense of European identity is not necessarily bad, but merely a sign of rhetorical work in progress.

References

Billig, Michael. 1991. *Ideology and Opinions. Studies in Rhetorical Psychology.* London: Sage Publications.

Billig, Michael. 1996. *Arguing and Thinking.* 2nd edition. Cambridge: Cambridge University Press.

Bruner, Jerome. 1986. *Actual Minds, Possible Worlds.* Cambridge: Harvard University Press.

Calame, Claude. 1999. "The rhetoric of muthos and logos: Forms of figurative discourse". In *From Myth to Reason?*, R. Buxton (ed.), 119–144. Oxford: Oxford University Press.

Corbett, Edward P. J. and Connors, Robert J. 1999. *Classical Rhetoric for the Modern Student.* 4th edition. Oxford: Oxford University Press.

Corvino, William and Jolliffe, David. 1995. *Rhetoric. Concepts, Definitions and Boundaries.* Boston: Allyn and Bacon.

Delgado-Moreira, Juan M. 1997. "Cultural citizenship and the creation of European identity". *Electronic Journal of Sociology* ISSN: 11983655 Available at <http://www.sociology.org/content/vol002.003/ Delgado.html>. Accessed 8 January 2007.

Dosenrode, Søren. 2002. "The Danes, the European Union and the forthcoming presidency". *Research and European Issues* No. 18. Available at <http://www.notre-europe.asso.fr/etud18-fr.pdf>. Accessed 8 January 2007.

Eurobarometer 37. 1992. Available at <http://ec.europa.eu/public_opinion/archives/eb/eb37/eb37_en.pdf>. Accessed 8 January 2007.

Eurobarometer 51. 1999. Available at <http://ec.europa.eu/public_opinion/archives/eb/eb51/eb51_en.htm>. Accessed 8 January 2007.

Eurobarometer 65. 2006. Available at <http://ec.europa.eu/public_opinion/archives/eb/eb65/eb65_en.htm>. Accessed 8 January 2007.

European Commission. 2000. *How the Europeans See Themselves.* Luxembourg: Office for Official Publication of the European Community.

Fentress, James and Wickham, Chris. 1992. *Social Memory.* Oxford: Blackwell.

Hardt-Mautner, Gerlinda. 1994. "How does one become a good European?: The British press and European integration". *Discourse & Society*, 6(2): 177–205.

Hesse, Douglas. 1989. "Persuading as storying: Essays, narrative rhetoric and the college writing course". In *Narrative and Argument*, R. Andrews (ed.), 106–117. Milton Keynes: Open University Press.

Hug, Simon. 2002. *Voices of Europe.* Lanham: Rowman & Littlefield.

Jacobs, Dirk and Maier, Robert. 1998. "European identity: Construct, fact and fiction". In *A United Europe. The Quest for a Multifaceted Identity.* M. Gastelaars and A. de Ruijter (eds.), 13–34. Maastricht: Shaker.

Johnstone, Barbara. 1996. *The Linguistic Individual.* New York: Oxford University Press.

Kennedy, George. 1998. *Comparative Rhetoric. An Historical and Cross-Cultural Introduction*. Oxford: Oxford University Press.

Kirchhoff, Hans. 2002. *Samarbejde og Modstand under Besættelsen*. Odense: Odense Universitetsforlag.

Kølvraa, Christopher. 2003. "Discursively constructing Europe: Culture, history, values and the other". *Kontur*, 7: 25–31.

Mumby, Dennis. 1993. "Introduction: Narrative and social control". In *Narrative and Social Control: Critical Perspectives*, D. Mumby (ed.), 1–12. Newbury Park: Sage Publications.

Nash, Walter. 1989. *Rhetoric. The Wit of Persuasion*. Oxford: Blackwell.

Poulsen, Henning. 2002. *Besættelsesårene 1940–1945*. Aarhus: Aarhus Universitetsforlag.

Rapp, Christof. 2002. "The topoi of the Rhetoric" [online]. *Supplement to Aristotle's Rhetoric, Stanford Encyclopedia of Philosophy*. Available at <http://plato.stanford.edu/entries/aristotle-rhetoric/supplement2.html>. Accessed 8 January 2007.

Reflection Group. 2004. *The Spiritual and Cultural Dimension of Europe*. Brussels/Vienna: European Commission/Institute of Human Sciences. Available at <http://ec.europa.eu/research/social-sciences/pdf/michalski_ 281004_final_report_en.pdf>. Accessed 8 January 2007.

Robyn, Richard. (ed.). 2004. *The Changing Face of European Identity: A Seven-Nation Study of (Supra)National Attachments*. New York: Routledge.

Scott, Robert et al. 1971. "Report of the committee on the nature of rhetorical invention". In *The Prospect of Rhetoric*, L. Bitzer and E. Black (eds.), 228–236. Englewood Cliffs, NJ: Prentice-Hall.

Siune, Karen, Svensson, Palle and Tonsgaard, Ole. 1992. *Det Blev et Nej*. Aarhus: Politica.

Staub, August. 2001. "Rhetoric and poetic: Aristotle, the enthymeme and the discovery of dramatic troping in contemporary theatre" [online]. *Didaskalia* Vol. 4(2). Available at <http://didaskalia.open.ac.uk/ issues/ vol4no2/ staub.html>. Accessed 8 January 2007.

Too, Yun Lee. 1995. *The Rhetoric of Identity in Isocrates*. Cambridge: Cambridge University Press.

Van der Veen, Maurits, A. 2002. "Determinants of European identity: A preliminary investigation using EUROBAROMETER data". Available at <http://www.isanet.org/noarchive/vanderveen.html>. Accessed 8 January 2007.

Van Dijk, Teun. 1993. "Stories and racism". In *Narrative and Social Control: Critical Perspectives*, D. Mumby (ed.), 121–142. Newbury Park: Sage Publications.

Van Dijk, Teun and Wodak, Ruth. 2000. (eds). *Racism at the Top: Parliamentary Discourses on Ethnic Issues in 6 European States*. Klagenfurt: Drava Verlag.

Vickers, Brian.1998. *In Defence of Rhetoric*. Oxford: Clarendon Press.

Welch, Kathleen. 1999. *Electric Rhetoric*. Cambridge, MA: MIT.

Narratives of Greek identity in European life

Ekaterini Nikolarea
University of the Aegean

Introduction

This paper will venture to understand the reasons of a paradigm shift which occurred in Greek society and culture at the end of the twentieth century and the
beginning of the twenty-first century (1994–2001), and will try to capture moments of the (trans)formation of Greek identity in relation to its European 'other'
within this shift. The shift in question is that of a slow but steady change from
an agricultural country into a commercial and technocratic one. Otherwise un-
noticed, this paradigm shift can usually be discerned either during periods of
crisis or in various manifestations of everyday Greek life vis-à-vis a supranational
European identity, society and culture.

Drawing on Bakhtinian notions of discourse, it will be examined how official
Greek economic and political discourses, policies and political practices not only
intermingle with everyday narratives, discourses and demands as presented in the
media, but also influence each other and assume each other's voice and point of
view when facing their European other. I will attempt to show through the discussion and interpretation of written and visual texts that, despite many instances of
multi-voicedness and multiple points of view in the representation of Greek identity vis-à-vis European identity, there are moments of single-voicedness when the
Greek voice or 'I' narrates itself and expresses its opinion in harmony with its
European 'other' and moments of single-eyedness when the Greek point of view
or 'Eye' (i.e. as a focaliser) views the world through the European 'view'. These
instances are especially noticeable in visual and written texts (original and translated) on the Economic Monetary Union or EMU and the Euro. It is through
these national and supranational cultural processes that the remodelling of Greek
society, culture and history takes place.

In conclusion, it is proposed that a better view and understanding of a wider European life can be attained only when functions of various discourses within different European countries at given historical moments are examined, compared and contrasted. Only through this comparative and contrastive analysis, can one examine if and how these discourses are able to generate 'identical' EU policies and political practices, and in so doing construct an EU of multiple, identical European identities.

Theoretical considerations

Following Bakhtin (1981: 276), language will be considered to be dialogic:

> The living utterance, having taken meaning and shape at a particular historical moment in a socially specific environment, cannot fail to brush up against thousands of living dialogic threads, woven by socio-ideological consciousness around the given object of an utterance; it cannot fail to become an active participant in social dialogue.

Dialogue can be external and internal. On the one hand, the external dialogue presupposes an interaction between two distinct subjects: an 'I' who is the author of the utterance and an 'Other', who is the addressee and who is expected to respond to the 'I'. Note, however, that in responding, the 'Other' ceases to be an addressee and becomes the author; in other words, the positions of the subjects change in a dialogue. On the other hand, the internal dialogue is seen as a form of inner speech when an earlier self encounters a later self (Bakhtin 1986). This later self can be seen as an 'I' who views the earlier self as an 'Other', since the intervening time has altered both the perception of self and the self itself.

Applying these concepts to the Greek situation, I seek to explore:

1. When and where Greek identity ("Greekness") as an 'I' (the author of an utterance) expects a response from its addressee; or when and where as an 'Eye' (the focaliser) it perceives the 'Other' as a different subject or self and so engages in an external dialogue.
2. When and where Greek identity as the author and the focaliser is similar to, but not identical with, the European Other and assumes the latter's characteristics, attributes and discursive practices. In this case, an internal dialogue is involved.

If this tension and these dynamics hold true, then Greek Identity as 'Self' belongs to more than one collective group or system; it is involved in many heterogeneous, and often conflicting, regional, supraregional, cultural, linguistic, political and economic activities in which this 'Self' takes several positions and uses different socio-ideological languages which are (re)presented in its everyday narratives.

The everyday and narratives

The dialogic activities noted above take place in the everyday, that is in the space and time that is mundane, ever-present, and yet materially invisible (i.e. it is so obvious that it ceases to be visible anymore). It is a *topos* (a meeting place or site) of various powerful discourses (such as politics and economics) and discursive practices (as exercised by institutions, centres of decision-making and decision-makers) which, although repetitive, cyclical and mundane, may hold unexpected economic and political reversals and surprises.

In the context of this chapter, the temporality of everyday Greek life is the 7-year span of 1994–2001 and spatiality is considered to be the agglomeration of different spaces and discourses in which the everyday takes place. These spaces are conceptualised in terms of three environments: the local/familiar environment of Greece; the global/unfamiliar environment of the EU and international scholars and agencies; glocal/quasi-familiar environment of Greece vis-à-vis the EU and/or local scholars and agencies interacting with their international counterparts. In the local environment, discourses include those of various centres of decision-making (government and ministries); the national print, broadcast and electronic media; and the responses of Greeks, which are mediated by the media in Modern Greek. For example, see Appendix 1, which consists of primarily Greek news commentaries and publications on the EMU and Euro. In the global environment, discourses include those of various centres of decision-making (the EU and international agencies, such as the World Bank) and the directives or criteria for the EMU; the foreign print, broadcast and electronic media; and the responses of non-Greeks and specialists (academics, economists, politicians etc), which are mediated by the media in English or in any other European language. In the glocal environment, discourses include those of various centres of decision-making (Greek and European) which meet, creating discourses expressed either in Modern Greek, English or any other European language; Greek and foreign media discussing Greece in Modern Greek, English or any other European language; and responses of Greeks and foreigners, which are are mediated by the media in Modern Greek, English or any other European language. Note the term "glocal" has been borrowed from Gray (2002) who defines it in the context of English language teaching, as an English coursebook that aims at straddling the *global*/lo*cal* divide, trying to strike a balance between the local world of the learners and the global world of Standard Englishes. Glocal environments are an impact of globalisation on local environments – a phenomenon that is not new; it is rather as old as the Tower of Babel and is usually produced in geographical locations (environments) where whole societies are in transition. In these kind of environments, there is not necessarily a balance in the use of the various local languages and the global language. The complex nexus of the interrelation of English as today's global language and local languages and the need for the mobility of individuals in an ever-increasing globalised environment is discussed in Nikolarea (2003, 2004a, 2004b).

It will be examined how people make sense of their local, global and/or glocal environments and the situations they experience through a variety of narratives, which can unravel how everyday beliefs and practices, can shape, transform and remodel an identity as individual, national or supranational. In this paper, although aware of a variety of theories of narratives of everyday life (Berger 1997) and analyses of everyday texts (Stillar 1998), everyday narratives will be interpreted as texts or utterances in Bakhtinian terms. These narratives will be (1) written or visual texts or a combination of both, and (2) originally written in English or in Modern Greek. If the texts are written in Modern Greek, both the original text and an English translation will be provided. In the analysis, we will try to explore how the author of the utterance is positioned in relation to wider, everyday discursive practices and how this 'I' views (thus becoming an 'eye') and interprets the specific situation. Furthermore, we will discuss how various authors of various utterances are related to their own utterances and show how power relations emerge in the texts.

Of particular interest will be Bahktin's (1981) notions of authoritative discourse and internally persuasive discourse. Authoritative discourse is not conceptualised as one's reply to a dialogue. It enters the situation (context) from without as a voice of authority, as a command which one can neither enter into a dialogue with nor doubt. This kind of discourse ignores or even excludes answerability; it is the kind of discourse in which single-voicedness dominates. Examples of authoritative discourse are (a) legal directives coming from above to which we have to conform (at least for a certain time); (b) summaries of historical periods of countries about which we know nothing and thus we take the knowledge provided at its face value (see my own recounting of the political and economic situation of Greece below); and/or (c) translated passages, which we have to take at their face value if we do not know the original language. In this chapter, the original Modern Greek texts, when available, are provided so those who can read Modern Greek can compare their own interpretation of the texts ('utterances') with mine.

Internally persuasive discourse is a "retelling in one's own words" (Bakhtin 1981:341) and can produce either single-voicedness or multi-voicedness. Both of these can be characteristic of heteroglossia, which refers to different styles or genres within a language as well as their use in the literary domain. It is through heteroglossia that differing points of view about the world are produced. Closely linked to the notion of heteroglossia is that of hybridisation, which involves a mixing of (socio-ideological) 'languages' within "the limits of a single utterance, an encounter, within the arena of an utterance, between two different linguistic consciousnesses, separated from one another by an epoch, by social differentiation or by some other factor" (Bakhtin 1981:358). Concepts such as 'utterance', 'heteroglossia' and 'hybridisation' can be used to highlight not only the interrelation between linguistic means and discursive practices, but also the reciprocal relationships between discursive action, institutional structures and decision-making on national and supranational levels. For instance, utterances articulated in the Greek context embed and internalise the authoritative utterances of the Other; and the historical remodelling of Greece and Europe can be seen at times as the remodelling of multiple Selves (or multiple identities) in an interactive and, on occasion, resistance mode.

1994–2001: Authoritative discourses, dialogised heteroglossias and hybridisation in and of Greece

The remodelling of Greece is best understood within the context of the wider political and economic framework of Greece during the second half of the twentieth century and the beginning of the new millennium. Political and economic discourses, developed within and outside of Greece, contributed to a slow but steady transformation of the political and economic landscape of Greece and brought about a dramatic change not only in Greek identity, but also in the Greek perception of the 'Other', i.e. Europe.

Here we will present a variety of texts from the mid-1990s onwards, written in Greek and/or English by Greek or international authors. These will be situated in wider contexts to show how a remodelling of history and culture of a member state like Greece and a super-state like the EU have coincided – when the 'I' becomes the 'Other' and vice-versa – and the role academics, political institutions, organisations, news and mass media, stock brokers and the Athens Stock Exchange (ASE) played in that remodelling.

1994–1996: a prelude – The Economic Monetary Union (EMU)
and Greece: Stereotyping and viewing

We will consider this period in terms of local, global and glocal responses to the
EMU.

*Local responses to the EMU: Greek efforts to understand what it is
to be European*
By late 1994, there was such a consensus on Greece's membership of the EU that
all political parties represented in the Greek Parliament (except KKE: the Communist Party) ratified the Treaty on European Union (TEU or Maastricht Treaty)
in spite of the difficulties Greece was facing in meeting the five convergence criteria for full participation in the EMU (Barbour 1996; Corbett 1994; Sandholtz
1994; (the) *Single Currency and the European Parliament,* 1997 and (the) *European
Union 1998*).

Within the given historical context, we can discern two levels of an authoritative discourse permeating Greek identity and everyday life with an interim of a
hesitant, internally persuasive discourse. On one level, the five convergence criteria for full participation in the EMU enter into Greek politics and economics
as EU directives – an authoritative discourse, an "ultimate semantic authority"
(Bakhtin 1984: 189) – which cannot be disclaimed. If Greece were to disclaim
those criteria, then *never* would it be permitted to join the EMU. Thus, the Greek
government had to present the TEU and the five convergence criteria to the Greek
Parliament for discussion and approval.

It was when the Greek MPs were discussing the TEU and the convergence
criteria in the Greek Parliament that an interim of a hesitant, internally persuasive
discourse occurred. During the discussion period, when the Greek MPs were trying to understand the TEU and its impact upon the political, economic and everyday life of their fellow citizens, they were inevitably internalising the European
authoritative discourse.

Still, when the MPs agreed to ratify the TEU – although they were fully aware
of the difficulties that Greece would face in meeting the convergence criteria for
the EMU – that agreement started being effective and entered into the space of
everyday Greek life as an authoritative discourse, a top-down decision. In other
words, it was imposed on Greeks, who had to understand and, eventually, internalise what that unfamiliar TEU – that European 'Other' – was all about and how
it might affect their daily life.

Global responses to the EMU: Authoritative discourses – a stereotypical image of Greece

In the present context, global responses are understood to be utterances produced in English by international specialists (politicians, economists, political or economic analysts), and academics, responding to a wider politico-economic context. In focus here will be Sandholtz (1994), Baun (1996) and Nagle and Spencer (1996).

In a widely read article, Wayne Sandholtz (1994), seeking to explain why the twelve EC countries chose EMU over other possible methods, made some astute comments on Greek macroeconomic policy choices. These comments were destined to become a stereotypical image of Greek economics that would linger for years, as we will discuss in the sub-sections below. Sandholtz problematises the Greek economy, occasionally juxtaposing it with that of Portugal, stating that:

> *Greece* and Portugal remain *problematic*, in the sense that inflation rates remain high (about 12 to 14 percent in 1989) and *restrictive economic policies* could impose *high social and political costs*. ... *Greek* entry into the ERM [Exchange-rate mechanism] and any monetary union will be accomplished *after some sort of transition phase*. (266; *emphases* and [brackets] added)

Later, when discussing policy choices and the five convergence criteria for full participation in the EMU, he claims that:

> For some states (*Greece*, Portugal) that [to join the first wave of entrants into full EMU] *will be virtually impossible*, and they will make *the transition later*. (273; *emphases* and [brackets] added)

Two years later, two other publications on the EU, which made specific references to southern European countries, appeared. Michael Baun (1996), exploring political theories surrounding the TEU and trying to go beyond that treaty, makes some very interesting observations on national positions on the EMU and EC fiscal and monetary authority. Regarding national positions on the EMU, he asserts that:

> In addition, the *poorer* EC members, especially Spain, Portugal, *Greece*, Ireland, and, to some extent, Italy, had a specific set of interests, particularly how to avoid being left behind in a two-speed EMU. This configuration would confer on them a *"second-class"* status, when most of them had originally coveted EC membership as *a means of modernizing* and *catching up* with the more economically advanced countries of northern Europe. (61; *emphases* added)

As for EC fiscal and monetary authority, Baun (1996) states:

> There was also considerable sympathy among other Community countries for
> EC fiscal and budgetary controls. Weaker countries such as Italy and *Greece,*
> which traditionally ran *high budget deficits* and *often found it difficult for domestic*
> *political reasons to rein in public spending,* were anxious to gain *external support*
> *for more restrictive national policies.* (70; *emphases* added)

What is striking in the above statement is the claim that the EMU and the wider
EU context would become a pretext for governments of countries like Greece to
adopt more restrictive national policies. How true this statement was proven to
be, and how the two consecutive governments of Simitis (1996–2000 and 2000–
2004) would implement it, will be discussed below.

Nagle and Spencer (1996), whose concerns are geographical, devote some
space to evaluate issues in, at least at the time, less familiar areas, such as Greece,
Portugal and Spain. They claim that:

> Each country is locationally disadvantaged within the EU:....
> 3. *Greece* has developed *outside the core areas of North West Europe* and *is poorly*
> *linked to* the EU: unlike Spain and Portugal it suffered a fall in prosperity during
> the 1980s.
> … But Greece also has structural disadvantages. It is *peripheral* within the EU
> *with no common border with another member state.* (146; *emphases* added)

The authors further assert that, although these three countries are politically, economically and culturally different, they encounter three similar problems, one of
which is that all three countries must meet the convergence criteria for full participation in the EMU by the end of the decade (i.e. 2000).

From a Bakhtinian point of view, these three global responses of academics enter into the wider European and Greek context as authoritative, scholarly
discourses – written and published texts expressed in an objective way. Their apparent scientific objectivity is based on hard facts of politics, economics, statistics
and geopolitics. The voices and the viewpoint of the authors (i.e. the 'I's' and 'Eyes'
of the above utterances) are those of an outsider.

Greek politics and Greece's geopolitical position result in Greek identity being viewed as the 'other' in relation to the EU, represented as one of the poorest
countries in the EU, which needs to catch up with the other northern European
member states, adopt restrictive economic policies and make a transition to meet
the convergence criteria for the EMU. Moreover, Greece is represented as outside
the core areas of North West Europe and poorly linked to the EU, meaning that
it is peripheral within the EU with no common borders with another member
state.

It can only be understood how powerful these scholarly discursive practices
are and what stereotypes they convey if the thread of polarities (the binary terms

the authors use) are identified in order to make sense of what (polarised) texture they form as illustrated in Table 1.

Table 1. Europe views Greece: An outsider's point of view.

Europe as 'I'/'eye' (Subject: the analyser)	Greece as 'other' (Object: the analysed)
Most of the countries are richer than it.	One of the poorest European countries.
Northern European countries are modern and economically advanced.	One of the southern European countries, which is old-fashioned and not economically advanced.
North West Europe is the core of the EU.	South East Europe is the periphery of the EU.
The core of the EU is well-linked to other EU member states and has common borders with them.	The periphery of the EU is poorly linked to other EU member states and has no common borders with them.

Interpreted in Bakhtinian terms and from a cultural perspective, these discourses and discursive practices represent 'outsideness', the eyes of other cultures (nations and academics included) that view and analyse 'objectively' what Greece and Greek identity is (Bakhtin 1986:7). In doing that, however, these discursive practices weave unflattering textures and project stereotypical images of Greece which, in turn, would become a *topos* where glocal discourses and discursive practices of the 1990s would be uttered and would partly mirror Greek economic policies, political decisions and everyday life – in other words, the (collective) Greek identity – for at least seven years.

Glocal responses to the EMU: A dialogised heteroglossia
In this context, we take glocal responses to signify the responses of local specialists (with contributions of international (global) scholars, at times), who produce their texts/utterances in English, in order to make local perspectives known to a wider, global readership; these utterances otherwise would have been left unknown, unfamiliar and thus 'unuttered'. The text analysed will illustrate how Greek academia perceived Greece vis-à-vis Europe at that specific historical moment; and how they narrated that perception. In doing this, we will venture to show that these utterances are good examples of heteroglossia and produce different views/selves/identities of Greece (a local context), which tries to make sense of itself by finding itself in a dialogue with, and many times in struggle with, Europe (a global context). Only in this dialogue and encounter with the European Other can Greece view itself and utter and narrate its position(s), thus understanding

not only how it sees itself and the European Other, but how it itself is viewed by this European Other.

Greek academia: Kazakos and Ioakimidis (1994)

> No doubt Greece stands as a unique case among the member states of the European Community/European Union in practically every respect. It is a *peripheral country*, geographically furthest from the centre of the European Union ... It is a country located in a turbulent region, *the Balkans*, in a stage of nationalistic turmoil which in the case of one country, *Yugoslavia*, has culminated in armed conflict ... it is the only member state of the European Union which feels *an intense external threat* [ie Turkey] to its national sovereignty and territorial integrity, something which compels it to spend the highest percentage (7 %) of its GDP on military expenditure; ... in *cultural terms*, it is the only member state of the European Union which participates in two cultural formations, the *Western liberal tradition* and the *Eastern orthodox religiousness* ... Yet Greece is the member state which, by virtue of its classical cultural heritage, feels that *it is entitled more than anyone else to the name 'European'. After all, the name Europe is a Greek one.*
> In *European terms* too, *Greece* is the country with the lowest level of development as measured by per capita GNP ... a state whose *economy* has, since accession to the EC, steadily *diverged* from the European economy. (ixx; *emphases* and [brackets] added)

In this text, a complex web of interrelationships is apparent where Greek identity either views itself as an 'Other' or views itself as different from the 'Other', perceiving itself as unique. Considering the former perspective, Greece is first seen as a member state of the EU (Self$_1$) and as the ultimate European country (Self$_2$). Self$_1$ is an insider's and outsider's point of view and, although both views may coincide, they are not identical because the experience of positioning is different. Self$_2$ is an insider's point of view where 'I' is identical to the 'Other', since the experience of positioning is the same.

From the perspective of Greece viewing itself as different from the Other come five more selves, all representing an insider's point of view. Self$_3$, Greece as the periphery of the EU, may sometimes coincide with an outsider's point of view (see Table 1); yet, these points of view are not identical because the experience of positioning is different. Similarly, Self$_4$, Greece as a Balkan country, may coincide with an outsider's point of view, but again these are not identical because the experience of positioning is different. Self$_5$, Greece as an Orthodox country, cannot be understood by the 'Other' due to the lack of lived experience (unless, the 'Other' happens to belong to an Orthodox Christian country). Self$_6$, Greece as a threatened country, similarly cannot be understood by the 'Other' due to the lack of such experience. Self$_7$, Greece with an economy greatly divergent from the rest of the EU, may coincide with the outsider's point of view, such as those of Sandholtz, Baun and Nagle and Spenser's views (see Table 1). Nevertheless, they are not identical because the experience of positioning is different.

All these aspects of Greece are created from the authors' different positioning of this utterance – which is an extract from the Preface of an edited book – and from their effort to see and interpret their views. Therefore, we have dialogised heteroglossia on a variety of different levels.

At the level of the actual book, when writing the Preface, the authors are in dialogue with the utterances (i.e. the chapters) of the other authors and produce themselves an utterance (the preface and the book together); in other words, both the utterance of the preface and the utterances of the various chapters are embedded in the utterance of the book.

At another level, that of European geopolitics and economics, Greece partakes in different geopolitical areas (in South East Europe and in the Balkan Peninsula) and sometimes it is involved in many heterogeneous and, often conflicting, regional and supranational activities in political, economic and cultural arenas, all demanding diverse positions and discursive practices. Once Greece takes several and different positions, it gets and experiences several views of itself – thus assuming several selves or identities – which are themselves engaged in a dialogised heteroglossia expressed in a political, economic and cultural hybridisation. Yet, in the process of hybridisation (and while the centrifugal forces of several identities are fully fledged), the authors of this utterance search and yearn for a unified, centripetal force, which in this case is the EU 'Other'. This desire is uttered in economic terms. as can be seen in the last paragraph of the Kazakos and Ioakimidis (1994) text: "In *European terms* too, *Greece* is the country with the lowest level of development as measured by per capita GNP ... a state whose *economy* has, since accession to the EC, steadily *diverged* from the European economy" (*emphases* added). In this passage, Greece and its economy ('I'/'eye'; the local context) encounters Europe and European economy (the Other; the global context), is discussed by Greek academics who take an outsider's point of view (positioning) and is expressed in English, thus creating a glocal perception of Greek economy; that is an outside-in view of Greek identity and economy.

On yet another level, in the wider European (global) framework of the ongoing dialogue about the necessity of constructing and strengthening a European identity at the time (Panebianco 1996), the extract of the Preface of the book, as well as the book itself and its authors, are embedded within this discourse as utterances within other utterances; they partake in a dialogue which started with the TEU in 1992 and was still in the making – a process which later became known as the Europeanisation process (Lavdas 1997).

Finally, if we place this book in its Greek (local) context, we realize that the book was published just only a year after Andreas Papandreou – the leader of PASOK[1] at the time who was also well known for his hostility towards NATO and EC – had returned to power. Hence, the statement "Greece is our home, Europe is our future" made by one of the contributors to the volume (Wenturis 1994:237) could signal a visible change of attitudes of the Greek public (at least the Greek academic public) towards the EU.

1996–2001: The reformative phase and face of PASOK – aspects of the remodelling of Greek identity

Before we continue our journey, we should keep in mind Kazakos and Ioakimidis' utterance: "a state whose economy has, since accession to the EC, steadily diverged from the European economy" (1994:ixx), which utters explicitly the desire of Greek academics for the Greek economy to converge with that of the EU, a desire which was going to haunt Greece for the next eight years and force Costas Simitis' two consecutive governments (1996–2000 and 2000–2004) to take and maintain austerity measures in order for Greece to meet the criteria for full participation in the EMU and become a member of the Eurozone.

1996–2001: Greece – A European sleeping beauty who wakes up and is introduced to the "Euro" court

When Simitis (himself an academic and who represented the modernizing technocratic wing of PASOK) was confirmed in office in elections in 1996, he expressed his determination to make Greece one of the countries of the Eurozone, participating in the third stage of the EMU. This third stage would consist of the fixing of exchange rates of the member states which would participate in the EMU, and the adoption and conduct of a single monetary policy (i.e. the adoption of the Euro) under the responsibility of the European Central Bank (ECB).

Once the Simitis government expressed their intention that Greece would join the European single currency, they took two steps simultaneously. The first was to make known to the wider Greek public the convergence criteria for full participation in EMU with two publications in Modern Greek, i.e. *The Single Currency and the European Parliament* (1997) and *The European Union: A Brief*

---

1.   PASOK is the Greek acronym for the Panhellenic Socialist Movement, a left of centre party which was founded by Andreas Papandreou in 1974.

Travelogue to its History, Institutions and Basic Policies (1998). The second step of Simitis' government was to embark on a very harsh austerity programme in order for Greece to qualify for EMU entry. This represented a rude awakening to the realities of European integration.

The response of the Greek public to these two steps, nevertheless, was mixed. On the one hand, most Greeks seemed to ignore the publications on the EMU and all discussions and negotiations surrounding it, since both the circulation of the two aforementioned texts was very limited and the issue of the EMU was not promoted by the newspapers or the TV channels. On the other hand, the public reacted to the government's tough budget cuts by calling strikes, which flooded the front pages of all newspapers and preoccupied the news of all TV channels at the time.

2000–2001: Greece – towards a European and Greek identity or Greek identity vs. a European one?

The Greeks' attitude towards the EMU was destined to soon change. On 2 May 1998, the Council of the EU and the ECOFIN made known that 11 member states, Belgium, Germany, Spain, France, Ireland, Italy, Luxembourg, the Netherlands, Austria, Portugal and Finland, had fulfilled the necessary conditions for the adoption of the single currency on 1 January 1999. Greece had failed to meet any of the EMU criteria, but it would try to fulfil them by 1 January 2001 (Kantas and Durand 1998).

After that rejection, all manner of publications, relevant to both the EMU and Greece's ability (or not) to meet the convergence criteria for its participation in the EMU, and also the introduction to the Euro, kept appearing in Greece (see Appendix 1 for examples). At the time, Greeks seemed to become more fully aware of their European partners, having mixed attitudes towards those European Others.

On 19 June 2000, the EU Council decided that Greece would participate in the third stage of the EMU – that is, the irrevocable fixing of exchange rates – because it fulfilled the convergence criteria. On 1 January 2001, Greece officially joined the third stage of the EMU thus becoming the 12th participating member state in the Euro. In the April of the same year, PASOK under Simitis' leadership had narrowly won the national elections of 2000 and the pro-European discourse continued to permeate Greek everyday life and society in the form of not only texts, but also symbols of the EU.

Co-identification of European and Greek identity
In order to ascertain when and where a European and Greek identity coincide and identify with one another, three instances of the written and visual discourse referred to above will be presented. These, despite their extrinsic differences, share some commonalities (and intrinsic values) and can be interpreted on at least four different levels.

The first example is from *Ekfrasi (Έκφραση: Expression)*, the official journal of PASOK. As shown in Appendix 2, the cover page of volume 27 of *Ekfrasi* consists of a large Euro symbol (€) in a yellowish colour, with the heading (in upper case) GREECE IN THE EMU (*Η ΕΛΛΑΔΑ ΣΤΗΝ ONE*) and underneath "Progressive governance in the 21st century" ("Προοδευτική διακυβέρνηση στον 21° αιώνα"). The image of the Euro and the short headings are imposed on a waving, blue EU flag.

The remaining two examples relate to materials produced by government and banks, aimed at making the Euro a daily reality for Greeks before its introduction to the Greek market on 1st January 2002. In December 2000, a booklet entitled *National plan for the introduction of Euro notes and coins (Εθνικό σχέδιο εισαγωγής τραπεζογραμματίων και κερμάτων ευρώ)*, issued by the Ministry of Economics and Finances and the Bank of Greece, was circulated in the Greek market. The text is easily readable and explanatory, with banknotes presented on specific pages and images of Euro coins scattered throughout the book. From 1st January 2001, all cashier desks in Greek banks posted images of Euro banknotes and coins and their equivalence with the drachma.

In 2001 the Bank of Greece and the European Central Bank (ECB) produced promotional material about the Euro. The front page (see Appendix 3) pictures a young female team of gymnasts where three are gazing at a purple ball held by one of the others, while another stares directly out as she performs a pirouette holding a 20 Euro banknote. They appear to be saying the phrase "EURO. *Our* OWN *currency*" (ΕΥΡΩ. *το* ΔΙΚΟ ΜΑΣ *νόμισμα*). At the bottom of the picture, there is an admonition in upper case: BE PREPARED FOR THE EURO (*ΠΡΟΕΤΟΙΜΑΣΤΕΙΤΕ ΓΙΑ ΤΟ ΕΥΡΩ*) and an explanatory sub-heading: Your guide to Euro banknotes and coins (*Ο οδηγός σας για τα τραπεζογραμμάτια και τα κέρματα ευρώ*). On the top, right-hand corner is written DAY OF €: 1 JANUARY 2002 (*ΗΜΕΡΑ €: 1 ΙΑΝΟΥΑΡΙΟΥ 2002*). The logos of the Bank of Greece and the ECB appear in Modern Greek at the bottom of the page, on the left and right side, respectively.

The second page is a Preface written by Willem F. Duisenber, President of the ECB, and Loukas Papadimos, the Governor of the Bank of Greece; it is written in Modern Greek – *our* OWN *language*. The Preface is about the historical aspects of 1st January 2002, when the third stage of the EMU will be complete, and the

Euro will become the currency of all Europe and, of course, Greece, since Greece is one of the 12 member states of the Eurozone. This Preface ends "Euro. Our own currency!" (*Ευρώ. Το δικό μας νόμισμα!*).

The remainder of the booklet is easily readable and attractively laid-out, making the presentation of the banknotes easy to understand and remember.

If a picture is a thousand words, then the images that were displayed in Greek banks, and the promotional material (as shown in Appendices 2 and 3) are as talkative as they can be; they are images of a unified EU identity. They are all visual utterances which, when combined with written texts, express and reinforce the idea of belonging and also entail multiple interpretations. On one level, there is dialogised heteroglossia in that Greek identity is seen vis-à-vis its European Other: the Euro and European flag uttering the attainment of its initial desire to become a European Other. However, at the moment when Greek identity identifies itself with the Euro and European Other(s), that identification itself can be read on other levels, within the European context.

In the wider European (global) context, all specific visual and textual utterances go along with, firstly, the efforts of the Italian EU Presidency in 1995 to promote European identity in areas of great symbolic value, thereby contributing towards an enhancement of shared community values (Delgando-Moreira 1997); and, secondly, the efforts of the EU in 1998 to prepare citizens and companies for the Euro by funding member states (among them Greece) through a programme called PRINCE (see http://www.europarl.eu.int/euro/press/euronews/doc1en_en.htm).

On another level, and in Bakhtinian terms, these visual and written utterances can be interpreted as a particular stance of their authors and their efforts to assimilate the word of the European Other by retelling it in their own words. Therefore, all pictures and texts can be interpreted as the internally persuasive discourse of the Greek government, which eventually becomes multi-voiced and thus heteroglot.

On yet another level, however, the authoritative discourse of the European Other – filtered through the internally persuasive discourse of the Greek government, which is itself a centre of specific power and ideology – enters into the space of the everyday life of the Greek identity as a *xenos*, that is a strange or foreign utterance. This *xenos* may be internalized, whereby the European Other becomes the voice and point of view of Greek identity (i.e. its 'I' and 'eye'); or, alternatively, it may be parodied or even ignored. During the time an authoritative discourse is becoming internalized, single-voicedness and single-eyedness occur. The voices of the Greek 'I' and the European 'Other' utter in unison and narrate their views in harmony. The 'eye' changes its focus and tries to see through the eyes of the 'Other'. At that specific moment, the Greek 'I' and European 'Other' feel that they "understand" each other perfectly and, momentarily, 'I' becomes the 'Other' and vice-versa.

This can occur and be discerned both in collective and individual everyday Greek life. As we have tried to discuss above, the images of the Euro promoted by the Greek Banks and the ECB – initially an internally persuasive discourse – were transformed into an authoritative discourse of the European Other and, as such, entered into the private space of Greek citizens. Once the citizen tried to learn and internalise what the Euro looked like and its equivalence to the Greek drachma, the initial purpose of the EU to promote the Euro and familiarise citizens with it was, at that specific moment, achieved.

Greece had the sense that it was one of the 12 member states of the EMU and Greek citizens felt that they belonged to the EU; the euro was to become *their* OWN currency, as the above-mentioned promotional material about the Euro (also Appendix 3) claimed, flooding the Greek market and the banks at the time. Greek identity was finally identical with that European Other, at least in relation to economic matters.

Non-identification of Greek and European Identity
When Greek identity finds itself in moments of crises due to its geopolitical and/ or cultural context and feels that the European Other cannot understand these, then the Greek 'I' tries to make the European Other understand its point of view by articulating its own uniqueness. During that process, however, the Greek 'I' produces a mixture of languages, i.e. it produces multi-voicedness, and takes different points of view, thus being divided into multiple Selves, assuming multiple identities. Eventually, Greek identity becomes a hybrid, whose European Other is only a part of itself.

Read how eloquently Costas Simitis expresses these multiple identities, not of a human being but of a country, in a speech delivered to the Council on Foreign Relations after the crisis in Kosovo in 1999.

> As is only natural, as a *European*, *Mediterranean* but also *Balkan country*, Greece has its share of perturbed history in South-East Europe. … Greece is … the only country in the region, which is a member of the *European Union* and in *NATO* and is expected as of 2001 to join the *Economic and Monetary Union* …
> Greece has a *double identity*. It is a European country, which participates in the *E.U.* and *NATO*. It is also a *Balkan country*, which can and must act as a factor of peace.
> Council of Foreign Relations (http://www.cfr.org/publication.php?_id=3132; italics added)

This utterance is similar to how Kazakos and Ioakimidis (1994) delineated the distinctiveness and uniqueness of Greek identity, being a Balkan country among its other identities or selves. In the light of Bakhtin's notions of heteroglossia and hybridisation, it can be suggested that the Greek 'I' claims its uniqueness only when it is involved in certain political or economic activities which, by its geopolitical position, are strongly conflicting with those of the European Other, and when an international situation brings into focus this (otherwise) internal conflict.

Under this lens, then, the above quotation reveals that the geopolitical position and political-economic engagements of Greece at that time lent it more than two identities (as Simitis claims): a European country and a member state of the EU which was trying to meet the criteria to join the EMU; a Mediterranean country; a Balkan country; a country in NATO. What this utterance illustrates is the willingness of Greece and its government to play the role of a peacemaker and contribute to the development of the wider Balkan region. However, what remains unuttered are the conflicting interests between the Balkan countries and NATO and the hesitant political stance of the EU in the Kosovo crisis. That hesitancy and aloofness created an identity crisis in relation to the European side of Greek identity and its European Others.

More recent examples, such as the Iraq conflict, have shown that Europeans as individual member states and/or persons will have a crisis of European identity whenever international politico-economical forces force Europeans to view themselves from both an insider's and outsider's point of view and these two views neither coincide with each other nor are in accordance with their value-systems or their expectations.

Conclusion: Towards which identity?

In contemplating how a Greek identity (be this collective or personal) narrates, interacts with and partakes in a wider European identity and life, I propose that, since we, as active participants in the making of a European identity, are deprived of historical distance, synchronic and diachronic investigations of how various discourses function within different European countries should be undertaken. Then it could be examined if and how these discourses, such as those of economics and politics which can generate 'identical' EU policies and political practices, are able to construct multiple, identical European identities.

For the time being, experience has shown that, while supranational economic policies, such as the EMU and the Euro, can regulate national economies – and thus function as a centripetal force creating a unified source of authority and an imaginary unified self (i.e. a European Other) – supranational politics function rather as a centrifugal force which, at times of crises, destabilises the illusory, constructed European identity into multiple national and cultural identities (i.e. into many Is and Eyes).

In order to survive and thrive in an increasingly globalised world, we (as Europeans) should search for models of identities and narratives of everyday life other than those we have been brought up with. We should find "something" – a value system – that can hold the centripetal and centrifugal forces together.

References

Bakhtin, Mikhail M. 1981. *The Dialogic Imagination: Four essays*. Michael Holquist (ed.). (Caryl Emerson and Michael Holquist, Trans.). Austin: University of Texas Press.

Bakhtin, Mikhail M. 1984. *Problems of Dostoevsky's Poetics*. C. Emerson (ed. and trans.). Mineappolis: University of Minnesota Press.

Bakhtin, Mikhail M. 1986. *Speech Genres and Other Late Essays*. C. Emerson and M. Holquist (eds.). (Vern W. McGee, Trans.). Austin: University of Texas Press.

Barbour, Philippe. (ed.). 1996. *The European Union Handbook*. Chicago & London: Fitzroy Dearborn.

Baun, Michael J. 1996. *An Imperfect Union: The Maastricht Treaty and the New Politics of European Integration*. Boulder, CO: Westview Press.

Berger, Arthur A. 1997. *Narratives in Popular Culture, Media and Everyday Life*. Thousand Oaks, CA: Sage.

Cohn-Bendit, Daniel, Duhamel, Oivier and Vissol, Tierry. 1998. *Small Dictionary of the Euro* (Trans. Magda Klavdianou). Athens: Polis [Μικρό λεξικό του ευρώ. Μετφρ. Μάγδα Κλαυδιανού. Αθήνα: Πόλις]. (The original title was *Petit dictionaire de l' euro*).

Corbett, R. 1994. *The Treaty of Maastricht*. London: Longman Current Affairs.

Delgado-Moreira, Juan M. 1997. "Cultural citizenship and the creation of European identity". *Electronic Journal of Sociology* (ISSN: 1198 3655).

European Union, The: A Brief Travelogue to its History, Institutions and Basic Policies 1998. [*Η Ευρωπαϊκή Ένωση: Ένα σύντομο οδοιπορικό στην ιστορία, τους θεσμούς και τις βασικές πολιτικές της*]. Athens: European Parliament and European Commission.

Gray, John. 2002. "The global coursebook in English Language Teaching". In *Globalization and Language Teaching*, D. Block and D. Cameron (eds.), 151–167. London: Routledge.

Kantas, Alexandros and Durand, Jérome. 1998. *EMU and Greece*. Prepared by the Directorate General for Research Economic Affairs Division. Available at <http://www.europarl.europa.eu/euro/country/general/gr_en.pdf>. Accessed 12 January 2007.

Kazakos, Panos and Ioakimidis, P.C. (eds.). 1994. *Greece and EC Membership Evaluated*. London: Pinter & New York: St. Martin's.

Lavdas, Kostas A. 1997. *The Europeanization of Greece: Interest Politics and the Crises of Integration*. London: Macmillan Press & NY: St. Martin's.

Nagle, Garrett and Spencer, Kris. 1996. *A Geography of the European Union*. Oxford: Oxford University Press.

National Plan for Introduction of Euro Banknotes and Coins. 2000. Athens: Ministry of Economics and Finances and Bank of Greece. [*Εθνικό σχέδιο εισαγωγής τραπεζογραμματίων και κερμάτων ευρώ*. Αθήνα: Υπουργείο Εθνικής Οικονομίας και Οικονομικών και Τράπεζας της Ελλάδος].

Nelsen, Brent F. and Stubb, Alexander C-G. (eds.). 1994. *The European Union: Readings on the Theory and Practice of European Integration*. Boulder, London: Lynne Rienner.

Nikolarea, Ekaterini. 2003. "Research methodologies and ELT at Greek universities". In *The Role of Research in Teacher Education*, B. Beaven and S. Borg (eds.), 71–75. Nottingham Conference Proceedings 2003. Nottingham, UK: IATEFL.

Nikolarea, Ekaterini. 2004a. "English vis-à-vis Modern Greek: New Methodological Approaches to EFL/ESP/EAP Teaching at Greek Universities". 2nd Symposium of TESOL Greece *New Directions in ESP and EAP* at <http://www.tesolgreece.com/nikolarea.pdf>. Accessed 12 January 2007.

Nikolarea, Ekaterini. 2004b. "Translation methods and methodologies in ELT for social sciences students". In *Choice and Difference in Translation – The Specifics of Transfer*, M. Sidiropoulou and A. Papaconstantinou (eds), 221–238. Athens: The National and Kapodistrian University of Athens.

Panebianco, Stefania. 1996. *European Citizenship and European Identity: From the Treaty of Maastricht to Public Opinion Attitudes*. Available at <http://aei.pitt.edu/384/>. Accessed 12 January 2007. [AEI University Library System, University of Pittsburgh].

Sandholtz, Wayne. 1994. "Choosing union: Monetary politics and Maastricht". In *The European Union: Readings on the Theory and Practice of European Integration*, B.F. Nelsen and A.C-G. Stubb (eds.), 257–290. Boulder, London: Lynne Rienner.

Simitis, Costas. Year not provided. "Prepared Remarks by Costas Simitis". Available at <http://www.cfr.org/publication/3132/prepared_remarks_by_costas_simitis.html?breadcrumb=%2Fregion%2F352%2Fgreece>. Accessed 12 January 2007. [Council of Foreign Relations].

Single Currency and the European Parliament, The [*Το ενιαίο νόμισμα και το Ευρωπαϊκό Κοινοβούλιο*]. 1997. Athens: European Parliament.

Stillar, Glenn F. 1998. *Analyzing Everyday Texts: Discourse, Rhetoric and Social Perspectives*. Thousand Oaks, CA: Sage.

Tsoukalis, Loukas. 1997. *The New European Economy Revisited*. Oxford: Oxford University Press.

Wenturis, Nikolaus. 1994. "Political culture". In *Greece and EC Membership Evaluated*, P. Kazakos and P.C. Ioakimidis (eds.), 226–237. London: Pinter & New York: St. Martin's.

Appendix 1. Examples of literature on the EMU and Euro

Chrysolora, E. "EMU: The path is opening". In *Ta Nea*. [Χρυσολωρά, Ε. *ΟΝΕ: Ανοίγει ο δρόμος. Τα Νέα*] [30/09/99]. Available at <http://ta-nea.dolnet.gr/print_article.php?e=A&f=16554&m=N47&aa=1>. Accessed 15 January 2007.

Chrysolora, E. "They spread the carpet for us". In *Ta Nea*. [Χρυσολωρά, Ε. *Μας έστρωσαν το χαλί. Στα Νέα*] [31/03/99]. Available at <http://ta-nea.dolnet.gr/print_article.php?e=A&f=16402&m=N44&aa=1>. Accessed 15 January 2007.

Chrysolora, E. and Antonakos, K. "European obstacles for the convergence". In *Ta Nea*. [Χρυσολωρά, Ε, & Αντωνάκος, Κ. *Ευρωπαϊκά εμπόδια για τη σύγκλιση*. Στα *Νέα*] [29/05/99]. Available at <http://ta-nea.dolnet.gr/print_article.php?e=A&f=16450&m=I04&aa=1>. Accessed 15 January 2007.

"Consistency and perspective. The traces of a year – by the Observer". In *Ekfrasi 21* (December 1999): 4–5. [Συνέπεια και προοπτική: Τα αποτυπώματα μιας χρονιάς του Παρατηρητή].

Corbett, R. 1994. *The Treaty of Maastricht*. London: Longman Current Affairs.

Euro and Enterprises of Tourism: An Analytical Guide of Preparation. 1999. Paris: Association for the Monetary Fund of Europe. [*Ευρώ και τουριστικές επιχειρήσεις: αναλυτικός οδηγός προετοιμασίας*. 1999. Paris: Association for the Monetary Fund of Europe].

Euro: Adaptations and Effects on the Greek Banking Sector from the Economic and Financial Union and the Introduction from the Euro. – Association of Greek Banks. 1998 Athens & Komotini: Ant. N. Sakkoula. [*Ευρώ: οι προσαρμογές και επιπτώσεις στον ελληνικό τραπεζικό τομέα από την οικονομική και νομισματική ένωση και την εισαγωγή του ευρώ. – Ένωση Ελληνικών Τραπεζών*. 1998. Αθήνα: Εκδόσεις Αντ. Ν. Σάκκουλα].

"Greece's steps toward the EMU are under the microscope". In *Ekfrasi 3* (June 1998): 42. [Στο μικροσκόπιο τα βήματα της Ελλάδας προς την ΟΝΕ].

"Greek Economy makes big strides". In *Embassy of Greece – Press Office* (August-September 1998):4(8).

"Hour of the Greek economy, The". In *Ekfrasi 21* (December 1999): 64. [Η ώρα της ελληνικής οικονομίας].

Hytiris, T. "The message". In *Ekfrasi 7* (October 1998): 3. [Χυτήρης, Τ. Το μήνυμα].

Hytiris, T. "Facing 2000". In *Ekfrasi 21* (December 1999): 3. [Χυτήρης, Τ. Μπροστά στο 2000].

"International Euro-mania despite the problems. A rendez-vous of the drachma with the Euro on 31 December 2000". In *Ta Nea*. [Διεθνής Ευρώ-μανία παρά τα προβλήματα. Ραντεβού 31–12–2000 δραχμής με ευρώ. Τα *Νέα*] [02–01–99]. Available at <http://ta-nea.dolnet.gr/print_article.php?e=A&f=16330&m=N01&aa=1>. Accessed 15 January 2007.

Introduction of the Euro and Local Government, The. 1999. Athens: Greek Association of Local Development and Self-Governance. [*Η εισαγωγή του ευρώ και η τοπική αυτοδιοίκηση*. 1999. Αθήνα: Ελληνική Εταιρεία Τοπικής Ανάπτυξης και Αυτοδιοίκησης].

Korliras, P.G. "Global economic crisis and its characteristics". In *Ekfrasi 7* (October 1998): 18–19. [Κορλίρας, Π.Γ. Η παγκόσμια οικονομική κρίση και τα χαρακτηριστικά της].

Kotsikopoulos, N. "The EMU, inflation and the ASE". In *Ekfrasi 21* (December 1999): 14–15. [Κωτσικόπουλος, Ν. Η ΟΝΕ, ο πληθωρισμός και η Σοφοκλέους].

Matziorinis, K. 1999. "On the verge of entry into the EMU: Greece, the challenge of convergence and a new beginning. An Investment seminar". Available at <http://www.hellascapital.ca/pdf_files/greece_on_the_verge.pdf>. Accessed 25 January 2007.

Mourouzis, N. "The Euro and the Greek banking system". In *Ekfrasi 3* (June 1998): 14–15. [Μουρούζη, Ν. Το Ευρώ και το ελληνικό τραπεζιτικό σύστημα].

Simitis, Costas. 1998. "Inaugural speech for the opening of the 63rd Thessaloniki International Fair". In *Embassy of Greece – Press Office* (August-September 1998) 4 (8).

"Waiting and hopes for recovery of the course of the Euro". In *Ta Nea*. [Αναμονή και ελπίδες για ανάκαμψη της πορείας του ευρώ. Τα *Νέα*] [01/06/99]. Available at <http://ta-nea.dolnet.gr/print_article.php?e=A&f=16451&m=N56&aa=1>. Accessed 15 January 2007.

"With EMU Membership in View: Tight Economic Policy Set for 1999". In *Embassy of Greece – Press Office* (August-September 1998) Vol. 4, No 8.

Appendix 2

Appendix 3

How to conceive of the other's point of view

Considerations from a Case Study in Trieste

Marina Sbisà and Patrizia Vascotto
University of Trieste

In memory of Sonia

Introduction

This paper[1] addresses the problem of how relationships among different linguistic, ethnic, cultural or "national" groups in Europe can best be conceived of and managed. Our primary concern is with majority-minority relationships in regions with a composite population. We consider management problems as reflected in discourse and exemplify them with reference to the province of Trieste (Italy), whose population comprises an Italian-speaking majority and a Slovene-speaking (but in fact bilingual) minority. We draw on a case study of representations of the Trieste territory conducted in Trieste and surroundings on a sample of boys and girls from the Italian-speaking and Slovene-speaking groups. We then attempt to draw more general conclusions about the requirements for a successful management of linguistic, ethnic, cultural and "national" differences, proposing that differences in the European population should be viewed in the light of a "family resemblances" paradigm. In so doing, we do not directly discuss European identity, least of all in its possible everyday narrative manifestations. No particular attention for European identity can be found in our data (after all, our case study was not designed to track the subjects' awareness of their being Europeans). But we deal with our subjects' differences in point of view and their emerging images of self and other as representative of attitudes towards collective identity which we take to be widespread in Europe. While these attitudes may hinder the formation

---

1. Patrizia Vascotto wrote the sections "Trieste: a historical and socio-linguistic outline", "Awareness of the composite nature of the population", and "Self- and other-images in Italian and Slovene discourse". The rest of the paper was written by Marina Sbisà.

of a self-conscious European identity, they may also be considered as providing a sort of paradoxical hallmark of the current "European identity" if indeed there is any (cf. Delanty 1995).

European identity, European differences and multiculturalism

It is commonplace that European natives belong to many different linguistic, ethnic or cultural groups. Several groups, characterized by linguistic, ethnic and cultural features simultaneously, have been called "nations" and some of them have given rise to political structures called states. The effort to make national borders match state borders was a source of conflict and war at least up to the First World War (the "Great" European war). The First World War and its consequences should have taught everyone in Europe that this goal is both beyond our reach and dangerous. But, as everybody knows, not everywhere in Europe are such matters settled, even in present times. After the defeat and disappearance of the old supra-national Austrian Empire, claims about the displacement of borders or creation of new national states have often been turned into disputes about the rights of national minorities or other minorities not perceived as national, but as merely linguistic, ethnic, or cultural, within existing national states. But from time to time some minority or other slips again into claiming its right to a modification of state borders or to a new state of its own (as if this were not bound to recreate the problem). Moreover, while most minorities aim at obtaining linguistic and cultural protection within the state in which they happen to live, legal protection is not always granted in the desired form and majorities do not always welcome it.

In many regions of Europe, the population is composite: it does not belong only to the linguistic-ethnic-cultural group that characterizes the national state of which the region is a part, but also includes people belonging to a different ethnic, or linguistic, or cultural group, who are in certain cases the overwhelming majority at the local level. This situation is natural enough: the dynamics of migratory flows and of linguistic or cultural influences between neighbouring peoples is certainly not guided by the ideal of the linguistic-ethnic-cultural homogeneity of each geographical area. But regions with a composite population cause problems within the framework of the national state.

The present situation is further complicated by the increasing presence in Western and Central Europe of migrants from Eastern Europe, Asia and Africa. We will not deal with the relationship between these various kinds of migrant groups and Western or Central-European linguistic-ethnic-cultural or national groups, but would like to point out that problems regarding it cannot be well understood and managed unless a successful management of differences among European identities is achieved. Insofar as we remain unable to manage intra-European differences adequately, it is either impossible or highly unlikely that we will discover sound ways to relate to migrants.

The existence of linguistic, ethnic and cultural differences among Europeans and the way in which they are managed influence European worldview and identity. The tendency has long been to consider linguistic, ethnic and cultural features together as amounting to "national" identity, but whether the latter is just a combination of the above or comprises some mysterious extra ingredient is unclear. In present times, the role assigned to nationality in the constitution of personal identity may vary: there are Europeans who in introducing themselves to unknown people in a new environment would foreground, explicitly or implicitly, their nationality over and above any other identifying feature, and others who feel it as rather marginal. However, the very existence of an (European) idea of nation influences a European's worldview and identity. Romantic nationalism, involving belief in a common mind or temperament shared by a whole people, is no longer consciously endorsed (except by isolated groups), but national stereotypes are still strong and active in everyday talk: they survive in short stories, jokes and the like and provide easy material for irony and insult (last but not least in the demagogic language of certain politicians). More positively, the general awareness and acceptance of there being many nationalities in Europe is integral to any seminal feeling of a European identity. This makes European identity not comparable with, for example, American identity. American identity in the US is felt as itself "national", albeit in the civic sense (since it makes reference to citizenship rather than ethnic and cultural matters and relies on loyalty to the Federal government). Whatever a European identity is going to be, it would be wrong to strive to model it on the American one. Rather, it should profit from a reshaping of the relationship among European nations or, in general, linguistic, ethnic and cultural groups.

The ideal of multiculturalism might seem to be a case in point. But the main proposals stemming from recent analyses of multicultural societies in political theory are not applicable, for various reasons. To illustrate this, we will examine here some influential ideas put forward by Will Kymlicka.

Kymlicka (1995) has proposed an interesting distinction between multinational and polyethnic states, claiming that different ways of coping with diversity are suitable for different situations. According to him, in those states in which more nations coexist (so-called multinational states), the management of diversity requires governmental autonomy to be granted to national minorities, while in the states in which there are large groups of immigrants belonging to ethnic groups other than the majority group (so-called polyethnic states), minorities should be granted special non-territorial rights (polyethnic rights). The basic idea

seems to be that linguistic-ethnic-cultural groups that are native (or autochthonous) to a certain region have a right to be considered as nations and being a nation entails a legitimate aspiration to forming a national state or, in consideration
of advantages deriving from participation in a larger geo-political unit, at least the
right to governmental autonomy within a multinational state. Migrant groups,
being non-native, have no entitlement to territorial claims, but wherever a group
is large enough, public recognition of its linguistic, ethnic or cultural identity by
means of the concession of polyethnic rights may enhance the integration of its
members in the social and political community of citizenship.

Kymlicka himself has recognized that his proposals are not immediately
applicable to the problems raised by different identities in Eastern and Central
Europe (Kymlicka and Opalski 2001). Nevertheless, he believes that they can be
adapted to cope with most of these problems. In our opinion, this is optimistic.
Neither of Kymlicka 's proposals fits European reality, and difficulties in their application pertain to the whole European continent.

It is dubious whether the multinational state solution has genuine applicabili-
ty in Europe. What does being "native" or "autochthonous" amount to here? There
are many European areas in which two linguistic-ethnic-cultural groups live side
by side, both feeling they have a right to count as native to the region. Whose
ancestors first came to the region belongs to centuries past and is quite irrelevant
to the present situation. No distinction between natives and colonists can sensibly
be drawn. Moreover, the concession of governmental autonomy clashes with the
difficulty, or even impossibility, of delimiting homogeneously populated areas. If
such autonomy is conceded, members of the former national majority inevitably
form a national minority within the autonomous region and oppression of the
new national minority by the former national minority is a concrete possibility.

In consideration of this, it seems that, in Europe, native national minorities
(and a fortiori linguistic, ethnic or cultural groups) should rather be dealt with
in terms of non-territorial rights (the polyethnic state solution). But protection
granted to minority languages and cultures might not succeed in getting minorities to better integrate in the political system of the state in which they happen to
live, too often a markedly national state. In fact, their problem is not resistance
to participating in the western way of life; they are already participating in it. So
native minorities, particularly if they consider themselves as national groups, may
refuse to collaborate with the national majority and its national state even when
granted substantive rights and instead insist on their claim to autonomy. [2]

---

2. Polyethnic rights might be an option in dealing with migrants, but only when these are
willing to integrate, which is not always the case for many reasons (e.g. short term immigration;

We need a European way for managing linguistic-ethnic-cultural differences as well as (hopefully) differences in nationality. Rather than striving to interpret our European realities through the results of analyses of non-European social and political contexts (USA and Canada in particular), we should reflect on the peculiarities of the European situation and the discursive tools for dealing with it that are available to us as Europeans. What are the discursive means by which we define our identities as well as those of our neighbours? At which point do our current discursive practices lead us astray, giving rise to conflicts and allowing for nationalism or even racism? One way to initiate such a reflection is to investigate how Europeans speak of linguistic-ethnic-cultural differences as well as of differences in nationality in the European population.

We approach this bundle of questions by commenting on the results of a case study concerning the relationship between the Italian-speaking majority and the Slovene-speaking minority in the province of Trieste (Italy).

Trieste: A historical and socio-linguistic outline

As a background to our case study and our subsequent considerations on the management of differences, we sketch a brief historical and socio-linguistic outline of the province of Trieste.

This province, one of the smallest in Italy, has, according to the 2001 census, about 240,000 residents, 211,000 of whom live in the city of Trieste. The Slovene-speaking minority, in fact a national minority, has traditionally lived in the area and can be estimated as approximately 10% of the population on the basis of the number of children enrolled in schools designed for the Slovene minority, give the absence of official statistics.

Fearing the influence of Venice, the city of Trieste, for a time an independent town in the Middle Ages, sought protection from the Habsburgs in 1382 and was ruled by the Austrian Empire up to the end of the First World War in 1918. Then it became part of Italy. The population of the city and its surrounding territory was linguistically and culturally composite already in the Middle Ages and comprised Italian, Slovene and Jewish communities. In the 18th and 19th centuries, the special status granted to the port by Austrian emperors attracted immigrants from many Mediterranean and European countries.

In the 20th century state borders in the area shifted more than once. Between the two World Wars, the borders of Italy extended to include Istria (a large penin-

---

familiar bonds in the country of emigration; deliberate will to create communities applying received rules of their own).

sula South-East of Trieste, now divided between Slovenia and Croatia) and part of present-day Slovenia. After the Second World War, a provisional Allied Military Government ruled the province of Trieste and the neighbouring area of Istria until 1954 when Trieste joined Italy again while Istria was left to Yugoslavia. Currently, the province of Trieste is bordered by Slovenia, which has recently joined the European Union. In 2008, the border is expected to be dispensed with.

From the linguistic point of view, Trieste is characterized by the presence of two languages, Italian and Slovene, each comprising several varieties (from dialect and colloquial standard to formal and literary language). The languages of the so-called historical communities (Greek, Serbian, Croatian, Jewish) and those of migrant groups are used only within each ethnic group (Hebrew has religious use only; cf. Lancellotti 2001).

Italian native speakers are themselves a composite group, comprising people whose families have lived in the Trieste territory for a long time, but also Italians from other areas of Italy (ranging from neighbouring Friuli to Puglia or Calabria) who have settled in Trieste in several waves of internal migration, and Italians from Istria who have left that region after the end of the Second World War. Several dialectal varieties of local or Istrian origin coexist with varieties of standard Italian (often affected in turn by the influence of local dialects). As for the Slovene language (cf. Vascotto 2001), Slovene-speaking residents mostly use the local dialect, whose varieties change across urban neighbourhoods and countryside villages. The standard variety is used in formal situations and for literary production, but some Slovene-speaking residents, particularly elderly people who had no Slovene-language schools to attend during the Fascist era, may have failed to master it. There is also an intermediate, colloquial variety of Slovene displaying some degree of morphological simplification. Notwithstanding a school system designed for the minority, a Slovene newspaper, a theater, a library, a radio station and some TV programs, all varieties of Slovene find it hard to resist the pressure exerted by Italian. Only recently have Slovene native speakers been granted the use of their language in communication with public institutions. The Slovene language, moreover, is visually absent from the city of Trieste and is only used in road signs, posters, etc. in traditionally Slovene neighbourhoods or countryside villages. In fact the Italian-speaking population is basically and traditionally urban, while Slovenes (many of whom by now participate fully in the urban environment and way of life) usually lived in villages on the Karst plateau or in peripheral urban neighbourhoods.

Italian-speaking residents have no obligation to learn the minority language and the number of those who actually learn and practise it is extremely low. Slovene native speakers are in general bilingual, to different degrees depending on personal circumstances. The city has a double cultural life, Italian and Slovene;

but while Slovene speakers have full access to Italian cultural life, Italian speakers have fewer opportunities of accessing Slovene cultural life and, moreover, due to deeply rooted prejudice and stereotypes, are often not interested in it.

As a whole, the relationship between the majority and the minority group is not completely smooth: conflict is latent and surfaces on occasion in various contexts and in various ways. Question that may be raised are: what exactly is the basis of the opposition between the two groups? Do they, for example, have different points of view on the territory in which they both live? If there are such differences, are they aware of any of them? How do they represent themselves and their "other"?

Our case study

With the collaboration of a group of teachers,[3] we explored how young members of the Italian-speaking majority and Slovene-speaking minority in the province of Trieste describe the territory in which they live, in order to check whether the images of the territory are different in the two groups and if so, in what way.

Our data were collected in written form in 6 middle schools and 3 high schools of the province of Trieste; 5 of these schools are regular state schools, while 4 are special state schools designed for the Slovene minority, in which most teaching is done in the Slovene language. In 12 classes, teachers of L1 (Italian or Slovene) asked their pupils to write a short but detailed description of the territory of the Trieste province. The task was described approximately as follows: "Imagine you are addressing a person who is not acquainted with the territory of the Trieste province and describe it to him or her in detail". 189 texts were collected, 89 in Italian and 93 in Slovene. The texts were first examined in order to decide, on an empirical basis, which themes were to be tracked in the analysis of the corpus. Then, for every theme so identified, explicit claims and implicitly indicated attitudes were listed and classified. Again, categories for classification were empirically derived from the array of claims and attitudes actually present in the corpus. Classification permitted us to calculate the frequency with which certain themes,

3.   The study was carried out in the framework of a workshop coordinated by Marina Sbisà in 1994–95 within the program "Multi and interculturality in the school of the '90s" of IRRSAE Friuli-Venezia Giulia. We are grateful to Valentina Goldschmidt for organizing the workshop and to Susi Pertot, Sonia Maizen, Patrizia Regalzi, Cristina Roiazzi, Iris Zocchelli for collaborating in the collection and discussion of the data. An overview of the results has been published as Sbisà and Vascotto (1998). The results concerning awareness of linguistic diversity are discussed in Sbisà and Vascotto (2001).

or certain claims and attitudes about them, appeared in Italian and Slovene texts. Similarity and difference in quantity and content enabled us to figure out how and when images of the territory differ. Awareness of the composite nature of the population and particularly of the presence of the other group in the same territory emerged as a side issue and the analysis of results concerning it shed some light on the image of self and other in the two groups.

The results of our study confirm that among the population of the province of Trieste there exist different points of view on the territory. They also strongly suggest that at least some of the differences in point of view correlate with the subject's belonging to the Italian-speaking or the Slovene-speaking group. The subjects' awareness of the composite nature of the population varies too (from a minimum among majority members to a noteworthy but not especially high rate among minority members), as do the contents of self- and other-images. We will now summarize our general results and then present in greater detail the results regarding awareness of the composite nature of the population.

Images of the province of Trieste

The analysis of the corpus produced findings as to how our subjects collocated Trieste from the geographical-political point of view, what images they offered of salient elements of its surrounding environment (particularly the sea and the Karst), and what episodes of its history they considered important. Various kinds of resemblances in the expressed images of the territory run through the whole corpus. Some differences correlate clearly with the subject's belonging to the Italian-speaking or the Slovene-speaking group.

Aspects of the territory in focus vary across the corpus. Italian subjects highlight features of the urban environment more often that Slovene subjects (93.2% vs 73.2%). Slovene subjects highlight the extra-urban, anthropized environment (e.g. villages in the Karst, cultivated fields) more often than Italian subjects (73.1% vs 23.6%). Conversely, wilderness is considered as prominent in the territory by 53.9% of the Italian subjects and 24.7% of the Slovene subjects. These findings may correlate merely with the fact that a good number of our Slovene subjects did not live downtown, while most Italian subjects did. But we suspect that the failure of Italian subjects to notice the extra-urban, anthropized environment is symptomatic of a more general attitude of understatement with regard to the Slovene minority and its traditional environment and activities.

The theme of the geographical location of Trieste was touched upon in 51.7% of the Italian texts and 29% of the Slovene ones. This suggests that the interest in this matter among Slovene subjects is even weaker than among Italian ones.

Those who specified the geographical location of Trieste, be they Italian or Slovene subjects, most frequently mentioned its lying on the border with Slovenia. In order of decreasing frequency, the Italian subjects describe Trieste as located in the Friuli-Venezia Giulia Region, on the Adriatic, in Italy, in Northern Italy and in Venezia Giulia (geographical denomination corresponding to the provinces of Trieste and Gorizia within the Friuli-Venezia Giulia Region). The Slovene subjects locate Trieste in Italy, on the Adriatic, in the Friuli Venezia Giulia Region, in the Primorje (Slovene geographical denomination coming from the old Austrian denomination *Adriatisches Küstenland*), in Northern Italy. That Trieste belongs to Italy is for Slovene subjects an accepted reality, but a significant one nevertheless, while the fact that Trieste is the administrative center of the Friuli-Venezia Giulia Region appears more interesting to Italian than to Slovene subjects. The denominations "Venezia Giulia" and "Primorje" are approximately co-referential, but apparently different in historical and ideological implications.

The theme of the sea appears in Italian texts more often than in Slovene ones (88.8% vs 59.1%). Among the texts mentioning the sea, several do so more than once and in different connections, but the extent to which this happens varies in Italian and Slovene texts. The rates of citations per text, that is, the average number of citations related to this theme that we could extract from each text, are 1.7 and 1.4, respectively. The sea seems to be more prominent an element of the Trieste environment, and a more interesting one to be talked about, for Italian subjects. However, there is hardly any difference in the content of the claims raised or attitudes displayed: we are not dealing with two different rhetorics. In both groups of texts, the sea is mentioned as a feature or a boundary of the Trieste territory, as an aesthetic feature of the landscape, as a source of economic activities, as a place for swimming and other sports. The only noticeable difference is that Italian texts pay greater attention to aesthetic aspects. Perhaps in connection with this, there is a greater inclination among Italian subjects (33.7% of the Italian texts vs 9.6% of the Slovene texts) towards following the landscape in contrasting sea and Karst.

The theme of the Karst appears with approximately the same frequency in both groups of texts (73% vs 74.2%). Here, though, the citations/texts rate is higher in the Slovene group (1.8 vs 1.4) and contents differ significantly. The Karst is mentioned in Italian texts more often than in Slovene ones in relation to its natural environment (geological processes, flora, wild animals, etc.). While both groups describe the Karst plateau as a place for hiking or biking, the aesthetic evaluation of the landscape and the description of typical villages, cultivated fields, churches are by far more frequent in Slovene texts. The description of the anthropized aspects of the environment is the most frequent approach to the Karst in Slovene texts. For Italian subjects, the Karst seems to be basically a natural environment providing relief from urban life, while for Slovene subjects it is above all the site of traditional culture and activities.

Some subjects in each group (23.6% of Italian subjects and 26.9% of Slovene subjects) mentioned events or phases of the history of the Trieste area. The degrees of descriptive detail are comparable, but again, contents vary. In order of decreasing frequency, the historical eras or events mentioned by Italian subjects are Roman times, the Habsburg domination, 20th century events, the Middle Ages, and Venetian occupations;[4] those mentioned by Slovene subjects are 20th century events, the threat of Turkish invasions, the Habsburg domination, Roman times, the Napoleonic occupation, Venetian occupations, and the Middle Ages. It is clear that historical memories do not coincide and that some past situations and moments that are still important for the Slovene group (Turkish invasions, the Napoleonic occupation) are unimportant for, or have been forgotten by, the Italians.

The picture emerging from our study is of an Italian-speaking and a Slovene-speaking group who share some cultural features, such as the awareness of living at a border, the habit of going swimming in the gulf during summer, some pride in the famous geological phenomena of the Karst or some memory of the Austrian empire, but whose points of view on the territory are different enough to explain how, on occasion, misunderstanding and even conflict arise. In the light of our results, for example, the difficulties encountered for decades by the project of a Karst National Park (never realized) seem no longer mysterious. Communication and cooperation between the Italian-speaking majority and the Slovene-speaking minority would greatly profit from some mediation as regards matters on which their points of view are different, but such mediation presupposes awareness of difference and recognition of each other's point of view. Unfortunately, as we will soon see, our study also suggests that these conditions are far from being realized.

Awareness of the composite nature of the population

The subjects' awareness of the composite nature of the population emerges here and there in our corpus. Its expression takes different forms and highlights different dimensions of diversity: linguistic, ethnic, cultural, "national" (whatever that means), and religious.[5] As evidence of the awareness of some kind of diversity,

---

4.   There were only two short Venetian occupations, but the Venetians started building the castle that still exists on the hill of S.Giusto in the center of the town.

5.   In our general introductory remarks, we did not consider religious identity as a separate category, taking religious beliefs and habits to be cultural facts. But some texts in our corpus

we have considered both straightforward assertions of the presence of a certain linguistic-ethnic-cultural or national or religious group in the province of Trieste and indirect references to such a presence (made, for example, by presupposing it or displaying its traces or influence).

There is remarkable disparity between the frequency with which awareness of the composite nature of the population is expressed by members of the Italian-speaking majority and of the Slovene-speaking minority (21.3% vs 48.4%). This disparity is mainly due to the different frequency in referring, explicitly or implicitly, to the fact that the Trieste province has both Italian and Slovene residents. As to other kinds of difference, such as religious differences (including the presence of a Jewish community) and the presence of migrants from outside Europe or from Eastern Europe and the Balkans, the sensitivity of each group is approximately equivalent, except for the slightly greater attention paid by Slovene subjects to migrants from the Balkans.

In Italian texts, only 12.4% display awareness of the Slovene minority and only 2.2% hint at the Italian identity of the majority of residents. In contrast, in Slovene texts, 35.5% thematize their author's belonging to the Slovene group explicitly and 30.1% display awareness of the presence in the territory of the Italian-speaking majority. A first observation is that the image of the Slovene minority plays hardly any role in the way Italian majority members talk about the place they live in. As for Slovene texts, the situation is a bit more complicated. The fact that Slovene subjects relatively often specify their own Slovene identity confirms the tendency to self-awareness that is characteristic of minorities. But such self-awareness does not guarantee analogous salience to the recognition of one's other. Awareness of Italian residents and of the Italian language is displayed more often in Slovene texts than awareness of the Slovene minority in Italian texts, but in about 12.9% of the Slovene texts, the writer's Slovene identity is affirmed in isolation, so that he or she might appear to be living in a monolingual Slovene environment.

As regards the diversity between the Slovene minority and the Italian majority, as well as other differences mentioned, there are different ways in which their awareness is couched. Groups are considered by our subjects as ethnic or national groups, as religious groups, as linguistic groups, or as not otherwise specified minorities. Italian subjects who express awareness of diversity most often use the nation or ethnic group lexicon, while Slovene subjects focus above all on language (as regards their own identity in contrast with that of the Italian majority) or on religion. The Jewish community is envisaged as an ethnic group or a not further specified "minority" in the Italian corpus (4 texts out of 6), while religious diver-

---

used the language of religious differences and the description of our findings has to reflect this.

sity is foregrounded in all the 7 Slovene texts that mention the Jews. The lack of sensitivity of Italian subjects for linguistic matters goes as far as to fail to recognize that in Trieste, or in some parts of its province, the Slovene language is spoken too (only 2.2% of the Italian subjects mention this fact explicitly). In contrast, Slovene subjects in displaying awareness of their own identity make use of the linguistic approach (present in the 60% of the Slovene texts that tackle the issue) rather than the ethnicity or nationality approach (44.4%).[6] Kaučič Baša (1997) has criticized the tendency to consider the Slovene minority in the province of Trieste as a "linguistic" rather than "national" minority, but as our data suggest, the prominence of language may be a psychological reality for the people involved.

Finally, it is fair to mention that in a small number of texts we found characterizations of the relationship between the Italian-speaking and the Slovene-speaking population. In Slovene texts, 11.8% attribute to Italians some negative attitude towards members of the Slovene group (from neglect and ignorance to hostility and scorn); 2.1% notice a positive attitude in at least some Italians; and 2.1% express implicit hostility towards those residents in their same neighbourhood who belong to the Italian-speaking majority, claiming, or implying, that they are not the original residents. In Italian texts, 4.5% express a negative attitude towards Slovene speakers by mentioning problems supposedly created by the very presence of the Slovene minority, including statements such as: "The only real problem of this town is the Slovene minority with whom cohabitation is becoming more and more difficult."

Self- and other-images in Italian and Slovene discourse

As we have seen, the self-image of Italian subjects in our corpus rarely receives any characterization of a linguistic, ethnic or national kind: the Italian majority's collective identity seems to be transparent to itself. Since Italian texts do not often mention other, diverse identities, we might simply conclude that nationality (and collective identities in general) are no hot topics for young Italian people in the province of Trieste. But our data might also be taken to reflect the lack of visibility from which the Slovene minority in Italy has long suffered in the eyes of the Italian-speaking majority (Stranj 1989). The Slovene minority is bilingual and on most public occasions in which Italians are involved, its members speak Italian (or some variety of the Trieste dialect), thus making themselves indistinguishable from local Italian native speakers. This makes it tempting for Italian majority

6.   Here as elsewhere, the total percentages exceed 100% because in some texts various approaches coexist.

members, whenever they feel uncomfortable about confronting the distinct identity of the Slovene minority, to get round the problem by forgetting about it.

The self-image of Slovene subjects is more elaborated upon and the image of
their others (Italians) is more present in their discourse. In our Slovene texts, we
found isolated, emphatic affirmations of national identity, but also widespread attention to linguistic difference and the tendency to deal with different identities in
linguistic terms. The sensitivity to the linguistic dimension is expressed in various
forms: as well as explicit references to the Slovene or Italian language, there is the
production of short narratives in which characters have a choice between speaking either Slovene or Italian, and last but not least, the use of code-switching or of
linguistic loans from Italian as expressive resources.

Our Slovene subjects seem to be very clear about the implicit rules for situ-
ational code-switching (that is, the language shift occurring in correspondence
with changes in the communicative situation, participants or in their relevant linguistic competence; cf. Gardner-Chloros 1997). In some Slovene texts, subjects
imagine themselves meeting a foreigner (in order to describe the territory to him
or her as requested by the proposed task). Dialogue with such foreigners regularly
begins in Italian, confirming the subjects' awareness of Italian as the majority language and granting it the role of main public language. A switch to Slovene occurs when it is revealed that the interlocutor not only can speak Slovene, but also
desires to speak it (thus showing linguistic loyalty, cf. Kaučič Baša 1997).

Awareness of the Italian language and of its public role is expressed in Slovene texts also by occasionally resorting to conversational or metaphorical code-
switching (Gumperz 1982), that is language shift prompted by expressive needs
internal to the ongoing linguistic production, often with evocative aims; in particular, Italian words are used for referring to sites and events of the urban context of Trieste. In other cases, words coming from Italian are treated as loans: the
implicit message is still recognition of language contact (cf. Myers Scotton 1990,
1997), but often Slovene morphology is applied, confirming that the language
meant to be spoken is Slovene.

Self- and other-images are both implicitly affected by these linguistic practices. The linguistic identity of the Slovene subjects in our sample includes awareness
of their Italian-speaking environment and tends to exploit it for communicative
aims. This notwithstanding, linguistic identity can still count as the major difference between Italians and Slovenes in the Trieste province: "Italianization", of
which some of our subjects speak with fear and scorn, does not consist of learning
the Italian language or of speaking it when needed or useful, but of abandoning
Slovene. Thus some subjects in our sample express pride in their bilingual skills
and contrast them with the monolingualism of Italians.

Again, the same sociolinguistic facts have different repercussions and elabo-
rations in subjects belonging to the two groups under examination. The extent to
which the subjects in our sample were found to be aware of diversity and the kind
of awareness displayed are of no help for solving problems that stem from their
differences in point of view.

Conditions for the recognition of the other 's point of view

The research results reported above strongly suggest that among the schoolchildren of Trieste and its province, at the time in which the corpus was collected
(1994–95), conditions for a real recognition of the other's point of view did not
obtain. The two groups do display differences in point of view as regards the Trieste territory and the way they define their self- and other-images (when they
define them at all). But the image of the other hardly plays any role in the way
majority members represent the territory and even among minority members,
the affirmation of one's own identity is not always accompanied by manifestations
of awareness of the presence of a diverse majority. Throughout the corpus, perhaps with the exception of two Slovene texts, whenever the distinction between
the Italian majority and Slovene minority is represented, it is conceived of as neat,
and those hybrid or complex identities, that contact cannot fail to produce, are
disregarded.

Insofar as these results can be taken as representative, or at least symptomatic,
of attitudes present in the population as a whole (at the time when the corpus was
collected, but also later on, since there have not been radical changes in the situation at issue over the last 12 years), they offer an explanation of the state of latent
conflict that still persists in the city and province of Trieste and point to what may
be considered a major source of trouble in mixed population areas: unwilling-
ness, or inability, to conceive of the other 's point of view. In the last part of this
paper, we turn to theoretical considerations again and discuss whether there are
remedies to this situation.

Only subjects have a point of view; therefore, in order for his or her point
of view to be recognized, the other has to be recognized as a (diverse) subject.
Moreover, since to identify a subject's point of view requires us to conceive of
or represent the place from which he or she sees the world, some conception or
representation of the subject's identity is also needed. But from these premises, a
dilemma arises. Either the other is recognized as other, but not as a full-fledged
subject, or he or she is recognized as a subject, but only insofar as he or she is
similar or comparable to us and can be included in the same world and order
of values. When we give a description of the other, defining his or her identity

and characteristic traits, we deal with him or her as *other*, but only apparently as *subject*, because the description defining his or her identity is given from our own point of view. When we recognize somebody as a subject and, therefore, as a thinking and acting being, we tend to model his or her supposedly autonomous thought and action on our own, so that he or she is no longer really *other*. Since the source of the dilemma seems to lie in the need to ascribe an *identity* to the alien subject in order to calculate where his or her point of view is collocated, the solution might be searched for in a closer investigation of the conception of identity we are employing.

Now, discourse on linguistic-ethnic-cultural identity and *a fortiori* on national identity is usually governed by what we may call an "ideal of perfect delimitation": we speak as if people could be classified and made to fall either into one linguistic, ethnic, cultural, or national category or into another. Linguistic, ethnic, cultural, national identities are held to be perfectly delimited by the sets of properties that define them. This supports the belief that any social community to which a specific concept of collective identity applies should also be perfectly delimited and (in the case of national identity) control, by means of its political expression, the national state, a territory with precise borders.

But all this is either false or not feasible. Individual identity is multidimensional: the linguistic, ethnic, cultural identities of one individual may be defined at least in part independently of one another and, moreover, may combine with professional, generational, gender and other features. The collocation of every individual along each continuum of identity is to some extent a matter of degree: no ethnic belonging is ever literally pure, no individual has a perfectly standard linguistic competence (and only that one), and no cultural heritage is the exact replica of a model. Collective identities are abstractions or inductive generalizations at best, if not stereotypes, and do not merit the normative force they acquire when real people are required to fall either within or outside any one of them. As to national identity, it is typically a bundle of features of the ethnic, linguistic, and cultural kind, which are considered as one unit in the light of the ideal of perfect delimitation. Perhaps the mysterious ingredient that is added to linguistic, ethnic and cultural features to yield nationality is just that ideal. But it is simply not true that a person either possesses all those features and therefore belongs to a certain nation, or fails to possess some of those features and therefore belongs to some other nation (possibly because of other features he or she possesses instead).

All these matters of identity can be more realistically approached within a paradigm of "family resemblances " inspired by the philosophy of Ludwig Wittgenstein. Wittgenstein's idea (1953: 31–35) is, broadly, that many words that we take to express concepts are not applied depending on whether the object at issue possesses certain features (and therefore belongs to the set referred to by the word expressing the concept), but on the basis of its collocation in a complex network of similarities. A game, for example, need not share supposedly essential features with all other games in order to be correctly so called. But every game which is correctly so called has at least one similarity with something else that is also correctly called a game because of its further similarities to other games.

On analogy with Wittgenstein's views on meaning, we propose to consider identity as based on chains of similarities, criss-crossing each other in a network (Sbisà 1999, 2006; see also Nicholson 1994 for a critical consideration of gender from a family-resemblances perspective). Each individual collocates him or herself, with respect to each of the main dimensions of his or her social identity, at some place along a chain of similarities or at the crossroad of various chains. Similarly, collective identity does not consist of a perfectly delimited set of features singling out the set of individuals who share them: the cohesion of a social group does not depend on the homologation of its members, but on their participation in a network of partial resemblances. As to the relationship between diverse identities, the family-resemblances perspective admits of similarities and overlaps as well as differences, because distinctions need not consist of contrasts between mutually exclusive sets of features.

The adoption of a family-resemblances perspective on identity facilitates acceptance of non-standard or hybrid identities both at the individual and at the collective level, allowing for their exploitation as transition areas. By enabling us to notice similarities across different identities, it enhances communication. In its light, we see that the defense or protection of collective identities should be aimed at granting everybody the right to express the identity he or she happens to possess, whether standard or hybrid, not at building up perfectly delimited collective entities.

It could be objected that the family-resemblances paradigm has obvious limitations: there are matters that need to be dealt with in terms of precise borders. State borders are one of these matters, as is citizenship. Who is a citizen of which state and with what rights and obligations must be precisely determined by law if the very notion of citizenship is to be of any use to society. But citizenship should not be confused with linguistic, ethnic or cultural identity, or with nationality. Unlike the kinds of identity we have already discussed, citizenship is of use only if it is a perfectly delimited concept. If we see this difference, we cannot fail to see also how mistaken it is to ground citizenship in linguistic-ethnic-cultural or "national" identity.

We thus wish to challenge the received idea that national identities should be the foundations of national states. It is because of this assumption that linguistic-ethnic-cultural groups that perceive themselves as national groups feel justified in staking claims for a national state of their own or for displacement of an existing

state border. Conflation of "nationality" and citizenship is in some cases reinforced by linguistic usage. While in some European languages, such as German
and Italian, there are distinct words for the two ideas, in others, including English
and French, the word "nationality" (or its relevant translation) seems to mean the
complex condition of being a *citizen* of a certain *national* state. But the family-resemblances paradigm suggests that this link should be cut. Citizenship, as a kind
of second-level identity, should find more realistic grounds in the participation in
the historically elaborated and politically modifiable rules of civic life that hold
within a certain geographical area and for a certain population.

Coming back to our problem, that is, conditions for the recognition of the
other's point of view, we believe that the family-resemblances paradigm makes it
conceivable that different identities, and therefore points of view, are present in
one and the same territory. The fact that the other is different no longer hinders
his or her recognition as a subject acting in our same environment, since diversity
is always a matter of degree. Moreover, the other's identity and point of view can
no longer be deduced from the stereotype of the relevant linguistic-ethnic-cultural or national group, but is more freely constructed on the basis of self-images
actually expressed in discourse and interaction by individual subjects belonging
(in the family-resemblances sense) to that linguistic-ethnic-cultural group.

Conclusions

Can we Europeans train ourselves to recognize the existence, subjectivity and
point of view of those *others* (Europeans belonging to different ethnic-linguis-
tic-cultural groups as well as non-Europeans) who happen to live (for historical
reasons as well as recent migration) in our same territory? We believe we can,
insofar as we are willing to modify current discourse about identities, abandon
what has here been called the "ideal of perfect delimitation" and adopt a family-
resemblances paradigm instead.

One obstacle along the way is worth mentioning here: the ideal of perfect
delimitation seems to be reinforced nowadays by the increasing demand for identity, which is stimulated by anxieties aroused by globalization processes. When we
conceive of ourselves as individuals facing the whole world, we may feel awfully
lonely. Belonging to a well-defined group and defining our identity by reference
to it would seem to help us entertain reassuring social relationships. But then the
perverse mechanism of the ideal of perfect delimitation comes in, imposing a
simplified view on identity and fostering conflicts.

However, it is simply not true that the more perfectly the identity-giving socio-cultural group is delimited, the stronger identity it provides to its members.

Identities based on inclusion in a socio-cultural group simply turn identity anxiety into the defensive closure or the aggressivity of the group as a whole. In the family-resemblances paradigm, an individual grounds his or her identity not in identifying with a stereotype, but in how he or she collocates him or herself in a network of relations. He or she allows his or her identity to be defined along multiple parameters and therefore as potentially composite. Although seemingly weaker, the sense of individual identity achieved in this way – an unrepeatable mixture drawing on various socio-cultural resources – can in fact be more secure and lower identity anxiety. Research on intercultural communication has shown that a secure sense of one's identity correlates with successful intercultural communication, while anxiety as regards one's identity reinforces the interlocutor's anxiety and lowers the quality of the interaction (cf. Ting-Toomey 1993). Hence, it can be expected that the refusal of the ideal of perfect delimitation makes people not only less prone to accept nationalistic ideologies and serve the interests lying behind them, but also more capable of successful intercultural communication.

References

Delanty, Gerard. 1995. *Inventing Europe: Idea, Identity, Reality*. London: Macmillan.

Gardner-Chloros, Penelope. 1997. "Code-switching: Language selection in three Strasbourg department stores". In *Sociolinguistics*, N. Coupland and A. Javorski (eds.), 361–375. London: Macmillan.

Gumperz, John. 1982. *Discourse Strategies*. Cambridge: Cambridge University Press.

Kaučič Baša, Majda. 1997. "Where do Slovenes speak Slovene and to whom? Minority language choice in a transactional setting". *International Journal of the Sociology of Language* 124: 51–73.

Kymlicka, Will. 1995. *Multicultural Citizenship*. Oxford: Oxford University Press.

Kymlicka, Will and Opalski, Magda (eds.). 2001. *Can Liberal Pluralism be Exported? Western Political Theory and Ethnic Relations in Eastern Europe*. Oxford: Oxford University Press.

Lancellotti, Giancarlo 2001. "Gli ebrei". In *Dentro Trieste*, C. Benussi (ed.), 21–45. Trieste: Hammerle.

Myers-Scotton, Carol. 1990. "Codeswitching and borrowing: Interpersonal and macrolevel meaning". In *Codeswitching as a Worldwide Phenomenon*, R. Jacobson (ed.), 85–105. Bern: Lang.

Myers-Scotton, Carol. 1997. "Code-switching". In *The Handbook of Sociolinguistics*, F. Coulmas (ed.), 217–237. Oxford: Blackwell.

Nicholson, Linda. 1994. "Interpreting gender". *Signs: Journal of Women in Culture and Society*. 20: 79–105.

Sbisà, Marina. 1999. "The ideal of perfect delimitation versus the reality of family resemblances". In *Tolerancija/Tolerance*, B. Jaksić (ed.), 53–63. Beograd: Republika.

Sbisà, Marina. 2006. "Against identity: A family resemblance perspective on intercultural relations". In *Kulturen: Streit-Anaylse-Dialog/Cultures: Conflict-Anayalsis-Dialogue. 29th International Wittgenstein Symposium*, Georg Gasser et al. (eds), vol. 14, 295–297.

Sbisà, Marina and Vascotto, Patrizia. 1998. *Punti di Vista su Trieste. Ricerca sulle Rappresentazioni del Territorio Italiane e Slovene*. Trieste: Editoriale Libraria.

Sbisà, Marina and Vascotto, Patrizia. 2001. "L'immagine dell'altro: Consapevolezza delle differenze linguistiche in ragazzi italiani e sloveni della provincia di Trieste". In *Lingue di Confine, Confini di Fenomeni Linguistici/Grenzsprachen. Grenzen von Linguistischen Phänomenen. Atti dell'VIII Incontro Italo Austriaco dei Linguisti*, P. Cordin, R. Franceschini and G. Held (eds.), 161–177. Roma: Bulzoni.

Stranj, Pavel. 1989. *La Comunità Sommersa. Gli Sloveni in Italia dalla A alla Z*. Trieste: Editoriale Stampa Triestina.

Ting-Toomey, Stella. 1993. "Communicative resourcefulness. An identity negotiation perspective". In *Intercultural Communication Competence*, R.L. Wiseman and J. Koester (eds.), 72–111. London: Sage.

Vascotto, Patrizia. 2001. "Gli sloveni". In *Dentro Trieste*, C. Benussi (ed.), 75–99. Trieste: Hammerle.

Wittgenstein, Ludwig. 1953. *Philosophische Untersuchungen*. Ed. by G.E.M. Anscombe and R. Rhees. With English translation. Oxford: Blackwell.

Narratives on lesser-used languages in Europe

The case of Ulster Scots

John Wilson and Karyn Stapleton
University of Ulster

Introduction

Continuing political integration in Europe has produced many new questions of identity, belonging and allegiance (see, for example, Carl 2003; Conant 2001; Kohli 2000; Paasi 2002). On the one hand, the European Union (EU) is becoming progressively centralised at the political and bureaucratic level, and there is, further, an emphasis on concepts of European citizenship, and European identity (Lehning 2001). Simultaneously, however, under EU regionalisation policy, ethno-national minorities and ethnically contested regions are increasingly claiming, and gaining, constitutional recognition. In this context, as Durrschmidt (2002:123) points out, "the interplay between social boundaries and territorially defined political borders becomes more complex in that they become increasingly delinked".

This centralisation/regionalisation dynamic is particularly well-illustrated by issues of linguistic rights and recognition. Both by formally legitimating minority languages (see below), and endorsing the official (national) languages of all member states in the European parliament, the EU affirms, at a bureaucratic level, its commitment to linguistic diversity. This move is countered, however, by an increasing reliance on English and French in less formal proceedings, such that these two languages have come to function as global 'European', rather than national, languages, within the Union (see Nic Craith 2000). In this chapter, we are specifically concerned with the issue of minority languages, and in particular, how official linguistic recognition and endorsement is perceived by members of the culture (s) on whose behalf such moves are made.

Focusing on the case of Ulster Scots, we propose a *narrative approach* to understanding the everyday 'meanings' of minority, or indeed contested, languages.

We argue that because bureaucratic linguistic decisions are experienced and constructed at an emic level within the communities themselves, these issues may be usefully examined through the narrative accounts of community members. Thus, the personal/biographical narratives offered by individuals about their language may be seen as contributing, in a constitutive way, to a larger social and cultural narrative of the language itself; and indeed to a narrative matrix of discourses and references, within which their own language is meaningfully located. Below, we outline both the sociolinguistic background to Ulster Scots, and the context of minority or lesser-used languages in Europe. We will then discuss the concept of narrative as a social and cultural phenomenon, before empirically analysing community narratives of the Ulster Scots language. Drawing on this analysis, we consider some of the linguistic and cultural identity issues raised by Ulster Scots, and attempt to relate these issues to the broader European context of regional language policy.

Ulster Scots: The sociolinguistic context

Over the last decade, Ulster Scots has emerged as a recognised cultural identity within Northern Ireland. Previously, the use of the term 'Ulster Scots' had been much more limited, being employed mainly to designate a specific form of linguistic use found in parts of Ulster (see Adams 1977; Gregg 1972; Harris 1984; Kingsmore 1995; Robinson 1997). This language use had developed originally from Scots, the language of many of the lowland planters who arrived in Ulster in the 16th and 17th centuries. Scots in turn is said to have developed from a mixture of Northumbrian English and Old Norse. The term 'Ulster Scots', then, may now be used to refer to those who see themselves as being of Scottish origin, or having close affinities with Scottish culture or its manifestations within a specific community in Northern Ireland; and it may also designate a specific form of language use. In both cases, there has been some element of controversy surrounding the use of the term 'Ulster Scots'. In the case of designating a specific cultural grouping, the issues have revolved around the perceived association of the term 'Ulster Scots' with the Unionist and Protestant population of Northern Ireland. Here, its recent prominence has been treated as reactive, as opposed to historically or culturally derived; hence the identity is accused of being 'invented' and non-'authentic' (cf. Stapleton and Wilson 2004). In the case of Ulster Scots as a form of language use, the issues revolve around the core question of whether Ulster Scots is a language or a dialect (Kallen 1999).

In this chapter our aim is to consider how those who view themselves as 'Ulster Scots' talk about and reflect on such issues. As indicated in the previous section, we will explore the general *narrative discourse* of members of the Ulster Scots community as they respond to questions of culture and language. Our specific reasons for using this approach in this context are twofold. First, Ulster Scots has received recognition within Europe as a minority or lesser-used language. In Northern Ireland, however, there is some debate about the extent to which it actually exists as a living language, even among those who might be said to be from an Ulster Scots tradition. What, therefore, is the relationship between language and identity for Ulster Scots? Second, we want to relate the discussion of Ulster Scots to general issues of European minority or lesser-used languages, and to consider this in terms of the broader European context. Hence this paper uses the narrative discourse of Ulster Scots as an example for consideration of more general issues of minority linguistic identity.

Minority languages in Europe

The European Union is a multilingual community, with 23 official working languages: Bulgarian, Czech, Danish, Dutch, English, Estonian, Finnish, French, German, Greek, Hungarian, Irish, Italian, Latvian, Lithuanian, Maltese, Polish, Portuguese, Romanian, Slovak, Slovenian, Spanish, Swedish. In addition, there are numerous parts of Europe where indigenous groups speak a language distinct from the official majority population. The term minority language is not in itself uncontroversial since who determines what is or is not a minority language may have more to do with political issues than a simple numerical assessment. Consider also that there may be no such thing as a majority language in the context of the EU; therefore the very designation of a minority language is a form of narrative in itself. Consider, for example, the case of Catalan. Catalan could be viewed as a minority language in either Spain or Europe, but with the expansion of the EU in January 2005, Latvia – to take one example – was entered as a member state, like France, Germany or the UK; hence, Latvian is an official language within the EU. Yet the speakers of Latvian number around two million while speakers of Catalan number some five or six million. There is also a further complication with the movement of European peoples where significant numbers of migrant workers may end up as a minority group in one state, but speak the major language of their own state. There are, for example, 2 million members of the Turkish and Maghreb communities in Germany, with a further 1.4 million in France (Extra and Gorter 2001: 14).

Under the *European Charter for Regional or Minority Languages*, which came into force in 1998, and which was ratified by 11 of the 41 members of the Council of Europe in October 2000,[1] Article 1a defines a 'regional' or 'minority language' as follows:

i.   traditionally used within a given territory of a State by nationals of that State who form a group numerically smaller than the rest of the State's population; and

ii.   different from the official language(s) of that State; it does not include either dialects of the official language(s) of the State or the languages of migrants. (from Extra and Gorter 2001:14).

Within the 25 EU member states, i.e. before the accession of Bulgaria and Romania, the following regional, minority and other languages were identified (as listed on the EU website Europa 'Languages and Europe'):

Austria:	Croatian, Czech, Hungarian, Slovak, Slovene
Belgium:	German
Cyprus:	Armenian, Cypriot Arabic, Romani
Czech Republic:	German, Polish, Romani, Slovak, Bulgarian, Croatian, Greek, Hungarian, Russian, Ruthenian, Ukrainian
Denmark:	German
Estonia:	Russian, Belorussian, Finnish, German, Latvian, Lithuanian, Polish, Romani, Swedish, Tatar, Ukrainian, Yiddish
Finland:	Saami, Swedish
France:	Basque, Breton, Catalan, Corsican, Dutch, German, Occitan
Germany:	Danish, Frisian, Sorbian
Greece:	Albanian, Bulgarian, Macedonian, Turkish, Walachian
Hungary:	Croatian, German, Romani, Romanian, Serbian, Slovak, Slovenian, Armenian, Bulgarian, Greek, Polish, Ruthenian, Ukrainian
Ireland:	Irish
Italy:	Albanian, Catalan, Croatian, Franco-provencal, Friulian, German, Greek, Ladin, Occian, Sardinian, Slovene
Latvia:	Belorussian, Polish, Russian, Ukrainian, German, Latgalian, Lithuanian, Livonian, Yiddish, Romani
Lithuania:	Polish, Russian, Belorussian, German, Yiddish, Karaim, Romani, Tatar, Ukrainian

---

1.   The *Council of Europe* was set up in 1949 and is a much larger organisation than the EU.

Luxembourg:	Luxembourgian
Netherlands:	Frisian
Poland:	Belorussian, German, Kashubian, Lithuanian, Ruthenian/ Lemkish, Ukrainian, Armenian, Yiddish, Karaite (or Kara- im), Roma, Russian, Slovak, Tatar, Czech
Portugal:	Mirandese
Slovakia:	German, Hungarian, Romani, Bulgarian, Croatian, Polish, Ruthenian, Czech, Ukrainian, Tatar, Czech
Slovenia:	Hungarian, Italian, Romani, Bosnian, Croatian, German, Serbian
Spain:	Aragonese, Asturian, Basque, Berber, Catalan, Galician, Oc- citan, Portuguese
Sweden:	Finnish, Saami
United Kingdom:	Cornish, Gaelic, Irish, Welsh

There have also been other initiatives linked to the recognition and support of minority language rights, for instance, the *Universal Declaration on Linguistic Rights*,
signed in Barcelona in 1996; and there have been a number of parallel activities
such as the Council of Europe's *Framework Convention on National Minorities*,
which supplement the policy provisions for minority groups. However, there is
some confusion here about the responsibilities of specific States in relation to the
Charter for Regional or Minority Languages. As Extra and Gorter (2001:20) note:

> ..the concepts of 'regional' and 'minority' languages are not specified in the Char-
> ter and...(im)migrant languages are explicitly excluded from the Charter. States
> are free in their choice of which RM languages to include. Also the degree of
> protection is not prescribed, thus a State can choose for light or tight policies. The
> result is a rich variety of different provisions accepted by the various states.

For example, Limburgian was perceived as a dialect of Dutch until 1998 when the
Netherlands gave it recognition as a regional language under the *European Charter for Regional or Minority Languages*. At the same time, however, in Belgium
where Limburgian is also spoken, the government has not taken a similar step
(Extra and Gorter 2001:10).

In the case of Ulster Scots, the language is recognised both by the European
Bureau of Lesser Used Languages (where it is designated a dialect of Scots), and
by the British Government who officially recognised Ulster Scots as a variety of
Scots when they became signatories to the *European Charter for Regional or Minority Languages* in March 2003. In fact, it could be argued that the 'language or
dialect' debate is now 'dead,' since Ulster Scots is recognised within the EU as a

minority language.[2] As can be seen above, this may be true at one level, but the case of Limburgian shows the complications of official recognition. Further, it is an interesting sociolinguistic point that if something is defined as a language or dialect by official edict, then what is a language today could become a dialect tomorrow and vice versa.

Narrative discourse

The term narrative is notoriously difficult to define. It is often seen as simply story telling, but structuralists and others would wish to separate the story from the telling, that is the narrative. The dualist perspective has been central throughout the history of the study of narrative. As McQuillan (2000) notes, dualism may be found in the work of Russian scholars on folklore, who distinguished between *fabula* and *sjuzhet*, the French tradition, which made a distinction between *historie* and *discours*, and the structuralists, who distinguished story and discourse. This type of thinking is matched by taxonomic efforts, dating from Aristotle's *Poetics* (1997 edition), which aim to determine specific set categories or forms of construction. For example, White (1973) suggests organising a series of texts, from historical to literary, as tragedy, romance, comedy, and satire (for application beyond formal genres, see Gergen and Gergen 1988, 1993; Murray 1989). The general structural orientation may also be seen in the highly influential work of Labov and Waletsky (1967), which distributes the structure and function of narratives in terms of the following set of categorisations: Abstract, Orientation, Complicating Action, Evaluation, Resolution and Coda.

The value of this scheme has been exemplified in a variety of different accounts of narrative (for example as applied to the media, see Bell 1998). As Derek Edwards (1997) notes, however, such structural delimitations are idealisations, and they may fit more easily to some selected modes of discourse than to others. Equally, he argues, it is possible to offer counter categorisations for what might be taking place in selected narrative examples. The important point is that narratives may be more than the sum of their structural categorisations. Consider this well-known example provided by Sacks (1992: 113):

---

2.   This view is expressed by a number of informants in our own research – both by those who advocate further 'official' support for the language, and by those who feel that the 'argument has been won', and thus suggest greater emphasis be placed on promoting other aspects of the Ulster Scots culture (Source: The Ulster Scots Identity Project, Institute of Ulster Scots Studies, 2002-2003).

1.   B: ...Well, she (((wife of B)) stepped between me and the child,
2.   I got up to walk out the door. When she stepped between me
3.   and the child, I went to move out of the way. And then
4.   about that time her sister had called the police. I don't know
5.   how she...what she...
6.   A: Did you smack her one?
7.   B: No.
8.   A: *You're not telling me the story, Mr. B.*
9.   B: Well, you see when you say smack you mean hit.
10. A: Yeah, you shoved her. Is that it?
11. B: Yeah, I shoved her.

One of the important points here is line 8, 'you're not telling me the story, Mr B' (in italics). As both Edwards and Sacks have commented, this is not a request for some structural reanalysis or for the inclusion of a missing structural element *per se*, rather this is an interactional challenge to the adequacy of the 'telling' at that point. It is the social action orientation that is interesting here, and this is also what interests us in this chapter. We want to consider the interactional work being done by narratives, but further, we want to use this work to comment on the way in which this interactional information links with narrative content to tell us something about the attitudes and beliefs of informants as they relate to specific cultural and other identifications.

In contrast to the use of formal models, Smith (1981) has argued that while a story may be retold, each narrative is unique. She argues, therefore, that each retelling reconfigures a new or different narrative. Hence there is no basic narrative, nor indeed any basic set of grammatical rules for generating one narrative from another; consequently, it becomes impossible to distinguish narrative from other forms of everyday discourse. Narrative, in this open post-structural sense, becomes more flexible and more relevant, we would argue, for considering narrative positionings within the semi-structured context of group interviews. While by their very nature, such interviews initially direct topic orientations, their open-ended format leaves room for informants to develop or introduce a range of structural and topical orientations. As we will see, responses often do take the form of storied examples within a narrated framework. Often, however, the responses are less articulated and seem to offer only positions or opinions. But these very types of responses are operating in the structural context of the group interaction, and may be interpreted in relation to a set of intertextual relations being displayed explicitly and implicitly within the intersubjective construction of the data.

Here what Bruner (1986, 1990) calls 'framing' takes place. Frames or schemas may be seen as cultural templates which assist community and individual understandings, and also assist in maintaining the folk memory of such understandings (see Mandler 1984). Smith's (1981) more volatile and fluid picture of narrative allows us to formulate not simply individual narrative discourse, but also those examples of narrative discourse within what McQuillan (2000) calls the 'narrative matrix'; that is, the system where all narratives touch upon each other. This is somewhat similar to the discourse analysts' use of the term 'intertextuality' where one text can call up, link to, or touch upon (directly or indirectly) other texts (see Fairclough 1992). For example, Ulster Scots informants tell of how school teachers or others would denigrate the use of Ulster Scots language as bad English. Such a narrative of the belittling of one's own language against a standard or societal norm touches on a narrative matrix of such experiences in other minority languages (and indeed, in one example, Welsh is invoked for this very purpose). It also forms a frame or schema of shared understanding where non-standard forms of language prove difficult to maintain within the context of formal education where the standard language dominates (see below).

Linguistic identity and cultural identity in Ulster Scots

The informants interviewed in this study are members of a range of community and cultural groups, some of which have an explicit Ulster Scots focus, while others incorporate aspects of the culture within their general remit of activities. These groups were contacted by post and invited to participate in a study of 'Ulster Scots identity'. The recruitment criterion was simply that participants *saw themselves* as being of Ulster Scots descent and/or felt themselves to 'be' Ulster Scots. As such, we view the members of such groups as self-designated Ulster Scots. These groups were interviewed on a range of topics related to their views of themselves as Ulster Scots, and in this chapter we will be specifically focusing on those responses, discussions, and stories which consider Ulster Scots language and its position within the general scheme of Ulster Scots identity. In considering this, we will explore a number of selected themes which the participants have targeted in relation to talk about Ulster Scots language; these include education, Europe, language and identity, and cultural maintenance.

Narratives of Ulster Scots language

As noted above, there has been a debate within Ulster about whether Ulster Scots is or is not a language, like English or Irish for example (see Kallen 1999; Kirk 1998; Mac Póilin 1998, 1999; Robinson 1997). This debate has often been quite heated and has been closely linked not only to cultural or linguistic aspirations, but also to political motivations (see McCall 2002, Nic Craith 2001). In some ways, this should not be surprising since it is something reflected in similar contexts across Europe. Consider the position of Walloon in Belgium, or Basque and Catalan in Spain, or indeed Irish in the context of Northern Ireland. When one considers the position of a minority or regional language in a political as opposed to a linguistic framework, there are often political consequences linked to such issues as power, resources and education. If all recognised minority or regional languages were the same, then all would have to be treated equally. However, since the *European Charter for Regional or Minority Languages* leaves significant room for interpretation on the part of states, one cannot even begin to debate resources or protection for a regional or minority language unless there is some form of state recognition under the Charter.

But what exactly is the issue with regard to Ulster Scots? The argument is predicated on the case that many Ulster Scots words and phrases look remarkably like English (e.g. more: mair, house: hoose, away: awa). In some ways, this is not surprising since, as noted above, Ulster Scots emerged from Scots, which was itself a form of language developed from Northumbrian English and Old Norse; hence both languages have similar roots. Linguistically speaking, languages are notoriously difficult to define in any unequivocal or formal manner, and dialects fare little better (see Billig 1995; Haugen 1966). What the general public view as languages are often national languages such as French, Spanish or English, but these are defined as national languages because they have been historically standardised from selected geographical and cultural variants. Therefore, what is assumed as the English language, the French language, and so on, were originally regional forms which gained standard language status. In the case of English, the dialect around the East Midlands was picked up and developed by merchants in the South of England. In the case of French, it was Parisian French that was developed as the norm and it is Castilian Spanish, as opposed to Catalan or Galician, that has emerged as the normative language of Spain.

Now since we are dealing in this chapter with everyday members of the community, we do not expect that they would debate the linguistic, sociological, or political issues as found in academic or political circles; so how do they view the position of Ulster Scots as a language? Consider the following extract.

Extract 1[3]

M3:   Well, you know (.) in school there, I studied Latin and French (.) And you
       could clearly see how…you had <u>all</u> your verbs to learn. You know. And there

---

3.   Transcription conventions are listed in the appendix at the end of the chapter.

was blah, blah, <u>blah</u> (.) blah, blah, blah, blah, <u>blah</u>? (.) And when I went through them all (.) it's a long time ago <u>now</u>. But (.) you could see the, clearly the structure of the <u>Latin</u>. And you'd see Latin language coming through in, in <u>English</u>. Right (.) y'know a lot of the verbs and that. And in French, you had <u>all</u> your verbs, and your nouns, and whatever <u>else</u>, subjectives and all. And in English (.) the <u>same</u>. (.) But, um, you know I see that as a clearly structured and set out language.

In this extract M3 tells us about his study of languages at school and emphasises the recurrent patterning one finds in learning different languages. There are the structural elements, the verbs, the nouns, and the subjects. M3's repetition of 'blah' is interesting here in that it has essentially no core meaning. It is generally used to indicate talk or talking which is irrelevant or uninteresting, and it may also be used to critically assess what someone else is saying as in responses such as 'yea blah blah'. In M3's case it seems that the term is intended to fill in for those obvious structural elements found in language teaching, which we have all experienced, and which therefore are uninteresting, repetitive and perhaps even boring. But while that may be true, the fact is that these obvious elements are found when one has a 'language'.

For M3 this is the point; when you learn a language you are taught about its various structural and component parts. His last comment seems to articulate a comparative base for the definition of a language; specifically, that it will have a clearly set out structure, containing many of the same things one finds in other languages (i.e. it will form a 'clearly structured and set out language'). There is an underlying logic being presented here. If something is a language, then it will have nouns, verbs, repetitions of structures and things. Consequently, we may say that if Ulster Scots had the structural features of a language (set A) then it is a language (B). (Equally, in this case, if B is a language, then it will have set A).

The interaction continues as follows:

Extract 1 contd.
R: Mmm.
M3:   Whether now (.) they say that Scots (.) some of the languages to be found in, in <u>Greek</u> manuscripts, and <u>Norse</u> manuscripts, and (.) these Germanic tribes (.) and whatever. The Belgiques, and whatever <u>else</u>. That it may have been a very <u>ancient</u> language. That it has been lost (.) and gradually absorbed into English. (.) Uh, you know. It used to be spoken (.) it was the, the language of the, the <u>Court</u>, the King's Court in Scotland, and the Royal Courts of Scotland
M2:   Aye, it <u>was</u> Scots.

M3:   Yeah. And (.) then when the two countries merged, or the <u>Union</u> of the two (.) then the King James I <u>Bible</u> was adopted. And (.) everything became <u>English</u> then. (.) And that gradually, the Scots was just (.) kept on as, as <u>words.</u> But (.) they weren't in schools, they weren't used, like. Like <u>I</u> remember in, in school, if you said (.) if you were asked a question, and you said 'aye' instead of 'yes', you know (.) that was (.) <u>terrible</u>. You know.

M3 continues with some general comments on the issue of what is a language. He begins by situating the use of Scots in an 'ancient context', and then provides a reasonable historical summary of the use of Scots at the Court of Scotland, and its demise through the Union of the Crowns and the adoption of English for the King James Version of the Bible. The second part of M3's account accords with much that has been claimed in the literature on Scots. The first set of comments is more oblique in interpretation, but perhaps not in objective. It is often the case that we cite evidence for the existence of something by its historic positioning. This is a particularly useful strategy if a category X is accused as being a recent phenomenon or an invention. This is sometimes referred to as a 'myth of origin strategy', basically the use of historical or folk narratives to position and strengthen a modern case as one of simply historical lineage. If one can quote history then it takes the argument out of the here and now and offers historical proof of the existence of the category under debate. In M3's second set of comments he seems to be paraphrasing existing knowledge, but he also seems to be mixing together the story of Scots and Ulster Scots. Once one proves the existence of Scots, Ulster Scots follows; the troubles faced by Scots are the troubles faced by Ulster Scots. All that is left now are the 'words', and they are being suppressed by education. The term Scots is jointly constructed with another informant who picks up on the drift of the argument (M2: Aye, it was Scots).

Nowhere in the narrative, however, is there any clear or formal claim by M3 that he believes Ulster Scots is a language. What he has done is lay down threads within the narrative matrix of languages such that if Scots has the same set patterns as other languages, that is, has a history and evidence of historical use, then it would, or should, be defined as a language. Further, what M3 also seems to be involved in is 'framing' in Bruner's terms; that is, he is drawing on a set of shared knowledge about Ulster Scots and Scots. The argument draws on both explicit and implicit texts and arguments within the public domain of debate on Ulster Scots. This is perhaps not unusual, however, and one might expect a member of an Ulster Scots group to have a general awareness of the frame within which Scots and Ulster Scots are positioned in relation to each other and to the language debate.

Before we discuss the informants' comments about 'school', let us add some further examples of the discussion of Ulster Scots as a language. In this extract, the informants are discussing the link between language and Ulster Scots culture:

Extract 2

R: So, do you think that the Ulster Scots language is an important part of the movement?
  (...)
M2: An important thing. But <u>not</u> necessarily overly important to the people in <u>this</u> area.
M3: No.
M2: Because they've <u>used</u> the words (.) they <u>continue</u> to use the words...And I mean, words that we (.) I mean if you come down around the harbour and listen to the fish being auctioned (.) those boys <u>there</u> (.) when they're talking about 'crans' and everything, and all their weights of fish, and everything <u>else</u>. It's all still using the old Scots terms.
M1: Well, I, I don't think it's a <u>defining</u> feature, but it's very important, because (.) if you have an identity, part of that identity, or one of the big things about it, is <u>language</u>. Uh, language and then, then <u>culture</u>. And culture can be a whole <u>pile</u> of things. Like (.) we talked about it before, but (.) culture can be the way somebody has a <u>wake</u> (.) uh, marriage, Churches, and (.) a whole (.) y'know, even the way you <u>pronounce</u>
M2: A <u>panoply</u> of things.

There are several points of interest here. First, note how M2 picks up on the general point that speaking Ulster Scots as a language, of whatever form, may not be the only criterion for having an Ulster Scots identity, but it is conceded that it is 'important'. This notion is later taken up by M1, who explains that there are many elements involved in having a specific identity. M2 gives a brief narrative account of the 'boys' who work at the harbour; 'those boys', presumably those working in the fishing industry, make use of specific 'words', 'crans and everything', which, he then comments, is 'still using the old Scots terms'. So there are those who still use the 'words', and this is evidence of the language in some form, but not evidence for the people that Ulster Scots language is the primary marker of Ulster Scots identity. Consider again M2's claim that those boys use the 'words'. This mirrors M3's earlier comments that the language elements that are surviving are the 'words'. This general point arises again and again throughout the discussions, as illustrated in these brief exemplar comments, drawn from different group interviews.

M2: People don't (.) a lot of people <u>use</u> the *words*, and they don't appreciate they're <u>not</u> English. (.) They're <u>Scottish</u>.

M1:   But you know (.) you got away with the *words*. (.) I think in my <u>ma's</u> time you didn't even get away with the words. I think then, they were a lot more harsh.

M1:   But, uh, <u>he</u> didn't mind you using the *words* (.) cos he always said (***), like, was <u>fine</u>.

M3:   But, um (.) it is very (.) you know (.) it's <u>incredible</u> really that the language and *words* <u>have</u> remained

The 'words' seem to represent for the informants the very concept of the language 'Ulster Scots'. It is here that is made real for them and where they can relate to stories of experience of using the 'words', both themselves and their families, particularly in areas such as education where, as M3 noted in Extract 1, to use the word 'aye' as opposed to 'yes' in school could be seen as 'terrible thing'. There are several examples of this (discussed in more detail below) and the following offers an interesting narrative about the school experience of family members who used the 'words'.

Extract 3

M3:   Well, I remember kind of, uh (.) my <u>grandmother</u> (.) on my <u>mum's</u> side, the [NAME] side (.) always had a, a kinda distinct Belfast <u>dialect</u>, just on certain (.) certain pronunciations of <u>words</u>, and stuff like that there. And my mother as well (.) within the <u>family</u>. I remember they were all (.) <u>caned</u> (.) and stuff in school. To speak the Queen's <u>English</u>. So, the language, to a certain extent, or the dialect, whatever you want to call it (.) a distinct language or a dialect, I'm not too sure (.) there's a <u>debate</u> about that. (.) It was caned <u>out</u> of them in school. (.) Speak the proper Queen's English, and stuff like that there. Which I always thought was unfair. (.) And I remember, I lived in London for a while (.) and I'd be saying, um (.) the <u>grammar</u> would be the same as English, but there'd be certain words, or phrases, I'd be coming out with, that they wouldn't <u>recognise</u> (.) and I started recog-<u>realising</u> that…

Here M3 gives a narrative account of his family's and his own experience of using what he sees as Ulster Scots 'words'. The main narrative is about the consequences of using Ulster Scots. Although that term is not specifically used, it seems reasonable to infer the reference from the short 'embedded' comment about language vs. dialect, which is the thrust of the discussion related to Ulster Scots. Although M3 refers to Belfast dialect, again, we assume that he means the 'words' located in Belfast speech, which he believes arise from the influence of Ulster Scots. Here we can begin to see why the term 'words' appears to be the representative form for Ulster Scots usage. First, M3 admits that the debate about language and dialect is one he is not sure of, and second, he suggests that the grammar of Ulster Scots would have been the same as English. The hint here is that for M3, and for most of the informants, Ulster Scots is most readily recognised within the broad context of an Ulster Scots community, many of whom, as we shall see, would not even claim to speak the language, but may be aware of the 'words'. Consider the following extract:

Extract 4

M: (…) I do a class with a Youth Club in the (TOWN) area, and part of it was about culture, and (.) focused on Ulster Scots. (.) And we went through a list of words that you would use, for (.) your head, your arms, parts of your <u>body</u>. And they were quite young teenagers, but they were able to identify almost <u>all</u> the words, what they <u>meant</u>. (.) And that was coming from an (.) <u>urban</u>, situated in an <u>urban</u> area. (.) So, there is a <u>latent</u> sense of it there.

Here we see that even the modern youth have a sense of 'words' that are different from Standard English, but no understanding that these very words are from Ulster Scots. At this level, there is little debate or controversy, either amongst academic or lay people. There is a general acceptance that the English spoken in Northern Ireland has been influenced by Ulster Scots (Kallen 1999; Mac Póilin 1999). The question is, is this enough for the revival of a minority language? Here the answer is less clear since, as the examples above show, there is a consistent view that speaking Ulster Scots is neither a necessary nor sufficient condition for being Ulster Scots. Here is another example of discussion on this point.

Extract 5

M1:   Well, it's certainly a very important part of the whole culture (.) you know I'm talking about the whole Ulster Scots <u>tradition</u> in Ireland. It's just part of that whole heritage, y'know with all the other customs that we've carried on from Scotland. But I wouldn't say it's the <u>most</u> important thing. (.) Because there's other very strong traditions, for example in this county, we've a strong tradition of piping, (.) fiddling, and all that end of things. You know?

R: So the language is an important part of the Ulster Scots identity then?

M2:   Oh definitely. I think it is.
(General agreement)
(…)

F1:   Well, as I said before, <u>I</u> don't speak Ulster Scots myself. You know, the area that I come from wasn't a particularly strong, um, Ulster Scots speaking area. So, I don't actually speak the language. (.) (.) But that doesn't mean that I'm not Ulster Scots, or that I don't feel that that's my own identity. So, no, I don't think that you do need to speak it, to <u>be</u> Ulster Scots in that sense.
(…)

M3:   I mean there's lots of Ulster Scots speakers around here who wouldn't consider themselves to be of Ulster Scots descent at all. But they'd be, probably fluent speakers of the language

M4:   In fact there's lots of people who speak Ulster Scots who <u>aren't</u> actually from that tradition. Y'know historically, their people wouldn't have <u>been</u> Ulster Scots. But they're from here as well, and (.) I suppose in that sense, it's like a <u>shared</u> language.

What is clear from this extract is that

a.   Ulster Scots language is important to Ulster Scots culture and identity
b.   You don't have to speak Ulster Scots to be Ulster Scots
c.   There are those who can speak Ulster Scots who would not see themselves as Ulster Scots

Such factors are not unusual for minority language contexts. There are many members of the population in the Republic of Ireland, for example, who have limited knowledge of the Irish language but who clearly see themselves as Irish, and also clearly see the importance for Irish identity that there is an Irish language. This context is a reflection of the fact that in some minority language contexts the working language of the state is distinct from the national language of the state. Ireland is one example; Luxemburg would be another. In the present case, the working language of Northern Ireland is English, but the language of the Ulster Scots community is what may be termed an ethnic language linked to Ulster Scots as an ethnic identity; and it would seem to be represented in most cases by the historical legacy of the 'words' as opposed to a living and actively used language. We are using 'ethnic identity' here, following John Edwards (1995: 10):

> Ethnic identity is allegiance to a group-large or small, socially dominant or subordinate-with which one has ancestral links. There is no necessity for a continuation over generations of the same socialisation or cultural patterns, but some *sense of group boundary must persist.* (emphasis added)

There certainly seems to be a sense of group boundary for the Ulster Scots, not just in terms of language, as they say, but over a range of cultural dimensions.

Returning to our core point, since Ulster Scots has no operational state basis like that of the Irish language in the Republic of Ireland, where Irish can be encouraged, legally and otherwise, for example within the national education system, it is harder to see how the language of Ulster Scots can be maintained alongside English as a working language. Clearly, there are advocates of Ulster Scots who would like the language to be given a recognised position within a state-based context. In such a context, there should then be opportunities to study the language in schools. However, if our informants are representative, there would be no general call for a radical language teaching policy, involving masses of people learning to speak Ulster Scots, but rather an increased sensitivity to the historical existence of the language and the maintenance of the 'words'.

The importance of this is highlighted in school narratives (some already noted above) where, as in many minority language contexts, the use of Ulster Scots (words) was a punishable action:

Extract 6

R: That's (.) <u>very</u> common, isn't it, that experience at school?

M2: Aye.

M1: You know, I see me going to the Headmaster of the Primary School, and, and (.) him asking me two questions. I said '<u>aye</u>' (.) aye, aye. And he said (.) 'From now on (.) if I, if I ask you any more questions, you must answer and say <u>yes</u>'. And I says 'aye'.

R: *(laughs)*

M1: And he says, he just shook the <u>head</u>, and says 'go <u>on</u>'.
     (Laughter)

M1: But, um (.) it is very (.) you know (.) it's <u>incredible</u> really that the language and words <u>have</u> remained. With all the, you know, the <u>suppression</u>, and uh (.) everything that was used against it. And (.) it had to be <u>pure</u> (.) English. But now these things are, everything's a wee bit more liberal.

Extract 7

M5: (…) I, I think it's a pity that the old culture has been destroyed. Even the, you mentioned there the Ulster Scots language. (.) (.) Well most of that was, in our schools, battered <u>out</u> of us.
     (General agreement)

M5: Y'know the youngsters went to school and they talked in the broad Ulster dialect. This is not the way you're supposed to talk in the <u>school</u>. And then, when you went out in the world (***)

F1: When you went to work, you were called a culchie.

M5: <u>Yeah</u>. That's <u>right</u>.

F1: The 'aye' and the 'noo' and all that. *(General laughter)*

M2: You were taught the Queen's English.

Extract 8

M3: We, we had a very <u>bad</u> experience in the school that <u>we</u> went to. The primary school in (***). The primary teacher there was from the Gaeltacht in Donegal. A fluent Irish speaker. Born and bred. But her English…like, Gaelic was her first language, her best language. Y'know? But Ulster Scots or Laggan (.)

Laggan English, or whatever you want to call it (.) she could not understand it.

M1: Right

M3: And when we went we spoke Laggan, or Ulster English. And she was adamant that we would sort of (.) have to go back to the drawing board again and learn to <u>speak</u>. But she started hammering Gaelic into us. And we endured that for uh (.) she was there three years. And then we got a boy who was Eton-educated from Blessington in Co. Wicklow. And he taught us, what d'you call it, the Queen's…

F1: The Queen's English.
(General laughter)

M3: So, I went with Ulster Scots I learned two languages while I was there. And I was master of none.

Extract 9

M2: Yes. I think at primary school, teachers should teach where the roots of the words an' all <u>came</u> from. Whenever they're teaching them where such (.) say a word like 'anorak' came from. (.) Iceland or somewhere, wasn't it? Eskimos. (.) <u>Well</u> (.) they should be saying that 'fornenst' came from Ulster <u>Scots</u>. (.) And they should have a list of words and show them the roots of all those words. Because Ulster Scots is an important part of our language.
(General agreement)

M4: Yeah, because a lot of youngsters, and even <u>myself</u> (.) I have to confess, grew up thinking that (.) you know, that your father or your grandfather wasn't speaking properly. (.) Y'know, they were mispronouncing this word, because they'd had a bad <u>education</u>. (.) But then, when you become a bit older, and get a bit <u>wiser</u>, you realise <u>oh</u> (.) but that's not an <u>English</u> word. It comes from Ulster Scots.

R: Yeah, I, I think, again that that's quite common in people's experiences.

M4: Yeah. Yeah, now I don't know (.) as I <u>say</u>, I don't know how the educational system can marry the two, the two <u>together</u>. (.) But I would still like to see the, the <u>words</u>. (.) Because there are words again, like in a <u>lot</u> of languages (.) you can't actually replicate, or transfer exactly <u>into</u> English. And they have (.) they have their own particular (.) meaning or, or <u>feeling</u> to them.

There is a common thread in all of this; specifically that schools functioned to eliminate all forms of language other than English, or 'the Queen's English' as it is sometimes referred to above. This elimination was often violent with people being 'caned' (beaten across the hands with a bamboo stick). Although there is a suggestion that the context may have improved over the years, the informants' narratives nonetheless present a general cultural stigma attached to the use of Ulster Scots.

In some cases, this may lead to one being defined as a 'culchie'; that is, somebody from a rural background who may not be too intelligent or sophisticated. In Extract (9), however, there is a suggested solution to this problem, and, interestingly, one that brings us back to the 'words'. If schools could teach about the history of the 'words', the children would naturally learn about the influence of Ulster Scots on Northern Irish language use. Learning this alongside standard English, teaching would provide not only an understanding, but would give Ulster Scots its own place where its words have their own specific function. As one informant states, Ulster Scots words may provide functional communication alternatives not always replicable in English.

This is an interesting point and one that suggests producing a form of bi-dialectalism/bilingualism. After all, it is not only minority languages that suffer at the hands of state languages; other dialect variants, often referred to as 'non-standard' dialects, are also frowned upon, and this has been a centre of debate as much as minority/majority language differences (see for example Lippi-Green 1997; Mesthrie et al. 2000). This brings us back to the language/dialect debate, but in a different way. Here we can see it is not a matter of a dialect or a language, it is a matter of linguistic rights. To imagine that someone is beaten for using words that belong to their culture seems strange to modern ears. Yet it need not always be physical violence. The standards of literacy and school examinations are set within the dominant language of the state. Most parents will still encourage their children to avoid non-standard forms simply because their use will often lead, in formal contexts particularly, to a negative stereotyping of their children (see e.g. Giles and Powesland 1975, 1997). So there is family and community pressure on children to conform to standard language norms, but at the same time, there is also an almost contrary pride in the use of alternative local language forms such as Ulster Scots.

So far, we can see that the narrative discourse around Ulster Scots language presents an initial ambivalence. Most of the informants do not speak the language, they do not suggest they should, nor that speaking the language should be a requirement for being Ulster Scots. Equally, they believe the language is important to the Ulster Scots identity, that it has been suppressed in the past and that, now, some effort in education should be made to recognise its influence and value. Presumably this would fall short of core Ulster Scots Language courses, but rather encourage Ulster Scots awareness programmes alongside, perhaps, the study of English and other forms of Northern Irish speech.

This position, interestingly, is somewhat different from the perceived view of what support for Ulster Scots means. The controversial dimensions of Ulster Scots are not always seen as the reasonable suggestions of the informants above, but rather as the formation of what Mac Póilin (1999:2) calls "maximally differentiated Ulster Scots". Here there is an attempt to draw a clear distinction in form and comprehensibility between English and Ulster Scots. Historically, Ulster Scots and English have a similar root, and, as noted above, many forms and constructions are very similar such that the general population of Northern Ireland often see Ulster Scots as simply a form of English. But as Mac Póilin observes, Swedish, Danish and two varieties of Norwegian could be said to be the same language from a linguistic perspective, but the governments have designated that they will be seen as independent languages. Equally, one could accept that while Ulster Scots and English are very similar, nonetheless, both the UK and Europe have designated them as separate languages. For some Ulster Scots language advocates, however, this may not be enough, since they also see Ulster Scots as a separate language from Scots. Further, as our informants comment in Extracts 10–12 below, recognition by Europe may be useful for funding, but because of sceptical views of Europe itself, European recognition of Ulster Scots may not make much difference to the general public.

Extract 10
    M2:   Well, I don't know if it has much clout coming from <u>Europe</u>. Because <u>they</u> keep <u>everyone</u> happy. (***)
    F2:   <u>I</u> think there's (.) a bit too <u>much</u> coming out of Europe. *(laughs)*
    M2:   They just keep everybody happy, so…
    R: So that isn't really…?
    M2:   It doesn't really cut much clout.

Extract 11
    M2:   I, <u>I</u> think that Europe's more akin with <u>Ireland</u>. (.) Like with, with the <u>Irish</u>. And I don't honestly think they've much time for people like (.) Ulster Scots. (.) Presbyterians.
    R: Why (.) do you think that's because it's…
    M2:   Because Europe was mainly <u>Catholic</u>. (.) And I still think there's a big, um (.) bias towards, y'know, the Irish. The <u>real</u> Irish, the <u>green</u> Irish.

Extract 12
    M2:   Well, I think, um, I think there are <u>opportunities</u>. Like there's a European programme called Culture 2000. And that offered (.) people like Ulster Scots opportunities (.) in conjunction, I think, with two other member states (.) to go and take your culture to the other countries that you'd teamed <u>up</u> with. (.) Which is all a great idea to (.) transport your culture for a day, or two days to <u>other</u> countries. (.) But the way that was designed, I suppose like a <u>lot</u> of

European things, it was (.) quite a big undertaking for what's (.) what could be described as a culture with a low <u>infrastructure</u>.

These brief examples suggest scepticism of European judgements, alongside a recognition that the EU may at least try to assist in certain contexts. In the first case, we have a stereotyped view of EU actions, and this touches on a range of implicit 'narrative matrix' forms: e.g. that the EU is weak, that the French always get what they want, that the Germans run Europe, and that the Irish make as much out of it as they can. In such a context of potential interpretation, utilising the argument that Ulster Scots is a language because it is recognised in Europe may be taken simply as Europe giving people what they want, or as just an administrative rather than a cultural or political statement.

Discussion

In this chapter, we have looked at some of the issues and debates surrounding European regional and minority languages through a focus on Ulster Scots, which has only recently been granted formal language status. Notably, we have examined these issues and debates from a *narrative perspective* and through the voices of *Ulster Scots people themselves*; i.e. the community on whose behalf we expect official endorsements to be made. In this way, we have examined the narrative matrices, within which Ulster Scots is discussed and positioned; and how community members make sense of their language and identity within this framework.

The importance of the Ulster Scots language to the maintenance of the Ulster Scots culture is a recurring theme in the recordings. This link between language and culture is articulated through a range of narrative forms, including biographical and family experiences, historical accounts and 'myths of origin' and narratives of social/political life in Ulster. It would seem, then, that the Ulster Scots language is a central component of Ulster Scots culture, and, by implication, of Ulster Scots identity. However, in these narratives, there is *no* essential connection between *actually speaking* Ulster Scots and participating in Ulster Scots culture/having an Ulster Scots identity. In fact, within the emergent narrative matrix, it could be claimed that speaking the language is neither a necessary nor a sufficient condition for Ulster Scots identity. That is, most of the participants themselves – who do claim an Ulster Scots identity – are not, in fact, Ulster Scots speakers; while they readily admit that there are others who, by virtue of geographical origin, do speak the language, yet would not be seen as/claim to be Ulster Scots.

There is another potential paradox in relation to official linguistic recognition – and, specifically, recognition by 'Europe'. In general, the participants' articulated position is not one of active promotion of Ulster Scots *as* a language. Indeed, a number state that they are unsure as to whether it *is* a language (as opposed to a dialect), while others suggest that this question is of little relevance to them, anyway. However, this is not to say that the speakers wish the language to go unrecognised – or derided, as was the case in the past. On the contrary, they are enthusiastic about increasing public recognition of Ulster Scots language (and in particular 'the words') as an index of the wider Ulster Scots culture. What seems to be less important is the push for *formal linguistic* status/endorsement for Ulster Scots – especially if such endorsement is seen to come 'from Europe'.

If we consider the recurring 'education' narrative above (in which Ulster Scots was, in the past, derided and 'caned out' of pupils), we can see that the problem is framed primarily in terms of a lack of cultural recognition on the part of teachers and the educational establishment more generally; i.e. a failure to understand that this was the way in which the participants/their families spoke and/or that many of the 'words' they used derived, historically, from a source other than English. Arguably, then, such a problem is more likely to be remedied by an increased awareness of Ulster Scots as a distinct cultural and linguistic tradition than it is by a formal, bureaucratic recognition of Ulster Scots as a language; a recognition which, in itself, may do little to change people's negative perceptions.

Hence, there is ambivalence, within the emerging narrative matrix, regarding formal linguistic recognition for Ulster Scots. On the one hand, formal status, endorsement and promotion in official contexts, would seem to be tangential, and sometimes even antithetical, to the aims of a people who simply ask for a heightened awareness and understanding of their culture, and of their way of speaking – which many of the community are even reluctant to label a language. On the other hand, the very fact of (official) linguistic recognition raises public awareness of Ulster Scots as a cultural, linguistic and historical tradition, while also legitimising the speech variety; i.e. the very things that the participants bemoan having lacked in the past. The issue is further complicated by the way in which Europe (and, especially, it might be assumed, the EU) is itself narrativised. As well as the view – relatively common among our participants – that 'Europe' is not, historically or politically, a natural ally of the Ulster Scots (preferring, instead the 'green Irish'), there is also the perception that what takes place in Europe does so merely at an administrative or bureaucratic level, and hence, is of little cultural or political significance. At the very least, however, official linguistic recognition creates the narrative space to conclude that that particular debate is dead ('it is *de facto* a language because it has been recognised as such') and then move on to talk about the wider context of cultural, linguistic and identity recognition.

Conclusion

The context of Ulster Scots is not specifically a unique one, either in minority language or dialect difference terms. The question for Europe is how it deals with the many various contexts in which such issues arise. If the aim is to safeguard minority languages, Europe runs into the problem of deciding what is and is not a minority language. In general, it seems to avoid this as a linguistic question and tends to deal with it rather as a political question. There may be good reason for this. Despite the multilinguistic aspirations of Europe, with each member state having recognition in their official language, the fact is that the bulk of the EU's work is carried out in only one or two languages (see Nic Craith 2000). There seems to be a level of pragmatic process here where efficiency and reality interact. Given this, why then support so many other minority languages? Perhaps because there is also a level at which centralism seems less negative and distant when your individual and minority linguistic rights, as well as your national linguistic rights, are seen to be given recognition and support. Interestingly, however, in an ever-growing EU, what is a national and a minority language may actually begin to blur in itself.

References

Adams, G. Brendan. 1977. "The dialects of Ulster". In *The English Language in Ireland*, D. O'Muirithe (ed), 56–70. Cork: Mercier Press.

Aristotle. 1997. *Poetics* (tr. G. Whalley, ed. P. Atherton and J. Baxter). Montreal: McGill/Queens University Press.

Bell, Allan. 1998. "The discourse structure of news stories". In *Approaches to Media Discourse*, A. Bell and P. Garrett (eds), 64–104. Oxford: Blackwell.

Billig, Michael. 1995. *Banal Nationalism*. London: Sage.

Bruner, Jerome S. 1986. *Actual Minds, Possible Worlds*. Cambridge, MA: Harvard University Press.

Bruner, Jerome S. 1990. *Acts of Meaning*. Cambridge, MA: Harvard University Press.

Carl, Jenny. 2003. "European integration and multiple identities: Changing allegiances in post-devolution UK?" *Perspectives on European Politics and Society* 4(3): 475–500.

Conant, Lisa. 2001. *Contested Boundaries: Citizens, States and Supranational Belonging in the European Union*. San Domenico di Fiesole: European University Institute.

Durrschmidt, Jörg. 2002. "'They're worse off than us': The social construction of European space and boundaries in the German/Polish twin-city of Guben-Gubin". *Identities: Global Studies in Culture and Power* 9(2):123–150.

Edwards, Derek. 1997. *Discourse and Cognition*. London: Sage.

Edwards, John. 1995. *Multilingualism*. London: Penguin Books.

Europa: Languages and Europe. (no date). <http://ec.europa.eu/education/policies/lang/languages/langmin/euromosaic/index_en.html>. Accessed 10 January 2007.

Extra, Guus and Gorter, Durk. 2001. *The Other Languages of Europe: Demographic, Sociolinguistic and Edicational Perspectives*. Clevedon: Multilingual Matters.

Fairclough, Norman. 1992. *Discourse and Social Change*. Cambridge: Polity Press.

Gergen, Kenneth J. and Gergen, Mary M. 1988. "Narrative and the self as relationship". In *Advances in Experimental Social Psychology*, L. Berkowitz (ed), 17–56. New York: Academic Press.

Gergen, Mary M. and Gergen, Kenneth J. 1993. "Autobiographies and the shaping of gendered lives". In *Discourse and Lifespan Identity*, N. Coupland and J.F. Nussbaum (eds), 28–54. Newbury Park: Sage.

Giles, Howard and Powesland, Peter F. 1975. *Speech Style and Social Evaluation*. London: Academic Press.

Giles, Howard and Powesland, Peter F. 1997. "Accomodation theory". In *Sociolinguistics: A Reader and Coursebook*, N. Coupland and A. Jaworski (eds), 232–239. London: Macmillan.

Gregg, Robert J. 1972. "The Scotch-Irish dialect boundaries in Ulster". In *Patterns in the Folk Speech of the British Isles*, M. Wakelin (ed), 109–139. London: Athlone.

Harris, John. 1984. "English in the north of Ireland". In *Language in the British Isles*, P. Trudgill (ed), 115–134. Cambridge: Cambridge University Press.

Haugen, Einar. 1966. "Dialect, language, nation". *American Anthropologist* 68(4): 922–935.

Kallen, Jeffrey. 1999. "Irish English and the Ulster Scots controversy". *Ulster Folklife* 45: 70–88.

Kingsmore, Rona. 1995. *Ulster Scots Speech: A Sociolinguistic Study*. Tuscaloosa: University of Alabama Press.

Kirk, John 1998. "Ulster Scots: Realities and myths". *Ulster Folklife* 44: 69–93.

Kohli, Martin. 2000. "The battlegrounds of European identity". *European Societies* 2(2):113–137.

Labov, William and Waletsky, Joshua. 1967. "Narrative analysis: Oral versions of personal experience". In *Essays on the Verbal and Visual Arts*, J. Helm (ed), 12–44. Seattle: University of Washington Press.

Lehning, Percy B. 2001. "European citizenship: Towards a European identity?" *Law and Philosophy* 20(3): 239–282.

Lippi-Green, Rosina. 1997. *English with an Accent*. London: Routledge.

Mac Póilin, Aodán. 1999. "Language, identity and politics in Northern Ireland". *Ulster Folklife* 45: 106–132. Available at <http://www.bbc.co.uk/northernireland/learning/history/stateapart//agreement/culture/support/cul2_c011.shtml>. Accessed 10 January 2007.

Mandler, Jean M. 1984. *Scripts, Stories and Scenes: Aspects of Schema Theory*. Hillsdale, NJ: Erlbaum.

McCall, Cathal. 2002. "Political transformation and the reinvention of the Ulster-Scots identity and culture". *Identities: Global Studies in Culture and Power* 9(2):197–218.

McQuillan, Martin. 2000. "Introduction: Aporias of writing: Narrative and subjectivity". In *The Narrative Reader*, M. McQuillan (ed), 1–34. London: Routledge.

Mesthrie, Rajend, Swann, Joan, Deumert, Andrea and Leap, William L. 2000. *Introducing Sociolinguistics*. Philadelphia: Benjamins.

Murray, Kevin D. 1989. "The construction of identity in the narratives of romance and comedy". In *Texts of Identity*, J. Shotter and K.J. Gergen (eds), 176–205. London: Sage.

Nic Craith, Mairead. 2000. "Contested identities and the quest for legitimacy". *Journal of Multilingual and Multicultural Development* 21(5):399–413.

Nic Craith, Mairead. 2001. "Politicized linguistic consciousness: The case of Ulster-Scots". *Nations and Nationalism* 7(1): 21–37.

Paasi, Anssi. 2002. "Regional transformation in the European context: Notes on regions, boundaries and identity". *Space and Polity* 6(1):197–201.

Robinson, Peter. 1997. *Ulster-Scots: A Grammar of the Traditional Written and Spoken Language*. Belfast: The Ullans Press.

Sacks, Harvey. 1992. *Lectures on Conversation, Vol. 2* (ed. G. Jefferson). Oxford: Blackwell.

Smith, Barbara Herrnstein. 1981. "Narrative versions, narrative theories". In *On Narrative*, W.J.T. Mitchell (ed), 209–232. Chicago IL: Chicago University Press.

Stapleton, Karyn and Wilson, John. 2004. "Ulster Scots identity and culture: The missing voices". *Identities: Global Studies in Culture and Power* 11(4):563–591.

White, Hayden. 1973. *Metahistory: The Historical Imagination in Nineteenth Century Europe*. Baltimore: John Hopkins University Press.

Appendix: transcription conventions

(.)	Brief pause (less than one second)
(***)	Unintelligible material
(...)	Some omitted material
____	(underlining) Prosodic emphasis on word or phrase
R:	Researcher
M1:	Male 1 (etc.) (focus group)
F1:	Female 1 (etc.) (focus group)

Index

In the series *Discourse Approaches to Politics, Society and Culture* the following titles have been published thus far or are scheduled for publication:

27   **VERDOOLAEGE, Annelies:** Reconciliation Discourse. The case of the Truth and Reconciliation Commission. *Expected January 2008*

26   **MILLAR, Sharon and John WILSON (eds.):** The Discourse of Europe. Talk and text in everyday life. 2007. vii, 200 pp.

25   **AZUELOS-ATIAS, Sol:** A Pragmatic Analysis of Legal Proofs of Criminal Intent. 2007. x, 180 pp.

24   **HODGES, Adam and Chad NILEP (eds.):** Discourse, War and Terrorism. 2007. x, 248 pp.

23   **GOATLY, Andrew:** Washing the Brain – Metaphor and Hidden Ideology. 2007. xviii, 432 pp.

22   **LE, Elisabeth:** The Spiral of 'Anti-Other Rhetoric'. Discourses of identity and the international media echo. 2006. xii, 280 pp.

21   **MYHILL, John:** Language, Religion and National Identity in Europe and the Middle East. A historical study. 2006. ix, 300 pp.

20   **OMONIYI, Tope and Joshua A. FISHMAN (eds.):** Explorations in the Sociology of Language and Religion. 2006. viii, 347 pp.

19   **HAUSENDORF, Heiko and Alfons BORA (eds.):** Analysing Citizenship Talk. Social positioning in political and legal decision-making processes. 2006. viii, 368 pp.

18   **LASSEN, Inger, Jeanne STRUNCK and Torben VESTERGAARD (eds.):** Mediating Ideology in Text and Image. Ten critical studies. 2006. xii, 254 pp.

17   **SAUSSURE, Louis de and Peter SCHULZ (eds.):** Manipulation and Ideologies in the Twentieth Century. Discourse, language, mind. 2005. xvi, 312 pp.

16   **ERREYGERS, Guido and Geert JACOBS (eds.):** Language, Communication and the Economy. 2005. viii, 239 pp.

15   **BLACKLEDGE, Adrian:** Discourse and Power in a Multilingual World. 2005. x, 252 pp.

14   **DIJK, Teun A. van:** Racism and Discourse in Spain and Latin America. 2005. xii, 198 pp.

13   **WODAK, Ruth and Paul CHILTON (eds.):** A New Agenda in (Critical) Discourse Analysis. Theory, methodology and interdisciplinarity. 2005. xviii, 320 pp.

12   **GRILLO, Eric (ed.):** Power Without Domination. Dialogism and the empowering property of communication. 2005. xviii, 247 pp.

11   **MUNTIGL, Peter:** Narrative Counselling. Social and linguistic processes of change. 2004. x, 347 pp.

10   **BAYLEY, Paul (ed.):** Cross-Cultural Perspectives on Parliamentary Discourse. 2004. vi, 385 pp.

9   **RICHARDSON, John E.:** (Mis)Representing Islam. The racism and rhetoric of British broadsheet newspapers. 2004. vi, 277 pp.

8   **MARTIN, J.R. and Ruth WODAK (eds.):** Re/reading the past. Critical and functional perspectives on time and value. 2003. vi, 277 pp.

7   **ENSINK, Titus and Christoph SAUER (eds.):** The Art of Commemoration. Fifty years after the Warsaw Uprising. 2003. xii, 246 pp.

6   **DUNNE, Michele Durocher:** Democracy in Contemporary Egyptian Political Discourse. 2003. xii, 179 pp.

5   **THIESMEYER, Lynn (ed.):** Discourse and Silencing. Representation and the language of displacement. 2003. x, 316 pp.

4   **CHILTON, Paul and Christina SCHÄFFNER (eds.):** Politics as Text and Talk. Analytic approaches to political discourse. 2002. x, 246 pp.

3   **CHNG, Huang Hoon:** Separate and Unequal. Judicial rhetoric and women's rights. 2002. viii, 157 pp.

2   **LITOSSELITI, Lia and Jane SUNDERLAND (eds.):** Gender Identity and Discourse Analysis. 2002. viii, 336 pp.

1   **GELBER, Katharine:** Speaking Back. The free speech versus hate speech debate. 2002. xiv, 177 pp.